THE ART OF
PORTRAIT
PAINTING

By the same author
        Bird Flight
        Yacht Racing Rules and Tactics
        Start 'Em Sailing
        Treasury of Sea Stories

Coauthor with Gordon C. Aymar, Jr.
        Second Book on Sailing

Coauthor with Peggy Aymar
        Michael Sails the Mud Hen

GORDON C. AYMAR. *Gordon C. Aymar, Jr.* 1941. Water color

THE ART OF PORTRAIT PAINTING

*Portraits Through the Centuries as Seen
Through the Eyes of a
Practicing Portrait Painter*

GORDON C. AYMAR, A.W.S.

CHILTON BOOK COMPANY

Philadelphia   New York   London

DEDICATED

to those, past and present, who have created a perceptive interpretation of a human being and, at the same
time, an enduring work of art.

PREFACE

IT may be well at the start to state what this book does *not* intend to be. It is not a manual on the techniques of painting a portrait. It does not tell how to transfer a sketch to canvas, nor what colors are suitable for making flesh tones. It is also not a history of painting, in spite of the many reproductions of portraits through the centuries which are included to illustrate various points. There will be no documentation as to the authenticity of the attribution of a painting to this or that artist. This fascinating and complicated study will be left to the experts.

John Constable, in a lecture at the Royal Institution in 1836, said that he was "anxious that the world should be inclined to look to painters for information on painting." This book is, in some measure, a response to his desire. It is a book on the *art* itself, as seen through the eyes of a practicing portrait painter.

Portrait painting is an art, not only in revealing the skill of a painter in representing the outer man objectively and the inner man subjectively, but also because, in so doing, it offers the opportunity to create an object of beauty per se.

This last point is a primary concern of the true artist. Achieving a likeness, important though it is, is not sufficient. Many paintings which may have been faithful likenesses have not come down to us through the years because they were uninteresting as *pictures*. They have been stored in the attic and, eventually, have been disposed of. Some have escaped this unhappy fate solely because they depicted a historical character, but these are the exceptions.

Naturally, many portraits have been, and are today, painted

primarily to obtain a possible likeness. The matter of creating a work of enduring beauty has been, too often, a secondary consideration. If a rather large portion of this book appears to the reader to be devoted to this latter aspect, it is because the author is, for better or worse, deeply involved in this struggle. My contention is that both goals, the likeness and the *art*, are not mutually exclusive.

One of the problems which faces the author of a book such as this is the selection of paintings to be reproduced. With the thousands of great works available today, this is difficult. I have chosen primarily those which illustrate a specific point. Some of the great painters have, inevitably, been omitted. I have also tended to favor those paintings which are not reproduced again and again in the many splendid books on art which are now available.

I hope that I may take the liberty of showing some of my own portraits and discussing them, without any implication that I am presenting them in the same category as the masterpieces which appear beside them. This took considerable courage. They are shown to demonstrate various aspects of portrait painting, and, since I am more familiar with the details involved in their creation than I could possibly be with those of masters of the past, they may be useful in this respect.

I might add that this book does not aspire to be a literary monument. It is a manual for artists by an artist. I sense in the writings of certain authorities on art something of the gourmet who passes the glass of wine solemnly back and forth under his nose, inhaling its bouquet, ruminating on its ancestry and vintage, all in preparation for one tingling sip. An artist, on the other hand, when viewing a great painting, suggests a hungry man who lays an avid hand upon a second joint and devours it wholeheartedly. "Quelquefois le gourmet; toujours le gourmand." This may serve as an explanation, if not an excuse, for the detailed analysis of the composition of many of the illustrations.

There is one more point I would like to make: the fact that my own paintings may seem to tend in a particular direction does not mean that I consider this to be the one way toward "art." I believe firmly in the uninhibited approach to beauty, and in the independence of each artist to declare himself in his own manner. Trivial movements inevitably die sooner than fundamental ones. Beauty refuses to remain in one school of art, but presses on into eternity. Leonie Adams has expressed it in "Caryatid":[1]

> There is no clasp which stays Beauty forever.
> Time has undone her, from porphyry, from bronze
> She is winged every way and will not rest. . . .

[1] Leonie Adams, *Poems, a Selection* (New York: Funk and Wagnalls, 1954)

ACKNOWLEDGMENTS

THE author and publisher wish to express their gratitude to the following for permission to reproduce the paintings listed below, and also to the owners of the author's paintings:

Albertina, Vienna: pl. 27.

Albright-Knox Art Gallery, Buffalo, N. Y.: pls. 54, 83, 151.

Art Institute of Chicago, Chicago, Ill.: pls. 25, 29, 43, 55, 97, 104, 144, 148, 162, 163.

British Museum, London: pl. 61.

Brooklyn Public Library, New York, N. Y.: pl. 80.

Busch-Reisinger Museum, Harvard University, Cambridge, Mass.: pl. 91.

Cleveland Museum of Art, Cleveland, Ohio: pls. 31, 35, 62, 78, 100, 116, 120, 122, 124, 126, 142.

Fogg Museum of Art, Harvard University, Cambridge, Mass.: pls. 32, 66, 68, 70, 81, 95.

Frick Collection, New York, N. Y.: pls. 6, 18, 38, 47, 73, 112, 161.

Isabella Stewart Gardner Museum, Boston, Mass.: pls. 5, 44, 60, 134.

Louvre, Paris: pls. 42, 72, 86, 130.

Marine Historical Association, Mystic Seaport, Mystic, Conn.: pl. 21.

Metropolitan Museum of Art, New York, N. Y.: pls. 1, 9, 11, 20, 26, 36, 45, 52, 56, 69, 71, 84, 89, 90, 114, 118, 129, 135, 146, 159.

Middlebury College, Middlebury, Vt.: pl. 51.

Museum of Fine Arts, Boston, Mass.: pls. 4, 75, 113.

Museum of Modern Art, New York, N. Y.: pls. 24, 41, 85, 92, 102, 105.

National Gallery, London: pls. 63, 94, 136, 137.

National Gallery of Art, Washington, D. C.: pls. 15, 115.

New York Historical Society, New York, N. Y.: pls. 132, 139.

Private Collection, Chicago, Ill.: pl. 150.

Mr. and Mrs. Joseph Verner Reed, New York, N. Y.: pl. 164

Royal Collection of Paintings in Britain, by Gracious Permission of Her Majesty the Queen. Copyright reserved: pl. 13.

Royal Museum of Fine Arts of Belgium, Brussels: pl. 109.

Shelburne Museum, Shelburne, Vt.: pls. 16, 50.

Smith College Museum of Art, Northampton, Mass.: pls. 39, 58, 64, 74.

Solomon R. Guggenheim Museum, New York, N. Y.: pl. 23.

Sterling and Francine Clark Art Institute, Williamstown, Mass.: pls. 10. 22, 34, 59, 67, 79, 88.

Tate Gallery, London: pls. 87, 93, 110, 155.

Vatican Museums and Galleries, Rome: pls. 107, 108.

Victoria and Albert Museum, London, Crown Copyright: pl. 8.

Yale University, New Haven, Conn., Gertrude Stein Collection: pl. 57.

Yale University Art Gallery, New Haven, Conn.: pls. 2, 14, 17, 19, 28, 49, 53, 65, 82, 96, 98, 111, 133, 153.

CONTENTS

Beauty is more than a fortress
Behind whose walls one cowers
To seal oneself from ugliness;
More than a balm to heal
The wounds of ignorance,
       Insensitivity;
More than a retreat from stringency,
       From boredom.
Beauty is positive,
Has her own breastplate
       And halberd;
Is courageous without injuring,
Bold without offending,
Mighty without misrule;
Has a million facets,
Aeons of time;
Does harm to no one,
Ne'er repeats herself,
Infects without disease,
Illumines as no other light.
Beauty is more than a fortress!

THE ETERNAL ART

THE REASON for the existence of portrait painting is man's natural urge to have his image recorded, for a witness during his lifetime and as a memorial to pass on to future generations—the lineaments of the body and, hopefully, the essence of the personality.

Through the centuries portraits have been painted to honor potentates, clerics, and those who were rich enough to afford the works of the great painters.

In addition, however, to the historical category, there is the vast group which is painted because of the affection of one human being for another. Parents want to capture the fleeting appearance of a child at some enchanting point in his or her youth; a husband wishes to preserve the beauty of his wife; a widow wishes to have the picture of her husband beside her.

One of the most important fields in the history of portrait painting is that in which the artist has devoted his energies to painting his family, his friends, and himself for no other reason than to use his art unrestrained, unguided, and uninfluenced.

And there is another outstanding category: the portraits that have been painted of plain, simple folk—farmers, workmen, peasants—by such painters as Velázquez, Goya, Bellows, Henri, and Andrew Wyeth. This entire phase was a revolt from strictly "social" portraits. It was a deep appreciation of the importance and meaning of *human beings* as such. The artists recorded these people with understanding, compassion, and, occasionally, with an overtone of humor.

The basic appeal of the portrait was stated by Samuel Johnson, who remarked, "I would rather see the portrait of a dog that I know, than all the allegorical paintings they can shew me in the world."

Each sitter's reaction to posing for his portrait is different. But, in spite of a possible unwillingness to devote so much time to it, in spite of an unconscious feeling that he may not be worthy, in spite of a natural fear of what the final painting may look like or what it may reveal him to be, there is still deep down within him a feeling of lasting satisfaction that he should be considered a proper subject for a portrait. This was demonstrated to me in a memorable way during World War II. A small group of artists went one evening a week to the naval hospital in Brooklyn to draw portraits of the patients. These were then photographed and given to the men to send to their relatives and friends. I was working down the line in the fracture ward and, as I moved from bed to bed, I noticed one patient some distance away watching me. When I came to his bed, I asked him if he would like to have me draw his picture. He nodded and I proceeded. When the picture was finished, he again nodded, this time in approval. The following week the nurse took me aside and said that this particular patient had been speechless for six weeks. After he had completed his sitting, he spoke for the first time and had been talking freely ever since. I am sure that a psychiatrist would be able to explain this in detail. All I have are the facts.

One thing is certain: the art of portrait painting will continue through the decades, the centuries, the aeons, as long as man inhabits the earth.

*   *   *

In order to have a proper perspective on the art of portrait painting, we must go back to the earliest relics of picture painting, those found in the caves of France and Spain, dating from fifteen thousand years ago. Their subjects were bison, wild horses, and reindeer. Today in certain tribes in Africa the natives do not want anyone to paint pictures of their cattle, their belief being that in so doing the cattle are being stolen from them. An artist friend of mine who has lived for many years in Guatemala told me that if ever she tries to make a sketch of a native, he will run away in terror, lest his soul be stolen from him.

Portraiture, however, is known to have existed in Egypt over four thousand years ago. Egyptian religious beliefs were its moving force. In Hesire's tomb there is a bas-relief portrait of him, carved on a wooden door about 2700 B.C. It has the typical profile treatment of head, legs, and feet, and the front view of shoulders, body, and arms.

Since each person was believed to have a double or ka which went with him to an afterlife, it was only natural that in the early days effigies of the dead were made in three dimensions, life-size, lifelike, and colored as well. They were literally simulacra.

The paintings in Egypt followed their traditional style for thousands of years. We think of them as being a continuing repetition of the full figure with the heads always in profile.

Not until the Graeco-Roman influence exerted itself did the revolution in their painting take place. It was then revealed to Egyptian artists that the human head could be painted from the front. They were shown that form could best be rendered in two dimensions by the use of light and shade. Thus there began the art of portrait heads, painted realistically in wax and resin colors on panels of wood or linen cloths. They were painted during the sitters' lifetime, were hung in their homes, and, after their death, were inserted into the mummy wrappings, as a covering for the head.

The encaustic technique, which consisted of pigments suspended in hot wax, has proved surprisingly durable. The mummy portrait (pl. 1) from the Fayum district of Upper Egypt dates from the second century A.D. It conforms to a pattern established at that time: the head is turned very slightly from fullface; the light casts a hard, narrow shadow from the nose; high lights are added boldly in the eyes, on the nose and lower lip; form is given the flesh by lights added to flat flesh tones on forehead, cheeks, and upper lip. The same painting formula appears in the second century A.D. in "Portrait of a Boy," also in the Metropolitan. It would appear that the head was intended to be a likeness, since this was of religious importance.

Oddly enough, there is a similarity in this manner of painting a portrait head and that used by the eighteenth-century American artists Joseph Badger and Robert Feke. As a matter of fact, James Peale's portrait of George Washington in the New York Public Library has certain touches, such as the stiff arm and wooden hand, which are more naïve and "primitive" than the details in this mummy portrait.

One noticeable characteristic is the sureness and directness of the brush handling. It suggests that this painting was done by an experienced artist who had undoubtedly developed this technique over the years.

Greece was an important factor in influencing the painters in Italy even as far back as the fifth century B.C. With the decline of the great cities of Athens, Corinth and Olympia in the third and second centuries B.C., this influence was transferred to Alexandria, Rhodes, and Pergamum. It is surprising to learn that Greek painting was important as late as the thirteenth century. During the lifetime of Cimabue (1240 - 1302) the rulers of Florence sent for a group of Greek painters in order to resurrect the art of painting which had almost ceased to exist.

3

Plate 1. EGYPTIAN MUMMY PORTRAIT from Fayum. Second century A.D. Encaustic on wood. Metropolitan Museum of Art, New York, Rogers Fund, 1909

We know from the writings of Pliny that even in the first century A.D. portraits were being painted. The gold-glass miniatures of the third to the sixth centuries A.D. in Italy provide us with significant examples of the almost sophisticated treatment of the face which characterized them. The modeling is more subtle than in the mummy portraits, and the impression of a true likeness is conveyed within a diameter of two inches, more or less.

In China portrait painting is mentioned as early as 1326 B.C. In the sixth century B.C. Confucius uttered a pronouncement to the effect that portraiture of the great should be encouraged, if only to furnish future generations with examples of nobility which might be respected and followed.

Through the centuries the handling of the brush in calligraphy was closely related to the handling of the brush in painting. When we stop to think that the vocabulary of educated Chinese involved the writing of thousands of different characters, it is easy to understand how important was the manipulation of the brush. The artist's skill in writing became an important factor in his painting. Once the stroke was made on the silk, it could not be altered. Lines were not made by control of the brush with the fingers or wrist. The brush was held vertically, and the elbow and even the shoulder controlled its movement. This placed emphasis on complete spontaneity.

Many years ago I had the opportunity of talking to a young Chinese artist about his painting, which was executed in the traditional manner. He described how direct and confident the execution had to be, and what great concentration was required to put on silk (or, in some cases, rice paper) the concept he had in mind. He added that, upon completing a picture, he was in a state of utter exhaustion.

The eleventh-century Sung-dynasty portrait reproduced herewith (pl. 2) is a typical example of this style. The artist's prime concern is with pattern and brushwork. The headdress and robe form the main element. Everywhere line is of prime importance; form is completely subordinated. The features are depicted in line, as are the folds of his garment. The decorative inscription reads: "Chu Kuan, Retired Secretary of the Third Rank of the Department of War. Eighty-eight."

My granddaughter, reflecting her appreciation and sensitive understanding of this type of Chinese painting, once expressed its essence in the following words:

> The delicate whisper of a brush,
> The Tao for mind and body.
> Soft mystery of color,
> Sharp miracle of line.

Of portraits in the Tang dynasty (618 - 907) we have outstanding examples in the scroll of the "Thirteen Emperors" in the collection of the Museum

5

兵部郎中致仕朱貫八十八歳

Plate 2. CHINESE, SUNG DYNASTY. Eleventh century.
Chu Kuan. Color and ink on silk. Yale University
Art Gallery, New Haven, Connecticut, Hobart
and Edward Small Moore Memorial Collection

of Fine Arts in Boston. Although this period was reputedly less sophisticated than the later Sung dynasty, these portraits bear all the characteristics of the finest Chinese painting.

We are inclined to think of Chinese art as continuing century after century without change. A closer look reveals the fact that there was a sharply different point of view between the literati (the scholars who were amateurs) and the painters of the Academy. There were schools that believed in the precise handling of the brush, and there were radical cults that used it in a splashy, unorthodox way, even employing their hands and hair to apply ink and color. (Contemporary artists, please take note!) In these Tang-dynasty paintings, as in some work today, the *method* of painting overshadowed the subject matter.

It may seem peculiarly insensitive to dismiss Chinese painting in a few paragraphs. The purpose of this chapter, however, is not to cover the entire art of a country, but simply to select an illustration which will symbolize the country or the period.

*   *   *

I have always been charmed by the mystery, the repose, the overtones, in Chinese painting. To appreciate and savor its atmosphere fully, one must be equally well acquainted with Chinese poetry, for each painting is a poem. In the poetry, as in the painting, one becomes an intimate part of nature.

When another granddaughter reached the age of six, I sensed certain characteristics in her which seemed in harmony with the feeling one has in contemplating this phase of Chinese art. Here was an opportunity to interpret her personality in terms that were spiritual rather than literal.

In the painting of her, "Deborah, Thinking" (pl. 3), I have endeavored to use the Chinese manner in a free and uninhibited way. It does not purport to be an accurate copy of that style, but it is rather a reflection of their point of view.

*   *   *

In Flanders in the fifteenth century the middle class was asserting itself and had achieved a freedom hitherto unknown. The growth of trade, the wealth of its citizens, had produced a magnificence in architecture, in furnishings, in daily life, that has scarcely been equaled. The guilds had established the arts and crafts as important components of their society. An Englishman, visiting Bruges for the first time, wrote, "By my troth, I heard never of so great plenty as there is, and as for the Duke's court, as for lords, ladies, and gentlewomen, knights, squires, and gentlemen, I heard never of none like it save King Arthur's court."

It was in this environment that Rogier van der Weyden (c. 1400 - 1464)

Plate 3. GORDON C. AYMAR. *Deborah, Thinking*. 1963.
Water color

lived and contributed much to the art of the north, which was to have a great influence all over Europe. "St. Luke Painting the Virgin" (pl. 4) was executed by him about 1440. There are replicas of it in Munich, Leningrad, and Vienna. In order to examine more closely the manner in which it is painted, we are reproducing only a detail. It has been a matter of controversy for years whether this is a self-portrait. The important point, however, is that, regardless of whether Rogier painted himself or used a model, he was attempting to show his concept of St. Luke. This, then, was his image of the person who had the divine privilege of drawing a picture of the Virgin. (Incidentally, it would be more factual to entitle the painting "St. Luke Drawing the Virgin," since he is using a silverpoint pencil on toned paper to make what is presumably a preliminary sketch for the painting.)

Van der Weyden has shown us a sensitive, intelligent, distinguished human being. Actually, he is not looking directly at the Virgin, but to the left and above her, which gives the impression of a mood of contemplation. Perhaps he was suggesting that the Virgin and the baby Jesus existed only in his imagination. After all, he is in a completely contemporary Flemish environment. The painter's mood is conveyed by the slightly self-absorbed stare and the indication of a frown and wrinkles in the forehead, both of which are the result of an expression which is not simply transient. The perfection of the rendering of these details, and that of his eyes and hair, is characteristic of this great master.

There are other things to observe in the painting. Even though this is only a section of the larger painting, the composition in it is impeccable. The dark column is placed directly behind the drawing, and thus forms the one point of strongest contrast, in order to focus attention on this important object. Even the lines of the carving on the column repeat and counter the angle of the pencil. The trees make a light and feathery pattern around his face, and their vertical trunks repeat the lines of columns and castle.

Over the centuries artists have disagreed as to whether or not one should draw directly from nature, or compose and execute a picture from memory. My firm belief is that nature is the true source of beauty; that constant, searching observation is necessary to appreciate this beauty while one is painting and to extract from it the secrets of how it comes into being. This second phase is what transcends the realism of photography and becomes a self-created art. Van der Weyden shows this in every square inch of his painting. Nothing could be more of an accurate representation of nature than certain aspects of St. Luke's face, but nature did not present his robe with such harsh, straight-lined shapes as the artist has painted in the folds of his coat and sleeve. It is these that give the painting character, and prevent the picture from looking oversoft in handling.

The artist's inborn sense of pattern is evident even in the minutely

Plate 4. ROGIER VAN DER WEYDEN. *St. Luke Painting the Virgin* (detail). Courtesy, Museum of Fine Arts, Boston

rendered flowers and grass below the saint's left hand. Just because we may prefer one school of painting, we are not bound to disregard the beauty of another school. We can enjoy the free handling of a Turner landscape, and at the same time admire the meticulous treatment of van der Weyden.

Rogier van der Weyden was born in Tournai, and, since the language spoken there was French, his name was Rogier de la Pasture. When he returned to the city of his birth in 1426, he became apprenticed, according to certain authorities, to Robert Campin. The records show that he was given a banquet, and was made a "master." He had been trained in the art of sculpture in his father's studio, and the title was probably the result of this study. His complete awareness of three dimensions in his painting was undoubtedly due to this original training. Six years later he was made a master again, and the award this time enabled him to sell his pictures to the public and to maintain a studio of his own. By 1435 he had moved to Brussels, where he was known as Rogier van der Weyden, and in that year he was appointed "Town Painter." He had made such a reputation for himself that within a year the announcement was made that no one was to succeed him in this capacity. The city also granted him annually one third of a bolt of cloth. He died in Brussels and was buried in state in the cathedral of St. Gudule. This man was recognized not only as a great artist, but also as a man of rectitude and piety.

* * *

The disparity between eleventh-century China and fifteenth-century Italy is not merely a matter of hundreds of years and thousands of miles. The entire social, religious, and intellectual mores are at different ends of the poles. Yet here is a Florentine artist, Paolo Uccello (1397-1475), whose portrait of "A Young Lady of Fashion" (pl. 5) is concerned primarily with pattern, and whose treatment of form is largely rendered in line as in the Sung-dynasty portraits.

Uccello has reduced nature to a rigid design, reserving what might be termed a likeness for the mathematical relation between the features of the face—a long nose, a small eye and mouth, and a noticeable joining of the chin and jaw. The lady's hair is arranged with great care; her headdress is a jeweled masterpiece. The long, slim neck was something to be envied then, as it appears to be today in the field of fashion. Her facial expression is that of an impenetrable mask. The whole picture suggests the goldsmith's equal interest in each jewel and the stained-glass designer's careful placing of strong patterns.

In those days artists did not have the long routine of a formal education before beginning the practice of art. Uccello was cleaning and polishing Ghiberti's Second Door of the Baptistery when he was only ten years old.

Plate 5. PAOLO UCCELLO. *A Young Lady of Fashion.*
Isabella Stewart Gardner Museum, Boston

He studied sculpture under Ghiberti and executed mosaics as well. It was his absorption with mathematical perspective which caused Vasari to say that Uccello's wife found it difficult to persuade him to sleep at night. Wrapped in its complexities, he would murmur, "Che dolce cosa e la perspettiva!" ("How sweet a thing is perspective!") He had many other interests, birds being one of them; this accounts for his nickname, Uccello (bird). His real name was Paolo di Dono.

Comparing his painting of "A Young Lady of Fashion" with similar portraits of ladies by Domenico Veneziano, Alesso Baldovinetti, and Pollaiuolo, one sees their unswerving adherence to a pictorial formula. Each lady faces in full profile to the left; each head touches or barely misses the top of the picture; each picture is about two and a half heads high; each background is a dark or middle blue, some with almost imperceptible indications of clouds; headdresses, jewelry, and gowns are uniformly elaborate, and modeling is reduced to a minimum. Pollaiuolo's portrait in the Metropolitan Museum indicates the beginning of a more tender approach. Although there is a conspicuous dark line defining the silhouette of head and body, the expression is gentler and there are variations in the flesh tones, notably, a charming pink in the cheeks and color in the ear. The pattern on the sleeve is also less strident.

One of the earliest departures from the profile portrait was painted at the end of the fourteenth century by an unknown Florentine artist. It is a picture of the three Gaddis, each one a head and shoulders, arranged side by side. Taddeo is shown in a three-quarters view; Gaddo, in full face. The profile was reserved for Agnolo.

Another example is found in the group portrait of Giotto, Uccello, Donatello, Massette the mathematician, and Brunelleschi the architect. Their heads all face in different directions, Brunelleschi alone being in profile.

Vasari, with his deep understanding of the problems of an artist, wrote of Uccello, "Never giving himself a moment's breathing-space, he was always struggling to bring off the most difficult and impossible feats in art; thus he was reduced to living in solitude, almost like a savage."

By the latter part of the fifteenth century portrait painting had become an important branch of the fine arts. It was a definite indication of man's changing regard for man. He was no longer a meaningless part of a rigid religious pattern. He had become a highly regarded part of life on this earth. The individual had begun to emerge, and with this new emphasis portraiture began its long and flourishing career. Italy, escaping the fate of the embattled French and English on the one hand and of Constantinople and the Turks on the other, became the center of cultural development and a patron of the arts in a sense and degree hitherto unknown.

* * *

Gentile Bellini (c. 1429 - 1507) was born thirty-two years after Uccello, but use of the profile in portraiture still existed. His "Portrait of a Doge" (pl. 6) is an outstanding example of three great requisites of a fine portrait: the likeness, the interpretation of character, and the expression of these through the language of design.

Bellini has certainly given us the impression of a physical likeness, so that we can be confident that it represents the Doge almost relentlessly. The Doge's character also is clearly written in his features. He was apparently strong-willed, bold, determined, fearless, and in his eye he has the uneasy expression of the potentate who has to keep a sharp watch on the people who surround him and on those with whom he is dealing.

From the point of view of design it is interesting to note the five rigid wrinkles in his forehead. Nature does not do this, but the artist sees in them a rhythm which he wishes to record. The outline of the ear flap of his cap and the cord that ties it under his chin is related to these wrinkles. The curved boundary line of the bulge under his eye repeats the curved line of his cheek in the same way. The textures of fur and embroidery are meticulously rendered.

Here we have an illustration of what strong light and shade can do in modeling form. Bellini could not have given us a sense of such acute realism if he had not used this method of painting.

He was the older half brother of Giovanni Bellini (c. 1430 - 1516). His father, Iacopo, already had established a reputation, and may properly be called the founder of Venetian painting. His sister married the artist Mantegna. With this solid artistic environment, and with a comparable talent, it is not surprising that he held a distinguished position in art. This is testified to by the fact that he was knighted by the Roman emperor when he was forty years old, and ten years later was sent to Constantinople by the authorities to paint the portrait of the sultan Mohammed II, who had asked for the leading portrait painter of Venice. His reputation has been overshadowed by the magnificence of the work of his brother Giovanni, but he can still be regarded as one of the foremost artists of his time.

*   *   *

Having admired from my early youth these portraits of the Italian Renaissance for their strong and simple design and forthright color, naturally I wanted to paint a picture in this manner. However, the costumes of today did not lend themselves to this style of painting. Fortunately, when I saw a beautiful young girl in her choir robe, the picture came into being— "Penrhyn Earle" (pl. 7).

I began at once an intensive study of the profile portraits of Ghirlandajo, Domenico Veneziano, Ercole Roberti, and Antonio Pollaiuolo. This

14

Plate 6. GENTILE BELLINI. *Portrait of a Doge.* © Frick
Collection, New York

Plate 7. GORDON C. AYMAR. *Penrhyn Earle*. 1960. Oil
on Renaissance panel

is one of the rewarding aspects of painting a picture "in the manner of. . . ." Eventually, one comes to feel like an apprentice in the master's workshop. No amount of gallery visits or reading is a valid substitute for this experience.

As I compared the portraits of these masters, it became evident to me that certain similar characteristics appear in many of their paintings. The caps of the men, for instance (from which girls' choir caps are derived), are rendered with little or no light and shade. They form merely a flat pattern which serves to emphasize by contrast the modeling of the features of the face. Another characteristic is the use of robes and garments as *design* areas. They are not painted with photographic realism, but are used as important elements in the decoration of the painting as a whole.

I feel that there is a limit to which it is desirable to follow all the mannerisms of a period. I wish to be free to express myself in my own way. In the painting of Penrhyn Earle I have avoided using the rather hard and precise outline of the silhouetted head which occurs in many of the Italian portraits. It seemed to me that following details of this sort would appear too contrived, and that it would place too much emphasis on the rendering rather than on the spirit of their painting, which is what I was trying to express. As a performing musician throws himself wholeheartedly into the soul of the composer he is interpreting, I try to do the same with any painter who has become my master.

In executing this picture, it seemed appropriate to me to consider the techniques of the Italian painters. While Titian prepared his canvas with a flat coat of tempera before applying his thin oil glazes, I was fortunate in living at a time when a well-nigh indestructible "Renaissance" panel could be especially made for this picture. It was treated with six coats of hand-rubbed gesso. I then applied the thin glazes which, in Titian's paintings, give a richness of color and an almost radiant light.

Incidentally, I have always been concerned about the inept and ignorant restorer's treatment of paintings which employed glazes. These are removed so easily when the restorer attempts to clean a painting, and yet the final and therefore uppermost glazes were the finishing touches of the masters in correcting color and unifying tonal effects. I am sure that many of the restored paintings of the great masters now exhibited in museums would be a shock to the artists who painted them.

* * *

One of the outstanding portraits of the fifteenth century is the familiar "Portrait of Smeralda Bandinelli" (pl. 8), by Sandro Botticelli (1444/5 - 1510). It was one of his early works, painted when he was between twenty-seven and thirty-one years of age. It offers one a constant challenge to understand its hidden beauty.

Plate 8. SANDRO BOTTICELLI. *Portrait of Smeralda Bandi-nelli*. Victoria and Albert Museum, London. Crown Copyright

In spite of many strongly defined elements which tend to compete with one another for attention, the focus is clearly on the head. The lines of the paneling converge toward the face; the harsh, dark wall line is directed toward it; even the small shadow outline in the upper left-hand corner points to the center of the head.

Botticelli was one of the greatest masters of line in all Europe, and here we see how he used the uniformly straight lines of the background as a foil to the curved lines of the figure—those of the head, the hair, the cap, the features, the necklace, the folds of the gown and its braid, and, finally, the hands. While he has designed severe, flat planes for the background, he has rendered the flesh and gown with subtle light and shade. He has invented a reflected light on the left sleeve which enhances the translucent quality of the material. He has not painted the high lights in the eyes (which undoubtedly were there), but has kept the pupils as dark elements without details.

Her expression is that of quiet melancholy, a mood that became one of Botticelli's noticeable characteristics as he grew older. She has the resigned look of a sitter who is patiently watching the artist at work, curious as to his procedures and instinctively making judgments as to his personality.

Botticelli (whose name was Alessandro Filipepi) became a pupil of Fra Filippo Lippi at the age of fourteen or fifteen and was deeply influenced by him, both as an idealist and as a realist.

He achieved fame at an early age, and, when he was still in his thirties, was summoned to Rome to help decorate the Sistine Chapel. His three frescoes there brought him considerable wealth, but he had little regard for money and, not long thereafter, it was gone.

Botticelli received great acclaim from his contemporaries and then sank into relative oblivion. It was not until the nineteenth century that he was "rediscovered." Ruskin, Pater, and Swinburne revived an interest in his work. Rossetti was deeply influenced by him. The portrait of Smeralda Bandinelli was one of his most precious possessions and later became part of the collection of the Victoria and Albert Museum.

To me the secret of Botticelli's stature lies in that rare combination of divergent qualities—the boldness and vigor of his composition and design, which is melded so equitably with the gentle subtlety of his rendering of form.

* * *

I have chosen Memling's "Lady with a Pink" (pl. 9) to reproduce because it represents a departure from this artist's best-known portraits. We think of these generally as a meticulous transferring of nature to two dimensions and the achieving of an indisputable likeness. But there are definite factors in this picture which are not associated with Memling's conventional portraits. In those which show the sitter's hands there is usually the almost mathematically accurate relationship between the size of the hands, arms, and head. In the "Lady with a Pink" this is not so. Her hands are small compared with the size of her head. Instead of being in a natural position, which characterizes so much of his regular portrait work, they are stiff, unreal elements of design. The width of each arm is noticeably undersized. There is an artificiality in the pose of the horizontal right forearm and the protruding left elbow, and an equally artificial framing of the flower in the space between elbow and body. It is mannerisms such as these which probably lead the art historians to classify him as a Flemish "primitive."

The oval head, the high forehead, the small eyes, mouth, and chin, all contribute to the impression of an imaginary character. The face, instead of being that of an individual, has come to represent an ideal type. This treatment suggests the handling of faces in his religious paintings. In all probability he took the above liberties because, in this instance, he may not have been required to make a literal likeness.

Incidentally, I learned from a museum curator that the flower, a pink, was a symbol of status, since it had never existed in Flanders prior to this time. Holbein used it in the portrait of Simon George of Cornwall.

The design, as usual, is of real substance. The arch is repeated in miniature by the artificial shapes of trees. The vertical lines of the pillars are repeated in the lines of the lady's veil. Horizontal lines occur in the table, her arm, the front of her dress, and in the wall, which leads directly toward her face. The necklace holding a jewel ends its V shape exactly at the edge of her dress. This last touch occurs in several of Memling's portraits of ladies.

The color scheme is simple—a graded green-blue sky, warm greenish-brown trees, a red velvet dress. The painters of Flanders were not so concerned with color, as such, as were their Italian contemporaries, who used it not only to represent objects but to satisfy an abstract beauty. The Flemish passion for realism of form outweighed their artists' interest in this quality.

Artists of that day were fortunate in living in an environment and during a period which gave them rare opportunities to produce some of the world's most attractive paintings. The clergy, the nobility, the wealthy, were their patrons. Flanders was flourishing on the weaving of wool which was imported from England.

The Flemish painters, practical, down-to-earth men by nature, developed guilds which required disciplined training for their members—a certain number of years of study with a recognized master, basic specifications for the materials used, and a strict supervision by the heads of the guilds to insure a standard of quality.

I do not wish to elaborate on the details of their craft. Suffice it to say

Plate 9. HANS MEMLING. *Lady with a Pink*. Metropolitan Museum of Art, New York, Jules S. Bache Collection, 1949

that we should be grateful to Leo van Puyvelde for his research as to the mediums they used. First, they applied a smooth white coat of chalk and glue to the wood panels. They used mineral powders for colors where possible. Apparently, egg whites *and* yolks was their binding medium. This was dense enough for a single coat of color and did not require glazes. The oil medium, which they did not use at that time to any extent, was invented years before Van Eyck began to practice. Over fifty references to the use of oil colors have been discovered in various documents of the fourteenth century. There is one reference as early as 1320, and a well-known authority believes that it was discovered in the twelfth century.

Hans Memling (c. 1433 - 1495) was born in or near Mainz in Germany. He moved to Bruges, and in 1480 his name was listed with those of the two hundred and forty-seven richest burghers in that city. By that time he had been able to buy three houses in the section inhabited by artists.

Flanders was filled with artists whose standing has lasted through the centuries—the Van Eycks, the Master of Flémalle, Petrus Christus, Dierik Bouts, Van der Weyden, Van der Goes, Van Cleve, Massys, Gerard David.

Among these, Memling was one of those outstanding artists who did not embrace either of the two extremes of the portraitist—the penetrating and ruthless approach which attempts to reveal the sitter's faults and weaknesses, nor the oversympathetic treatment which spares him and overlooks some of his failings.

* * *

Influenced by my appreciation for the portraitists of this country and period, I painted the picture of Gordon Aymar, Jr. (frontispiece), using the head-and-shoulders cropped closely above and on the sides, but allowing just enough room in front of him to indicate the familiar scene of the pond near his home. The colors are reduced to what might be considered an unnaturally green sky which contrasts with the warm orange lining of his hood. This is one of the advantages of painting form with complete realism. Color may then be used with freedom and without being merely representational. (Incidentally, the size of this painting is 9⅛ x 8⅛.) The restless shapes of the clouds are a foil for the quiet shapes in the rest of the picture. The painting is pure water color on hot-press board. I confess that I used a magnifying glass to paint the detail in the eyes.

* * *

The "Portrait of a Lady" (pl. 10), attributed to Domenico Ghirlandajo (1449 - 1494), was painted at a time when *style* was a pre-eminent factor in Italian art. Ghirlandajo was not merely interested in painting a resem-

Plate 10. Domenico Ghirlandajo (attr. to). *Portrait of a Lady*. Tempora on wood. Courtesy, Sterling and Francine Clark Art Institute, Williamstown, Massachusetts

blance to a person; he was also creating an ornament. (Incidentally, he was one of the first to make ornaments for girls' heads. These were called "garlands"—hence the name "Ghirlandajo.")

The lady's head is part of a bold, yet meticulously executed, pattern. These are characteristics which are seldom found together. The bold design is generally rendered in an equally bold manner, and the meticulous is associated with the serene. Yet nothing could be more carefully rendered than this lady's hair and eyes. In recording the glow of light on her blond hair, the artist has given us the extra quality of beauty of line in each hair. The bold landscape with its curling roads and prominent, dark trees forms diagonals which help to isolate the head.

One of the identifying features of Ghirlandajo's painting is the use of exceedingly small brush strokes to create form, not only in the flesh, but in the details of clothing and landscape.

Domenico Ghirlandajo was a very successful painter at a time when the arts were flourishing in Florence. He was heartily supported by Lorenzo the Magnificent, and by such patrons as the Tornabuoni and Sassetti families, for whom he painted large religious frescoes. He taught Michelangelo for a short time, and served with many other famous artists as an assistant to Botticelli in decorating the Sistine Chapel with outstanding murals. His son, Ridolfo (pl. 43), was trained by his father, and became a distinguished artist in his own right.

*   *   *

I have always been impressed by the courage it must have taken to design a painting like that of the "Portrait of a Lady" (pl. 11) by Lorenzo di Credi. Surrounding her head, which, naturally, is the most important element of a portrait, with the prickly, eye-attracting evergreen trees is an original approach, to say the least. My curiosity led me finally to a book in my own library on early Italian paintings published privately in 1926. Here was a reproduction of this painting when it was in Richard de Wolfe Brixey's collection, with the entire right side of the background a flat dark like that of her dress. Hold your hand over this, and imagine the entire side to be dark. It becomes an entirely different painting. I then found out from the Metropolitan Museum that the picture had been cleaned in 1957. At some time (possibly in the late nineteenth century) a two-inch strip of wood was added on the right side, presumably to place the figure more nearly in the center. Then the dark area was painted over this side of the landscape and also over the lower left-hand corner of the foreground. The picture as here reproduced shows it in its original condition and proportions.

Regardless of these details, the lady (who may possibly be Ginevra d' Amerigo Benci) is lovely to look at. Her necklace repeats the shape of the

24

Plate 11. LORENZO DI CREDI. *Portrait of a Lady* [Ginevra
d'Amerigo Benci?]. Tempora on wood. Metropolitan Museum of Art, New York, Bequest of Richard de Wolfe Brixey, 1943

lower part of her face; the neckline of her dress is well related to the adjacent areas; her diaphanous veil relieves the severity of her dress. The line of the foreground at the lower left-hand corner continues the lines of the fingers of her right hand. Her thumb and forefinger holding the ring meet exactly at the line of the sleeve.

Most Renaissance portraits tend to keep the background far off, but the tall, thin evergreen at the left, which finally points itself carefully into the corner of the picture, is a prominent part of the total composition.

When I went to the Uffizi Gallery some years ago, I was impressed with Di Credi's "Annunciation." It is one of the most sensitive, charming interpretations ever painted. The Virgin's surprise, her wonder, are beautifully expressed, as is the tenderness and concern of the angel. The landscape background is a work of art in itself.

The well-known self-portrait in the National Gallery of Art in Washington is as fine as any portrait of the period. His youthful face is the epitome of an artist's melancholy.

Lorenzo d'Oderigo Credi, more conveniently known as Lorenzo di Credi (1459-1537), was fortunate to be born near Florence at one of the peaks of the great periods of Italian art. He entered Verrocchio's studio when he was about twenty years old, and had the privilege of knowing intimately, among other great artists, Leonardo da Vinci, Botticelli, and Perugino. As he developed, he leaned more and more to the gentleness and feminine grace of Leonardo.

His standing today is nothing compared with that of his friends. He is not even mentioned in many books on Italian Renaissance art. Yet Vasari rated him very highly, and he must have been pre-eminently regarded by his teacher, who designated him in his will to complete his own "Colleoni." He also is known to have done most of the work on Verrocchio's altarpiece of Pistoia.

* * *

"Lady Margaret Butts" (pl. 12) is a typical example of Holbein's painting of people as they are, with a total objectivity which distinguishes him from so many portrait painters. He is making no comments about his sitter; she is speaking for herself. The eyes are not duplicates of each other. He has observed what Renoir believed in—that the secret of nature was her irregularity; that two objects are never identical. The artist has revealed this difference, not from ineptitude in draftsmanship, I am sure, but with a dedication to make each feature as it actually was. Holbein's portrait is not executed with strong chiaroscuro. It is the perfection of handling which makes each feature an almost tangible object. In order to make this third-dimensional quality even more telling, he has kept the dark areas of the

ANNO ÆTATIS SVE LVII

Plate 12. HANS HOLBEIN. *Lady Margaret Butts*. Isabella
Stewart Gardner Museum, Boston

lady's clothing flat and almost without detail. Again, in contrast to this simplicity, he has used infinite detail in the white areas and in the flower.

As a personality, this lady is unforgettable. The strength of character, the self-discipline, are immediately evident. She has the look of an aristocrat with an overtone of almost peasant ruggedness. She is obviously the strong and effective manager of her realm—the realm assigned to the women of that period, within which they were confined. She met her future husband, Princess Mary's physician, while she was serving her as a lady in waiting.

Many years ago the librarian of Windsor Castle showed me the Holbein drawings in the Royal Collection. To be able to examine portfolios of nearly ninety of these great works, to note the difference in execution, the subtlety of color, to spend an entire day in these surroundings, to be able to express my deep admiration for them to one who cared, was a great privilege.

When Holbein made a preliminary sketch for a portrait, he must have put this on paper as quickly as his technique and integrity would allow, so that his distinguished subjects would not be bound to sit any longer than was necessary. The English chargé d'affaires in Flanders arranged for a sitting with Christina of Denmark, Duchess of Milan, and, according to his report, "although he had only the space of three hours, he showed himself a master of the art, for the likeness is quite perfect." The final painting was made in London from this sketch, and was presented to King Henry VIII, who was interested in her as a possible queen. Holbein's portrait of Anne of Cleves, painted for the same purpose, was completed in one week.

He often made notes on these quick sketches—the color of the hair, the eyes, the material of the costumes, and certain intended alterations. His early drawings were done in silverpoint, which cannot be erased. Later he used colored chalks, and the effect was more of an impression and less meticulous in detail. At times he reduced the likeness to a strict outline, and occasionally this was further defined with ink. It is interesting to compare one of his drawings with the final painting and to discover how he strengthened the light and shade and redesigned details in the hair and clothing.

One of the reasons that Holbein's drawings are so satisfying is because they were done spontaneously, without self-consciousness.

Five years after Columbus discovered America, Holbein (Hans the Younger) was born in Augsburg, Germany. It is shocking to realize that this giant among artists died at the age of forty-six, when he was at the peak of his career. His death was probably due to the plague, which was rampant in London in that year. He and his brother Ambrosius moved to Basel at an early age. They had been trained in their art by their father, Hans the Elder, who enjoyed a very definite reputation as a painter.

The work of Hans the Younger is outstanding in many categories. His first recorded work was painted in 1515, when he was eighteen years old.

During the following years he produced in rapid succession religious paintings, witty book illustrations, woodcuts, silverpoint and water colors of animals, illustrated signboards, fashion drawings ("Basel Women's Apparel"), murals, designs for heraldic and religious glass windows, and, above all, masterful portraits. Working in such varied fields must have contributed substantially to his effectiveness in each one of them.

In 1523 he painted three portraits of Erasmus of Rotterdam, who wrote to his friend, Sir Thomas More, urging him to find work in England for his artist friend. Three years later Holbein left for London and was welcomed by Sir Thomas to his home in Chelsea. After having successfully painted More's portrait, he soon became involved with portraits of Masters of the Horse, merchants of the Steelyard, bishops, archbishops, Astronomers Royal, knights, earls, dukes and noble ladies, ambassadors, and, eventually, the Prince of Wales, King Henry VIII, and his wives.

I think that if I were condemned to knowing the works of only one portrait painter, I would probably select Holbein, not necessarily for the paintings as pictures, but because they are the epitome of the art of portraying human beings.

* * *

One of the portrait painters whose talents were well suited to the fashions of his time was Sir Anthony Van Dyck (1599-1641). "Portrait of Beatrix de Cusance, Princesse de Cantecroix" (pl. 13) was painted toward the end of his short life, and is a testimonial to his sensitive appreciation of character. She has all the air of dignity and social confidence of the aristocracy, but the artist has also sensed in her a naïve quality and an air of peace which is not generally associated with this type of person.

He has isolated the head and shoulders, not only by making them the lightest tones in the picture, but he has set them apart by the rectangle formed by the wall and column. The sumptuous detail in the silk and lace of the lady's gown is emphasized by the flat treatment of the dark portion of the dress. The excited lap-dog is a useful part of the composition. The ease and freedom with which Van Dyck was able to create his compositions was due to his innate ability as an illustrator and his training under Rubens, with whose elaborate designs he was in sympathy. The large number of religious paintings which he executed also had a definite influence on his bold treatment of shapes and patterns.

At this time in the artist's career he was overwhelmed with commissions from the entire English court. His practice was to arrange a time for a sitting, to work on this for exactly an hour, to bow his sitter out of the studio, and receive another. His brushes were then cleaned by a servant, and a new palette was prepared. He began a portrait by making a sketch with black

Plate 13. ANTHONY VAN DYCK. *Portrait of Béatrix de
Cusance, Princesse de Cantecroix.* Reproduced by
Gracious Permission of Her Majesty the Queen,
Royal Collection of Paintings in Britain. Copy-
right reserved

and white chalk on gray paper. His assistants then transferred this to the large canvases, and painted the drapery from clothes borrowed from the sitter. Hands, both male and female, were painted from models whom Van Dyck employed. He touched up the drapery and painted the remarkable series of heads which record the noble aspect of so many of these individuals.

The financial aspect of his life is suggested in an account finally paid by Charles I for twenty-three portraits, of which five were of the king and twelve of the queen. It is said that while the king was sitting for him, he asked Van Dyck if he needed money. Van Dyck answered: "Yes, Sire. When an artist keeps open house for his friends and an open purse for his mistresses, it is not long before he comes to the bottom of his money-chest." In spite of this, he left a very substantial fortune.

Van Dyck was born in Antwerp and, at the age of ten, was listed in the Guild of St. Luke. He was a pupil of Hendrik van Balen, and at nineteen became an "independent master" of the guild. While he was still studying with van Balen, he worked for Rubens as an assistant. In those days replicas of portraits were made by assistants so that the client could give them to family and friends, and Van Dyck had an appreciable share in this work.

Toward the end of his life he traveled to Paris to try to persuade Louis XIII to appoint him as the artist to decorate the large room in the Louvre with historical paintings. Unfortunately, he fell ill, but was able to return to his beloved England, where he died at his home in Blackfriars a few weeks later.

* * *

The picture attributed to Juan de Valdés Leal (1622 - 1690) (pl. 14) is surrounded with mystery. Various opinions have been offered as to the name of the Spanish ecclesiastic depicted. He was at one time thought to be St. Bonaventura finishing his life of St. Francis, but I have learned from George Kubler, of the Department of the History of Art at Yale, that he has now been identified as Fray Juan de San Bernardo, who wrote the lives of St. Peter of Alcantara and of Santa Rosalia of Palermo.

The fascinating part of the story is that he is here represented as completing his manuscript during a period of three days after his death. The inscrutable blankness of his expression, the veil drawn over his eyes, his pause in writing while he awaits the divine inner light, all express the legendary story of his soul's being able to carry on after his body ceased to be.

It is worth comparing the present state of this painting with the way it looked when it was in the Cook Collection at Richmond. The London dealer who transferred it to the Yale University Art Gallery had the painting cleaned, with the result that the scroll now reaches the floor. Before cleaning, only one third of the scroll was visible. The total effect then formed a far

Plate 14. JUAN DE VALDÉS LEAL (attr. to). *A Spanish Ecclesiastic*. Yale University Art Gallery, New Haven, Connecticut

better composition than in its present state. The inscription is badly rubbed, but at least it is possible to read that the subject was a Franciscan of the Third Order Regular who served as a familiar in the Inquisition in the seventeenth century.

The tall, slim shape of the painting (it is over six feet high), the thin, stiff figure of the ecclesiastic, both contribute to the feeling of self-discipline and asceticism. The light areas of the feathers on his cap, his face, his collar, hands, and manuscript are particularly well designed.

Valdés Leal was partly Spanish and partly Portuguese. He studied under Antonio del Castillo. He was an ardent, aggressive, and temperamental man, and was a bitter rival of Murillo. The Academy was founded in 1660 in Seville, and he was appointed one of the officers. As so often happens, the rise and fall of a school can be a matter of short duration, and before these two great artists died, Italian painters were invading the land.

* * *

I have chosen to reproduce the "Girl with a Red Hat" (pl. 15) by Jan Vermeer (Jan van der Meer, 1632-1675) because it is a close-up of head and shoulders, rather than one of his interiors, which often represent full-length figures at a distance. In this picture we can examine every brush stroke.

First, let us look at the over-all design. The girl's figure, being on one side, is balanced by the arm, hand, and carved lion's head on the chair back. Lines on the tapestry lead directly to this lion's head. Diagonally from this point, at the upper left-hand corner of the picture, there is a dark area on the tapestry which helps to balance the lion's head. Its restless, curved pattern contrasts with the straight line of the back of the lady's gown, a line which is emphasized by the light-beige detail of the tapestry. Do not think for a moment that any of this design is accidental or was simply a matter of reproducing a transient effect which the artist happened to see.

The color scheme, which at first appears simple, is extremely subtle — the red of the girl's hat is repeated in her lips; her face color is echoed in her hand; her gown stands by itself, with the light and dark areas carefully related. The tapestry background is in contrast with the reds, but even here there are warm reflections from the hat, which reduce what might have been too stringent a contrast. Part of the tapestry color is repeated in the shadow on her face. Each color is conscious of the presence of every other color.

Avoiding the commonplace and the obvious, Vermeer has reserved the lightest lights for her collar and the small lower portion of her cheek. What he is really expressing in the portrait, however, is the dreamy, almost trance-like look in her eyes, but he has painted these in the shadow from her hat, and it is only their high lights, coming from a reflected source of light, that draws them to our attention.

Plate 15. JAN VERMEER. *The Girl with the Red Hat.*
National Gallery of Art, Washington, D.C.,
Andrew Mellon Collection

The lights on the gown are painted in his usual manner. They give the impression of having been applied spontaneously, in a carefree handling. By the boldness of the strokes a contrast is formed with the softly rendered shadows. Perhaps this artist is using our eyes to *create* the crisp glow of light, as the impressionists use our eyes to mix colors.

I have often wondered whether Vermeer did not postpone the final application of *all* his high lights until the last moment. In many of his paintings they form a noticeable pattern. They are all related to one another. Study the placing of the high lights on the girl's eyes, nose, lips, earrings, collar, dress, and on the lions' heads. (Incidentally, these heads appear on this same chair in many of Vermeer's paintings.) He used the chair as a matter of design. Her arm is resting on the back of a chair, which faces outward. If more of it were seen, it would seem to be placed in a rather odd position.

The device of the girl's half-open mouth was often used by this artist. It appears in the "Young Girl with a Flute," the "Woman in Blue Reading a Letter," the "Girl with the Guitar," the "Lady Reading at Her Window," and several others. It imparts not only an air of tranquillity, relaxation, and unselfconsciousness, but also the ingenuous expression of the interrupted moment.

Perhaps it is just as well to admit at this point that Vermeer has been one of my ideals from the time I was a boy. I have studied his work with great care, heartily encouraged by my teachers at the Boston Museum School. I have the feeling that the secret of the satisfying quality of his painting is due to his all-inclusive perception of the beauty of nature in all its phases. His eye has absorbed the intrinsic beauty of light, color, texture, design, and from this, without an error, he himself was able to create nature's beauty. In this particular painting it is within a space of approximately 9 "x 7 ."

A century ago several articles were published on Vermeer. From the time of his death, nearly two hundred years before, no one had paid much attention to his work. Even today only a few facts are known about him. Born in Delft, he lived there inconspicuously all his life. When he was twenty-one, he was admitted to the Painters' Guild of St. Luke. Ten years later he was elected its president, and five years before he died, he was re-elected. He had eleven children, and died with many debts, some of which were settled by giving the creditors his paintings.

* * *

The "Portrait of Colonel Jacobus Van Slyke" (pl. 16) is attributed to Pieter Vanderlyn, who was born in 1687 in Holland but later lived in the outlying country near Kingston, New York. He lived to the ripe age of

Plate 16. PIETER VANDERLYN (attr. to). *Portrait of Colonel Jacobus Van Slyke.* c. 1730. Courtesy, Shelburne Museum, Shelburne, Vermont

ninety-one. This picture was painted about 1730. The colonel later became commanding officer at Schenectady in 1754 and a member of the Assembly in 1750 and 1771.

This picture is interesting as a formal and conventional portrait that is treated in a broad, free manner not generally associated with this type of painting. The artist has used bold brush strokes applied generously in the treatment of the hair and in the modeling of the sleeve.

The pose of the hand within the waistcoat is Napoleonic. The stiff right hand is perhaps the most primitive touch. Oddly enough, it could almost be the hand of a lady in its delicacy of form.

The landscape, which suggests that the subject's home was in the country, is inserted in a completely artificial manner without identifying the area as a window frame.

If we assume that the date of Colonel Van Slyke's birth inscribed in the lower left-hand corner is correct (1704) and that the date ascribed to the painting (1730) is also correct, he would have been twenty-six years old at the time his portrait was painted, although he looks considerably older. He has a rather searching gaze, and appears to be quite self-satisfied.

Pieter Vanderlyn should not be confused with John Vanderlyn, his grandson, who was a more sophisticated artist, born in Kingston around 1775. John's career was far more distinguished, and during its course he painted portraits of four of our Presidents.

*   *   *

Copley's "Portrait of Mrs. John Powell" (pl. 17) gives us an opportunity to drift back into the eighteenth century in Boston, to sense the environment, and to understand the quality of the people. Mrs. Powell was the daughter of the silversmith Jeremiah Dummer. Her brother was Governor William Dummer, her husband was a cavalier of Welsh descent, and her two sons ran a successful business with warehouses on Long Wharf, at a time when trade with the West Indies was flourishing. This gives us a glimpse of the kind of person who was likely to have a portrait painted. Craftsmen, statesmen, merchants were all intermingled.

To me, this is one of Copley's finest portraits. He has used many of his skills in representing this distinguished old lady. Her granddaughter has given us a succinct description of her which will help us to understand what the artist was trying to express. She said, "She was a little woman of sober conversation and strong Presbyterian faith." Copley has shown great ingenuity in making her appear small. This characteristic is revealed by the very large chair in which she is sitting, and by her relatively small figure in such a large area of background.

Plate 17. JOHN SINGLETON COPLEY. *Portrait of Mrs. John Powell.* 1764. Yale University Art Gallery, New Haven, Connecticut, Bequest of Stephen C. Clark, B.A. 1903

The chair is a dull red, which is repeated in the book binding; the background is a very dark brown. This was a much respected color scheme in those days, and harmonized with the beautiful wood paneling and furnishings of that time.

One mystery which I have not been able to solve is the meticulous handling of the subject's face compared with the sketchy, direct, almost careless application of the high lights on the chair. In Copley's portrait of Mrs. Thomas Boylston, the chair is finished in elaborate detail. Could the artist have left this picture of Mrs. Powell unfinished?

Copley once summed up the complete subservience of the artist to his eyes in the following words: "There is a kind of luxury in seeing, as well as there is in eating and drinking; the more we indulge, the less we are to be restrained."

John Singleton Copley (1737 - 1815) was born of Irish parents in Boston. His father died soon after his birth, and his mother supported the family by selling tobacco. Some years later she married Peter Pelham and this sympathetic and understanding stepfather encouraged young John in his efforts to draw and paint. He may have learned his refined English technique from Blackburn, who painted at least eighty portraits of wealthy colonials. It was not long before Copley was launched on his distinguished career. When he was twenty-three years old, he wrote to a friend, saying that he now made as much money as if he were a Correggio or a Raphael.

It is always interesting to know what was involved in the working time needed to produce the great paintings of the past. We are told that Copley generally required at least twenty-five sittings, each one of six hours' duration. It is astonishing to learn that a sitter would devote six consecutive hours to a sitting, and also that Copley's physical strength and mental concentration would not have collapsed long before that. The amount of time contributed by the sitter is testimony to the fact that when these people decided to have portraits painted, they were willing to give this much of themselves.

Nevertheless, Copley became discouraged with the New England attitude toward the fine arts. He complained that they looked upon portrait painting merely as a trade like that of a carpenter, shoemaker, or tailor. His father-in-law was driven out of town after fifteen thousand pounds of his merchandise were thrown overboard in the Boston Tea Party. Copley sailed for London in 1774 and lived there the rest of his life.

He was an outstanding success in England and became the second American painter to be honored by membership in the Royal Academy.

His standing in this country is such that he is today, as he was then, regarded as one of the leading painters of his time. In the show of "One Hundred Colonial Paintings" held at the Boston Museum of Fine Arts in 1930, forty-four of the hundred were Copleys.

* * *

When I selected George Romney's "Lady Hamilton as 'Nature'" (pl. 18) to reproduce, it was primarily as an example of the typical eighteenth-century English "pretty girl" picture. It would almost have qualified for a magazine cover of the 1920's, when magazine cover girls were painted instead of being photographed. Representing her as "Nature" seemed to me to be simply a device for making a romantic conversation piece out of a superficial portrait.

However, when I began to examine the circumstances surrounding the painting of this portrait, I was forced to modify my opinion that it was the ultimate in flattery. In this case the human element was a dominant factor. I had not realized that this was his first encounter with the actress Emma Hart, who, nine years later, married Sir William Hamilton, the British minister at Naples.

Apparently, Romney fell in love with her at first sight, and was inordinately devoted to her during his entire life. He had studied in France and Italy between 1773 and 1775, when neoclassic art was taking over from baroque and rococo. He had become enraptured with the ideal in the human form. He would sit for hours in his studio contemplating plaster casts of antique sculpture. Emma Hart brought this ideal to life. He called her "the most beautiful woman in the world," and, years after he had met her, he wrote to a friend: "At present, and for the greatest part of the summer, I shall be engaged in painting pictures from the divine lady. I cannot give her another epithet, for I think her superior to all womankind."

Romney (1734-1802) painted at least fifteen pictures of this actress, adorned with such names as St. Cecilia, Cassandra, Alope, Circe, et cetera, two of which were done for the Prince of Wales. In addition to the portraits by Romney, she was painted by Madame Vigée-Lebrun and Sir Joshua Reynolds, as well as by numerous Italian painters.

Perhaps part of her success as a model was due to her innate ability to act. Chauncey Tinker, in an essay entitled "Sitter and Portrait,"[2] has an interesting comment to make on certain classifications of people who sit for their portraits. He maintains that children, actors, and courtesans, being free of the restrictions and conventions of society, make subjects which stimulate the artist's imagination, "for they are all compounded of pride and eager at any moment to exhibit themselves. They are without the *mauvaise honte* that makes a person hateful to himself and repellent to the painter. These happy beings delight in dressing up and pretending, for an intoxicating moment, to be something they are not."

Romney's portrait of this actress as "Nature," painted in 1782, records her lovely features, her tender look, her charming mood. Her long hair blows

[2]Chauncey B. Tinker, *Essays in Retrospect* (New Haven: Yale University Press, 1948).

Plate 18. GEORGE ROMNEY. *Lady Hamilton as "Nature."*
1782. © Frick Collection, New York

gracefully out behind her. This line and those of her upper arm and hand are balanced by the opposing angle of her lower arm, the dog's leg, the mountain, the clouds, and the freely rendered branch of leaves over her head. These leaves repeat the soft auburn color of her hair. This, together with the strong, dark-blue sky and pale-red dress make a simple color pattern for the painting. (Incidentally, those who are portrait painters will notice that her teeth would have turned the smile into a grin if the artist had not subdued them to a point where they almost disappear.)

Romney captures in his portraits the ease, grace, and elegance of the eighteenth-century upper class in England.

* * *

We now go from the sophisticated to the naïve. The portrait of "Mrs. Hezekiah Beardsley" (pl. 19) is by an unidentified Connecticut artist. It was painted between 1788 and 1790.

In the manner of the "primitives," the folk artists, and the portrait limners, the dominating interest is in pattern. There is a definite relationship between the weaving and embroidery of that period and the strong and insistent design of the various elements in this painting. The major portion of the picture is busy with these arithmetically rendered items. The lady's arms, hands, and fingers are as unlike human flesh as though they were cut out of wood. Yet they are placed with great care as part of the total design, and the sharp angles of the book, of her waistline, and of the lace just above it are set purposefully to repeat one another. The flowers in her hand come at the crossroads of these various lines. The curve of her elaborate headdress is offset by the opposing curve of the front of her dress. The fringe on the curtain parallels her sleeve, and the other line of the fringe repeats the line of the path outside the window.

The composition of the painting, with very little adjustment, could survive without the introduction of the dog, but again, regardless of whether Mrs. Beardsley wished to include him, he is used to fill up space. The line of his back is not incompatible with the lines in the lady's skirt. The small "rest area" is limited to the wall. Incidentally, it is rather unusual to paint a picture that is almost exactly square (43" x 45"). The execution of her face is as direct and austere as the lady herself.

This entire approach is the reflection of the work of the group of artisans, often self-taught, who painted decorations on velvet and glass, on clipper ships, furniture, and trays. The crafts were an important part of the livelihood of an appreciable percentage of the New England population. There was little distinction between pewterers, braziers, and portrait painters. We are fortunate to have the work of these grass-roots artists, devoid of damaging sophistication and the search for status.

42

* * *

Plate 19. AMERICAN, CONNECTICUT SCHOOL. *Mrs. Heze-
kiah Beardsley*. 1788-1790. Yale University Art
Gallery, New Haven, Connecticut, Gift of Mrs.
E. A. Giddings

Japanese portraiture was most profuse in the color prints of famous courtesans, dancers, and, especially, actors and actresses. A noteworthy example of this is the fact that Katsukawa Shunsho, who was active in the latter part of the eighteenth century, made, over a period of many years, at least sixty portraits of the actor Danjuro.

Later, at the beginning of the nineteenth century, the production of prints became a conscienceless, commercial operation. Japanese artists copied parts of the successful prints of their rivals. It was a highly organized business. An artist would invade the actor's dressing room at rehearsals, make rough action sketches, and depart to complete his designs, after posting a spy in the theater to make notes on final costumes. A group of assistants would put these costumes on his action sketches. Block cutters would cut apart the artist's painting, each working on a section of the final woodcut. These pieces would be strapped together, and the printers would be on their way. Within a few days after the show had opened, runners would be frantically selling the prints on the streets, hoping to outsell those of a rival artist. It is not surprising that this approach was of no benefit to the quality of Japanese prints, which had been works of art through the centuries.

Since portraits of these actors and actresses are familiar to many people, I have chosen a somewhat different type to reproduce. While most of the courtesan-actor pictures are full length, with the accent on pose, pattern, and costume, this picture of "The Actor Otano Oniji III" (pl. 20) focuses on the man himself at some significant point in the play.

It has the splendid, lively design which is characteristic of the work of Toshusai Sharaku, who made this portrait. He was completely apart from the work of his time. With no training whatever he launched himself into the world of art in a spectacular manner. Being an actor in lyrical drama, he had all the inborn feelings of the men in his profession. Instead of restrained, Orientally calm moods, he depicted with frightening vigor the most tense moments of the actor's performance. He defines the faces and hands with lines that are applied spontaneously. They do not pretend to be the refined, decorative elements that were used in the prints of his great contemporaries.

After plunging into this work with the encouragement of Jusaburo, who printed them for him, the artist produced one hundred and forty-five pictures in a period of less then ten months, which averages about one portrait every two days. They were not a popular success and Sharaku left his workshop and was never heard of again. His only known period of working was in 1794 and 1795.

* * *

While the gayer aspects of society captivated the Japanese artists, the more serious side occupied the Americans of the nineteenth century. With

44

Plate 20. TOSHUSAI SHARAKU. *The Actor Otano Oniji III*. Metropolitan Museum of Art, New York, Bequest of Henry L. Phillips, 1940

the growth of whaling and trade across the seas, the important figures in these fields often had their portraits painted. The last time I visited the Mystic Seaport, I asked Edouard Stackpole, the curator, if he had in his collection a portrait of a sailing master with a typical seascape background. He escorted me to the basement storage area and drew out, from scores of other paintings, the "Portrait of Captain James Smith" (pl. 21). He later described the captain in the following words: "He was born in 1800 and died in 1877. He was one of five brothers who took out whaleships from New London. Captain Smith commanded the 'Commodore Perry' in 1825 on his first voyage as a whaling shipmaster. Upon retiring from whaling, he became a well-known master of ships sailing between San Francisco and Honolulu. He enjoyed a reputation of being adept at fisticuffs, and one story has him 'beating the tar' out of a British whaling master in a fight taking place ashore. The lighthouse in the background is New London light."

Captain Smith has the high forehead of an intellectual, the quiet gaze of a man of poise, the nose of an aristocrat, the firm chin of a man of determination and action. It is interesting to compare the composition of this picture with, for example, a Netherlandish portrait which includes a landscape background. The American painter assigns a far greater area to the seascape, while the Netherlandish artist's composition is more compact, with more emphasis on the figure. The drapery is a touch inherited from the English school. The strong wind blows the clouds and ships toward the figure. The captain's features are modeled clearly and distinctly, without resorting to strong light and shade.

The Frick Gallery has given me some notes on the artist, Frederick R. Spencer (1806-1875). He was born in Lennox, New York, and studied at the National Academy, where he learned to paint both portraits and genre scenes. He must have had considerable standing in his time, for he was on the board of directors of the American Academy, and became a full member of the National Academy in 1846. Two years later he returned to upstate New York and died at Wamponville. There are photographs of some forty of his portraits in the Frick Gallery.

*   *   *

One of Renoir's most pleasing portraits is that of the "Girl with Fan" (pl. 22) painted about 1881. I say "pleasing" with confidence, because Renoir himself would not have rejected it. He maintained—and he was often defiant about it—that a picture should be "jolie." He saw nothing that would prevent a painting from being great simply because it was full of happiness.

The composition of this picture is interesting. The fan, the girl's head and hat together, the bouquet of flowers, form roughly circular shapes.

46

Plate 21. FREDERICK R. SPENCER. *Portrait of Captain
James Smith.* 1839. Marine Historical Association,
Mystic Seaport, Mystic, Connecticut

Plate 22. AUGUSTE RENOIR. *Girl with Fan.* c. 1881. Courtesy, Sterling and Francine Clark Art Institute, Williamstown, Massachusetts

The vertical lines on the right side of the background are in direct contrast with the scattered circular shapes, which, with the impressionists' touch, blend one into the other. This blending of important elements is the exact opposite of the classic tradition where the head was isolated in value and color, and was carefully defined in its entirety. The casual, the accidental, the uncontrived, the informal, the unposed, the beauty of the unarranged, were what captivated this school and they were fanatical about it. The girl's hand, for example, looks almost stiff and awkward. With slight readjustments it could have become graceful. Yet Renoir would probably have defended the pose as being more childlike and unstudied. Actually, she now looks as though she were responding to the artist's request, "Hold it just a little higher, dear."

Renoir is inextricably associated with color, and this picture, painted in 1881, is a fine example of this. His color harmonies varied widely through his long career.

The "Girl with Fan" has the auburn hair which he called "adorable." The color is nearly repeated in the handle of the fan. Pinks run through her hat and swirl upward in the flowers until they take on a red tone. The cool colors are reserved for the background and for the girl's dress.

Pierre Auguste Renoir (1841 - 1919) began his career in art by painting pretty pictures à la rococo on porcelain, a factor which may have had a minor, unconscious influence on his later work. He always had a realistic eye on the picture market. He wrote to his dealer, Durand-Ruel, that his showing paintings in the Salon was simply a commercial consideration and did not necessarily imply his wholehearted approval of their position. He added that what he really wanted to do was to paint striking pictures which he could sell at high prices.

He was temperamental, captious, witty, completely involved in his painting, and at times severely critical and hopeless about his work; at other times firmly convinced that he had accomplished something truly great.

*   *   *

While Cézanne's primary interest was not that of portraiture, it would be wrong to omit the contribution of such a distinguished artist simply because he was more successful in landscape and still-life painting.

"The Clockmaker" (pl. 23), undoubtedly a personal friend who was willing to pose, is a fine representation of his style. It was painted between 1895 and 1900, toward the end of his career, when he had gone through the beginnings of impressionism with Pissarro, had been continually rejected by the Salon and the École des Beaux-Arts, had shown sixteen paintings in the impressionists' show in 1877, and had retired to a solitary life to work out his own individual theories on art.

Plate 23. PAUL CÉZANNE. *The Clockmaker*. 1895-1900.
Collection, Solomon R. Guggenheim Museum,
New York

The color scheme of this painting is subtle, beautifully planned, and justifies his contention that he did not "reproduce" nature but "represented" her by equivalents in form and color. All the main shapes are rather heavily outlined to define them as decorative elements. The white shirt focuses attention on this section of the picture. The cool gray-blue of the wall is echoed in the suit, the tie, and the hair. The warm tones of brown-gray of subtle variations are used in the overcoat, the waistcoat, the lower wall, the palette. The pale flesh tones turn to yellowish in the canvas stretcher. Then there are the bold touches of red in the cheeks, ear, neck, and chin, with soft blue-gray halftones added.

I wish I could sit down beside Cézanne and ask him why he distorted the angle of the eyes in relation to each other. Was it to follow the direction of the clockmaker's glance? Did he feel the necessity for a line to oppose the body and lower arms facing in the opposite direction? Or was it due to a certain clumsiness which he identified when he morbidly called himself a "Primitive," stumbling down an untraveled road?

Another version of this portrait is in a private collection, entitled "Homme aux Bras Croisés." The size is identical, the clothing is the same, as is the position of the arms and hands. The main difference is that Cézanne painted this one with the body facing directly forward, and with the head turned very slightly to the left. The palette and canvas stretcher do not appear. The distortion of the eyes is even greater. It is always rewarding to learn that the great artists strove so hard to satisfy themselves. This portrait also is recorded as having been painted between 1895 and 1900.

Cézanne was rigid in his demand for at least one hundred sittings for a portrait. (Vollard's took one hundred and fifteen of three hours each.) When it was finished, Cézanne made the famous comment that at least he was not entirely dissatisfied with the upper part of the shirt front. He had to absorb nature, understand her, digest her, recreate her, and place her on canvas. He said that one could not be too submissive to her, nor too scrupulous. He was like a composer of music who does not simply reproduce the notes of a cuckoo but, instead, expresses its mood, its character, and its environment.

Unable to persuade subjects to sit for these long periods, or unable to afford to pay them, he took photographs for some of his figure paintings, such as "The Bather." This photograph was found not long ago pasted on the back of one of his drawings.

Like so many artists, Cézanne was not acclaimed during his lifetime. After the Group shows of 1874 and 1877, a critic called him "a jackass painting with his tail." (Today painting with one's tail is far more highly regarded!) Whistler had the audacity to say of one of Cézanne's paintings, "If a child had drawn it on his slate, his mother would have whipped him."

51

The life of Paul Cézanne (1839 - 1906) is familiar to so many people that there is no need to go into detail. His banker father's opposition to his becoming an artist, his having an illegitimate son and concealing it from his father, his financial worries and generally uneasy relationship with people, could not have produced a contented, confident, and happy personality. We are fortunate that he was devoted to his art, slow in his work, conscientious in trying to live up to "the art of the museum." It is rather significant that he died from a fever which was caused by his painting a landscape in a downpour of rain.

* * *

It is only natural for Salvador Dali to adopt a mystical, psychological approach when he paints a portrait of his wife. It would not satisfy him, I am sure, simply to represent her in a conventional manner. In the "Portrait of Gala" (pl. 24), painted in 1935, he shows her staring at herself. While she is studying her replica intently, she also appears to be dreaming. Behind her head is Dali's distorted version of Millet's "The Angelus." Gala has become involved with the Millet by sitting upon a wheelbarrow and sack borrowed from "The Angelus."

The design of the "Portrait of Gala" is impeccable; the relation of the large figure to the smaller one, the tying together of the two by the severely rectangular shape of the Millet, the support of the wheel at the corner, the interesting line of the shadow side of the foreground figure—all these features are very satisfying. Depth is also emphasized by the cubelike seat compared with the flat rectangle of "The Angelus," which helps to define the plane of the wall. The line of the subject's forearm as she faces us is completed by the folds in the back of her foreground skirt, and repeated by the line of the seat.

All of the meticulous, shimmering details are made more brilliant by the bareness of the wall. I am sure that the old Flemish painters would have studied his rendering of her hair. The painting is only 12¾" x 10½".

The color is rich and glowing, with the wall a cool yellow with a green shadow, the cube and the far-off skirt a yellow, with warm and cool variation of yellows, browns, reds, and blues. The Millet repeats a series of these colors.

Salvador Dali (1904 -   ) was born in Figueras near Barcelona. When he was seventeen, he enrolled in the Madrid School of Fine Arts, but was expelled three years later for "unruly conduct." He was a conscientious draftsman when in school, and this quality has always remained in his work. In 1928 he met Picasso in Paris, and became completely absorbed in surrealism. During the growth of the movement of abstract painting, he ardently defended the surrealist as an artist who understood subtle tones of light and

Plate 24. SALVADOR DALI. *Portrait of Gala.* 1935. Oil
on wood. Collection, Museum of Modern Art,
New York, Gift of Abby Aldrich Rockefeller

gradations of texture, and could employ them if he wished to paint an abstraction, whereas the abstractionist was not capable of mastering these qualities, nor could he use them without opposing his theory of art.

* * *

"Sing unto him a new song; play skilfully with a loud noise." Whenever I read Psalm 33, I think of Picasso (1881-   ). His songs are continually new; they are skillfully played; and today they are a loud noise.

I remember reading, as far back as 1920, a remark made by Picasso to one of his pupils. He said, "It's time for a change." This could be interpreted in many ways: a conviction that cubism had run its course; a feeling that he wanted to stimulate himself with new objectives; or a look at the market that might exist for paintings with a new flair.

He had already gone through various stages in his painting, from the "Science and Charity," painted when he was fifteen in a late nineteenth-century manner almost reminiscent of Eakins, to the Toulouse-Lautrec-influenced sketchy, poster style of 1901. The Blue Period (pl. 55) of 1904 was quickly replaced by the Pink Period. In 1906 he painted the remarkable portrait "Gertrude Stein" (pl. 56) which might be classified as distorted realism. He then became absorbed by archaic African sculpture. This was followed by the cubist portraits of 1910 and later, in the early twenties, by the clean, almost classical, pencil outline drawings of his men friends. His restless, frantic nature then developed a style that was to be his obsession for many years. The "Self-Portrait" of 1929 combined a well-proportioned flat, silhouette profile with a mad nightmare of open mouth, flashing teeth, wild hair, and scattered eyes.

Picasso has been rather wary in discussing the overtones and inner meanings of some of these paintings. He never submitted completely to a movement. He watched Dada, he followed surrealism, but he always had to be himself. And he carried the skill of executing pictures of his different periods with him through the years. It is difficult to understand how the basic style with which he is generally associated today, and which he employed in the "Three Dancers" in 1925, could have held the interest of this tumultuous, volatile, and versatile personality for as long as forty years.

"Sylvette (Portrait of Mlle D)" (pl. 25) was painted in 1953. A photograph of Picasso in his studio, taken by Liberman, is very revealing in connection with this picture. He is standing, arms folded, staring at the photographer with that penetrating, tense look so often associated with Picasso. On his easel are two monochrome paintings, one of a head-and-shoulders profile of Sylvette; the other, a full face. These are rendered realistically in his early-twentieth-century manner. Behind them, with only a small area

Plate 25. PABLO PICASSO. *Sylvette (Portrait of Mlle D)*.
1953. Courtesy, Art Institute of Chicago, Gift of
Mr. and Mrs. Arnold H. Maremont through the
Kate Maremont Foundation

showing, is the unfinished "Sylvette." Leaning against the wall in the rear is a different version of this portrait.

The color scheme of the one here reproduced is simple—a clear, strong blue (right out of the can) in some of the lower shapes, a warm green across the bottom, reddish-purple in some of the middle areas, and blue-grays in the background and in what may be identified as the head. If we assume that the realistic paintings of the subject are reasonable likenesses, nothing could be farther from expressing, implying, or suggesting her physical resemblance. If these shapes are meant to symbolize any phase of her personality, she is then indistinguishable from the scores of women whom Picasso painted in this manner from 1925 until today.

It is interesting that he chose to paint two portraits of his young son, Paul, in a realistic manner—the first in 1924 as a harlequin; the second in 1925 as Pierrot. Both are handsome and bold in design, but have no connection whatever with the picture-puzzle style of the "Harlequin with Guitar" (1924) and the "Ram's Head" (1925).

* * *

I hope that this condensed picture of portrait painting through the centuries has at least given an impression of the breadth and depth and enduring qualities involved in making it an "eternal art." In all countries with a foundation of culture, during all periods, and in spite of the interruption of wars, political uprisings, disasters, famines, invasions, and the changing standards accompanying them, portrait painting has survived. Trivial motives undoubtedly exist, but they are overemphasized by the average writer. Even in the eighteenth century, which tended toward the fashionable rather than the fundamental, Tischbein, a distinguished painter and an intimate friend of Goethe's, stated his belief that the most important thing for mankind was to learn to know human beings better, and that man had "nothing nobler to cherish and honor than the cultivated, reasoning man." Portrait painting has certainly made its contribution in both these fields.

ACHIEVING A PHYSICAL LIKENESS

PAINTING a portrait involves rendering a likeness of the person—a representation of the outer image and a revelation of the inner spirit. In order to accomplish the first, an artist must be an able draftsman; the second demands a rare degree of perception and the ability to *create* in the visible face the various elements of character which are inherent in the individual.

I have always thought of a likeness, the physical representation, as the degree to which an individual departs from an ideal Greek head. I realize that this is a Western concept, and that such an "ideal head" to a Chinese artist would not be the same. However, since we are primarily concerned with Western art, let us take the head of the "Discus Thrower," by Myron, as our example. The original statue was in bronze and it is known to have been cast between 460 and 450 B.C., at the beginning of the classical period. Perhaps the most noticeable difference between this ideal head and one we would carve today is the Greek characteristic of the nose that runs directly into the forehead without any indentation.

In order to achieve a likeness by indicating individual differences, it is first necessary to know and understand the ideal figure. Mantegna pointed out that for *study* the ideal antique figure was better than the individual, since classic sculpture combined the perfections of nature gathered from many individuals.

Suppose we were to put a plaster cast of a Greek head beside the head of the man who is sitting for his portrait. We discover that the man's nose is longer, his ears stick out more, his mouth is wider, and the lips are narrower than those of the plaster cast. In so far as these differences are recorded in our painting of him, he has become an individual. No other individual will duplicate identically these variations from the Greek head. Think how few people whom you know look so like another person that they are continually mistaken for one another.

In this instance we are discussing form alone. And what infinite variety there is! The skull of an intellectual, together with its features, is one shape; the primitive skull of a brutish character is measurably different. There is the cunning, upturned nose of a child; the slightly arched, angular nose of a distinguished man. There is the Occidental form of an eye and the Oriental form; ears that are tall, thin, angular, standing out from the head, and those that are small, constructed of beautiful, interlocking curves, appearing to be almost set into the skull. (Incidentally, one of my greatest pleasures lies in painting an ear. It is, in itself, an object of fascinating interest in a purely abstract sense. Its form, the subtle rendering of light and shade, are most rewarding to paint. And few comments are made by the sitter about this particular feature.)

To render a satisfying representation of a human head requires intense observation. When one applies this concentration, strange things are sometimes revealed. In three separate instances I have been told by the parents of young children whose portraits I had painted that they were even more of a likeness today than when I painted them two or three years before. In trying to discover the reason for this, I have come to the conclusion that, by a continued examination of the face, certain incipient tendencies in facial structure were discovered and recorded, of which the parents had not been aware. In order not to have the facial form too soft, smooth, and characterless, I have found it necessary to emphasize these vaguely suggested planes.

In another instance, I painted the sixteen-year-old daughter of a friend. On seeing the picture for the first time, her uncle exclaimed that he had no idea that she looked so much like his brother who lived in Europe, whom I had never seen. Here again, it must have been the study of basic head structure that gave this impression.

A true physical likeness, then, represents the features as they are—departures from the ideal head. Caricature carries these departures to an extreme; it actually exaggerates a likeness. The portrait of his mistress by Amedeo Modigliani (pl. 53) illustrates this point. I do not say this in a derogatory sense. The rendering is handsome in design, very bold and satisfying in color, but the actual lines delineating the face, its elongated look, the small, penetrating eyes, the phenomenally long nose, give a distorted impres-

58

sion rather than a photographic record of her features. A nineteenth-century artist, in spite of his constant use of the camera, called it "a one-eyed liar." Through the centuries Chinese artists were taught to record not what they saw, but what they *felt* about what they saw.

But a likeness is not confined to the head alone. We are accustomed to think in these terms, since so many portraits are painted of only the head and shoulders. If a full length is used, the likeness will depend on the relation of the various parts of the body. Haven't you recognized a friend almost a city block away? If you were to hold a ruler at arm's length, the friend would measure perhaps an inch in height (his head being slightly over an eighth of an inch); yet within this minute dimension there is sufficient infor- mation to distinguish him from all the others around him. Not only his proportions but the motions of his body are important factors—how he swings his arms, how he moves his shoulders, and whether his feet point in or out.

The secret of making a true resemblance lies in the artist's eye. There is no sure way to succeed with other methods. An illustration of this is in the paintings of Henri Rousseau, which give the impression of distortions. Yet he is known to have measured the dimensions of his sitters with a ruler, and then to have transferred them to his canvas.

In addition to the need for a likeness to be suggested in three dimensions, there is the important element of color, with hair ranging from black through browns and rust color to a nearly white blond, and skin tones, even in Caucasians, from cool pink to tones of terra cotta and ocher. Within a single face there is an extensive range of color—the rosy cheek, the warmer color toward the end of the nose, the more yellowish temples, the subdued ocher of the neck, the violet tones around the eyelids, the orange or cool red of the ear as the light shines on or through it, and endless subtleties and gradations. Each individual exhibits differences in these variations.

What a pity that someone does not write a "Bible for Artists"! It might start like this: "In the beginning there was form. For without form nothing is or can be. And after form came light, that form might be revealed to the eye as well as to the touch. And with light came color to decorate form. Of these three was forged a union indissoluble."

Quite aside from objective draftsmanship, there is one detail which an artist may find it necessary to watch. An inborn tendency seems to dictate that he paint something of himself into the portrait of his sitter. Many years ago, after World War I, my father-in-law went as commissioner of the Near East Relief to a school for Armenian refugees. In gratitude for his services a young Armenian drew his portrait. It was an excellent likeness, except that my American relative had suddenly become an Armenian!

I remember also that when I was studying in art school, a fellow student, stocky and of Greek descent, drew every model, regardless of what he or she looked like, with an unmistakable overtone of himself. No matter how the instructor pleaded with him to relinquish his own hard and fast concept of a head, no matter how he pointed out that he must obliterate himself and accept what his eyes beheld, he continued his self-portraits.

André Gide once said that art is a collaboration between God and the artist, and the less the artist does, the better.

Perhaps a rather farfetched illustration of this—but one that I definitely noticed as I was walking through the Uffizi Gallery in Florence—was the similarity in certain features of Fra Filippo Lippi's self-portrait in his "Coronation of the Virgin," and the head of the Christ child in his "Madonna and Child with Two Angels." Why should there be a resemblance between an ideal baby's head and that of a man sixty-three years old? Yet the general shape of the skull, the small, round ear, the full, round cheek and jaw, the way the hair fits on the head, and something in the far-off gaze—all these are related, if we allow for the difference in age.

Aside from the matter of likeness, the painting itself is bound to reflect the personality of the artist. Samuel Butler once wrote, "Every man's work, whether it be literature or music or pictures or architecture or anything else, is always a portrait of himself, and the more he tries to conceal himself, the more clearly will his character appear in spite of him." This is as it should be, for the *art* of painting is an integral, inalienable part of the individual.

It may be well at this point to admit that the ability to record a likeness is a gift, separate, distinct, and recognizable. It can be cultivated like other talents, but the gift cannot be brought into existence through education, but only in the mother's womb. This is easy to detect in the paintings of the masters. You *know* that a donor in an altarpiece painted by Robert Campin (pl. 26) is a particular individual.

Horace Walpole appreciated this ability in the work of his contemporary, Thomas Beach. In a letter written from the fashionable resort of Hot Wells he said, "Beach is a painter, whose portraits never require the horrid question of 'Pray, whose is that, Sir?'"

Nearly everyone has a series of characteristic poses which are as natural to him as the color of his hair. Perhaps it is a typical cross-legged position when one is sitting in a chair, or it may be the hands folded one over the other in a resigned pose, or a habit of resting one's chin on the palm of one's hand.

Having observed the sitter's characteristics in form and color, the artist then has the problem of how to render them. If you are working in the manner of van der Weyden (pl. 4), you will record the form of each finger and eyelid with a line, regardless of the incidental effect of light and shade. This artist's attitude, and that of his Flemish contemporaries, must have been that form and its delineation were basic, and that light and shade were trans-

Plate 26. ROBERT CAMPIN. *Triptych (The Campin Altarpiece): The Annunciation with Donors and St. Joseph;* Left Wing: *Donors.* Metropolitan Museum of Art, New York, The Cloister Collection, Purchase

itory and impermanent factors which should not be allowed to minimize at any point the factual, almost statistical nature of the form.

If you intend to paint under the influence of Renoir (pl. 22) or Degas (pl. 69), you will be subordinating form, as rendered by light and shade, in favor of areas of shimmering color whose beauty is their interrelation and over-all pattern.

If your belief is that the ideal is nature's balanced whole, where no element of rendering it is rejected in favor of another, you will be looking at the sitter as Vermeer (pl. 15) did, taking into account what form and color contribute as revealed by light and as subdued by shadow. I know of no other artist who had such an objective understanding of the appearance of nature. Looking at his painting "Mistress and Maid" from a distance, one is conscious of the perfect relation of all its parts. If one studies the head of the Mistress alone from nearby, its marvelous simplification is revealed. The temptation to overemphasize each feature (two eyebrows, two eyes, two ears, two nostrils, two lips) was rejected by Vermeer. Instead of squandering colors, values, and accents in delineating each feature, he *related* all the lights and darks to the lights and darks in the rest of the figure and to those throughout the entire painting. The tendency to overemphasize reflected light is negated. Combined with this ability to see objectively is his feeling for designing such areas as the clothing. Folds in drapery have a sharp character that is pleasing to the eye.

Sir Joshua Reynolds has an interesting and rather typical approach to obtaining a likeness. In his "Twelve Discourses" he says, "Even in portraits, the grace, and, we may add, the likeness, consists more in taking the general air, than in observing the exact similitude of every feature."

Quentin de La Tour had the opposite approach. He believed in recording every detail, and he carried this to the point where he once said that it was necessary even to register the sitter's physical condition from head to foot, so that the observer could know the king's, magistrate's, or priest's state of fatigue.

Painting a perfect resemblance of a person is not necessarily a photographic treatment. Some painters can give a freely rendered impression that is much more characteristic than a photograph might be. Think of the times you have heard someone say, "I'd never recognize you in *that* snapshot." Or, of the more formal studio photographer's picture, "That's not *you!*" It therefore requires infinite perception in selecting the light, the pose, and the expression which will synthesize the sitter's physical characteristics.

* * *

Of all the schools of art through the centuries we can depend upon the Flemish to give us the truest bodily representation of the individual. Their abject devotion to recording nature is unsurpassed. Robert Campin (c. 1385 - c. 1438) is outstanding among these painters. He is also known as the Master of Flémalle and the Master of the Mérode Altarpiece. From this altarpiece we have chosen the left panel, on which the donors are placed (pl. 26).

With a manner that was an integral part of his school he has outlined their heads, and such features as the donors' noses. The modeling in their faces is very subtle. Each wrinkle on their foreheads and each hair of their heads is carefully recorded. One donor is looking through the door of the Virgin's typically fifteenth-century room, and his expression is full of reverence, concern, and curiosity as he watches the mystical Annunciation.

In restoring this part of the triptych, it was discovered through X-ray photographs that the lady's figure (and that of the man in the background) had been added to the original painting. The assumption is that these donors had been married after the altarpiece had been completed.

The painting of her head is different in technique from that of the man. It is even smoother and more refined in treatment. This mode of execution was more pronounced during Campin's later years. The light and shadow of her face is a work of art in itself. The folds of the material around her head and neck are not merely literal representations. They are beautifully designed and rendered with the accent on line rather than on modeling. Her expression is one of thoughtful submission—a fitting mood for a lady of her period.

There are other Flemish characteristics in this painting—the interest in depth and perspective. The viewer's eye is led across the courtyard to the figure standing beside the door, then through the doorway and across the square to the man on horseback and to the beautiful fifteenth-century buildings of what may have been the town of Tournai (Doornik).

Miniatures had been painted for several centuries before Campin was born. His meticulous handling of the brush in the faces of the donors and the exquisite flowers and grass could well be the result of training in this field.

The exactitude with which all the details in the faces are carried out results not only in a physical representation, but a visual record of the strains and stresses which have modeled the faces. In the words of Cowper, "Heaven held his hand, the likeness must be true."

Campin was known to have been recognized as a master painter in Tournai in 1406. He became a citizen of the town four years later, and his workshop was known throughout Flanders. He was elected dean of the Painters' Guild in 1423 and a council member of the town.

* * *

When an artist *draws* a picture of a person, he is involved solely in form. He is not dealing with the confusing complexities of color or even of value. In the portrait of Dürer the Elder (pl. 27) by his son, Albrecht (1471 - 1528),

Plate 27. ALBRECHT DÜRER. *Dürer the Elder, Picture of a Goldsmith*. Albertina, Vienna

the subject appears almost as though he had been drawn from a cast. There is no indication in his cap or jacket that they are any different in tone from his flesh. With this preoccupation with form, it is not surprising that the *individual* is most poignantly recorded. Dürer himself refers to portrait drawings as "counterfeits." On his self-portrait, drawn when he was thirteen, he wrote, "I did this counterfeit of myself from a mirror in the year 1484, when I was still a child."

Dürer used various media for his drawings—brush and ink, pen and ink, charcoal, and silverpoint. The strokes in each case are made in curving lines which help to suggest the shape of the form. When dark areas are required, these curved lines cross one another at suitable angles.

This manner of using line instinctively suggests its use as *decoration*. Notice how the rendering of Dürer the Elder's hair has become not only a detailed representation of each hair, but a design as well. This is a very important characteristic, and it is a simple step from a drawing of this kind to the engravings with which Dürer is so closely associated.

Dürer's father was originally Hungarian, and had studied extensively with the great Flemish artists. He came to Nuremberg in 1455 and worked in the shop of Holper, the goldsmith. He later acquired the title of "master" and officially became a citizen of the town.

Toward the end of his distinguished career Albrecht planned to write a series of books for students. Part of this project consisted of a "Doctrine of Proportion," but he succeeded in finishing only one of the planned four books on this subject. He felt that many artists of his day were mainly craftsmen, uneducated in matters of scientific study. In the preface to the "Doctrine of Proportion" Camerarius, director of the school at Nuremberg, says, "We admire Albrecht as the most zealous upholder of purity and good morals. . . ." He then describes Dürer's remarkable methods: "What shall I say about the firmness and sureness of his hand? One could almost swear that he had used rule and compass for what he had drawn just with the brush. He sometimes began a drawing of a composition or of a body in different places, wide apart, which yet, when he came to connect them, united so perfectly that nothing more coherent could be imagined."

Dürer was a rare combination of a craftsman and an essentially creative artist of endless fertility. His fame was firmly established during his lifetime, not only in Germany and Flanders, but also in Italy. He was much respected by Raphael, who exchanged works with him, which, he said, enabled him to "shew his hand."

* * *

When Frans Hals (1580? - 1666), who obviously enjoyed painting rogues, wastrels, and boorish characters, received a commission to paint middle-class burghers, he must have had to discipline himself to represent them in sober mien and with an assumed dignity. "Mevrouw Bodolphe" (pl. 28) was apparently one of those who could afford a portrait. At that time a good portrait sold for about sixty florins. It cost half again as much to buy an ox. From what Hals has told us through the structure of this subject's face, she would appear to have come from peasant stock. She has the hard, relentless look which is not transient, but is the result of an inborn attitude toward her fellow man. There is an overtone almost of scorn in her glance. We can feel confident that this was an accurate physical resemblance as well as a study of character.

The painting is not done in the splashy style which is associated with the latter part of the artist's career. It is carefully rendered, and there is little indication of the bravura of brush handling which is his most typical characteristic. He has even recorded the slight distortion in her eyes, and this effect was undoubtedly not the result of carelessness.

He has subdued the background, the dress, and the details of the chair so that the light areas are reserved for her face, hands, ruff, cap, and gloves. The three high lights on the chair add interest to the pattern of the lights.

The casual gallery observer who is not a trained artist would assume that the painting was an almost photographic representation of what actually existed, and would probably respect the artist for executing it so well. An artist, when studying it, would realize immediately that Hals had *understood* the appearances of nature so well that he could create a meaningful, well-organized painting which would qualify as a work of art.

Hals led the uncertain life of an artist whose commissions depended on the whim of fashion. His work was never so popular as we might suppose. When he was sixty years old, he was no longer fashionable; in another five years he was neglected. His financial difficulties finally necessitated his applying to the municipal almshouse for help. Besides his poverty, he suffered from such devastating problems as having a half-witted child who was committed to the almshouse and a fifteen-year-old daughter who was sent there because of her sins. How a man with this tragic background could reflect the gaiety and coarse enjoyment of his models is beyond comprehension.

* * *

Frans Hals painted "Mevrouw Bodolphe" (pl. 28) with firmness and care, but if we are to examine a likeness rendered with utter devotion to "finish," it should be the "Portrait of a Young Girl" (pl. 29), by Pieter Dubordieu (1609/10-1678). This degree of meticulous craftsmanship is well suited to the face of youth, with its smoothness and delicacy. Dubordieu was bent on making a facsimile of the jewelry and embroidery, as much as he was in rendering the girl's head as a living object. His understanding of the subtlety of light and shade on the face is remarkable. Each feature is an achievement

66

Plate 28. FRANS HALS. *Mevrouw Bodolphe*. Yale University Art Gallery, New Haven, Connecticut, Bequest of Stephen C. Clark

Plate 29. PIETER DUBORDIEU. *Portrait of a Young Girl.*
c. 1635. Courtesy, Art Institute of Chicago, Wilson
L. Mead Fund

in itself, but it is also perfect in its relation to the whole head. The light reflected from the collar into the shadow on her jaw is restrained and correctly adjusted to the full light on the rest of her face. The color scheme is very subdued, and the only touches to relieve it are the dull green of the belt and sleeves, the warm red in the flowers of the embroidery, and the gold of the necklace.

Dubordieu was born in Lille-Bouchard in France and died in Leyden, Holland. Little is known about his life, but he appears to have been trained in the Franco-Flemish tradition. Beginning in his early twenties, he was active as a portrait painter in Leyden and Amsterdam, where he came under the influence of the early work of Rembrandt.

*   *   *

Sometimes members of the family can be a real help in entertaining a young sitter while he is posing. When his son was posing for me, the father of Charles C. Hickox decided to sit in the back of the room and read one of his son's favorite books aloud (pl. 30). This created the quiet, thoughtful mood which I have tried to capture in the son's portrait. He is wearing a plain, dark-brown leather jacket, which had a texture that was interesting to render. The pale-buff lining adds two decorative stripes to the total design; the zipper provides a waving line which is echoed by the edge of the dark-blue flannel shirt. These curves are in keeping with the lines of his blond hair.

The farm buildings not only suggest his environment, but were worth while to include because of their design. Incidentally, since I try to avoid the use of any tempora in my clear water-color paintings, I was amused by the challenge offered by the infinitesimal white boards of the fence in the distant background, which I left as plain, untouched, white paper.

The color of the sky is a dark blue, darker and warmer at the top of the picture. The subject's blue eyes pick up some of this color. Here again, the high light is the paper showing through.

*   *   *

"Don Juan Antonio Cuervo" (pl. 31) was director of the Royal Academy of San Fernando. Goya painted this portrait of his friend in 1819. Cuervo was trained in neoclassical architecture and is shown here with one of the plans for the church of St. James in Madrid.

Undoubtedly, the stiff, erect pose was characteristic of a man accustomed to command. This demonstrates what an important factor bodily attitude is in making a physical likeness. His facial expression is determined, yet there is still a suggestion of sensitivity. A paradoxical contrast exists

Plate 30. GORDON C. AYMAR. *Charles C. Hickox*. 1948.
Water color. Collection of Mr. and Mrs. Charles
V. Hickox

Plate 31. FRANCISCO DE GOYA Y LUCIENTES. *Portrait of
Don Juan Antonio Cuervo.* 1819. Cleveland Mu-
seum of Art, Cleveland, Ohio, Mr. and Mrs.
William H. Marlatt Fund

between the luxuriously ornamented coat and the casual look of the uncombed hair. In this picture Goya refutes, to a certain extent, his statement that he never saw details such as the number of buttons on a man's coat. The complicated braid is rendered more sharply and with more emphasis than the man's features.

It was Goya's practice to try to complete a portrait in the course of one day. His sitters complained about his rigorous demand that they hold the pose for so long a period. They said that he worked in silence with complete absorption.

His extraordinary ability to invent all kinds of imaginative characters and scenes with complete abandon was undoubtedly a help in his approach to a physical likeness. He sensed these distortions in the human face instinctively, as we can see so well in his portraits of "The Family of Charles IV" and "King Ferdinand VII."

He rejected the use of "lines" and said that he saw only forms in light and forms in shadow; things that protruded and things that receded; planes in the foreground and those at a distance. His masters were Velázquez, Rembrandt, and nature—a really substantial triumvirate.

Francisco de Goya y Lucientes (1746-1828) at the age of fourteen became an apprentice in the studio of Luzán. After a few years he was able to take a trip to Italy to study the great masters in the country whose art had been far more outstanding than that of Spain. When he returned, he studied etching and particularly aquatint, a process in which tones are bitten into the metal by acid. Goya, like Hogarth, used his paints to preach against evil, and many pictures were painted simply to record fantastic nightmares.

His brother-in-law, the artist Bayeu, arranged for him to paint cartoons for Madrid's Royal Tapestry Works. Some of these, such as "The Parasol," have great charm and are far more idealistic than most of his later work. He was appointed court painter to Charles IV at the age of thirty-three. Toward the end of his life, having gone through the tragedies of the Napoleonic invasion, he retreated to Bordeaux, where he died.

Delacroix paid him the high compliment of describing an ideal style of painting as a combination of Michelangelo and Goya.

* * *

When Jacques Louis David (1748-1825) painted a portrait, one may be reasonably sure of the resemblance to the sitter. His absorption in classical art, not only in its ideals but in its subject matter, made him a meticulous craftsman and a conscientious artist. "Portrait of Emmanuel Joseph Sieyès" (pl. 32) was painted in Brussels in 1817 when David was sixty-five years old. I must confess that the sitter does not appear to be sixty-nine, as is indicated in the lettering at the top of the picture. However, the proportions of his

EMM. JOS. SIEYES.   ÆTATIS SUÆ 69.

Plate 32. JACQUES LOUIS DAVID. *Portait of Emmanuel
Joseph Sieyès*. 1817. Fogg Museum of Art, Harvard University, Cambridge, Massachusetts

face, the careful rendering of form by traditional light and shade, the expression in and around his eyes, make it easy to believe that this is exactly what his sitter looked like.

The eyes, in particular, not only are recorded in form and color, but there is an almost imperceptible squint, especially in his right eye, that suggests that while he was posing in the strong studio light and had to look directly at the artist, his expression was as David represented it. He has not only painted his basic appearance but this transitory expression as well.

Notice how the artist has been aware of the light reflected from Sieyès' collar into the shadow on his cheek and chin. This kind of light always is present on classical sculpture, whether in marble or on a plaster cast. The modeling of his coat is painted with as much care as his hands or face, but it is properly subdued by painting the lights and darks with little contrast. The hands are beautifully drawn, and there is a consciousness of anatomical form in every finger. The flat background, free from detail, serves to emphasize the modeling of the face. This unbelievably scrupulous examination and ability to render infinitesimal details in a face is very evident in his portrait of his uncle, Pierre Desmaisons, now in the collection of the Albright-Knox Art Gallery in Buffalo. It enables us not only to recognize the physical resemblance, but gives us a clue to the sitter's thoughts.

David, whose family were concerned with architecture and building, studied with Vien and Boucher; when he was only twenty-six years old, he won the Prix de Rome. His six-year stay there gave him the opportunity of studying classical art, which resulted in his allegiance to this style.

He became involved in politics, and was a member of the committee which sentenced Louis XVI to death. However, when the revolution was over, he became Napoleon's official artist and painted a number of portraits of him. With his newly acquired power he founded the Institute of France to replace the Academy of Louis XIV. One division of the institute was the Academy of Fine Arts, whose domination of nineteenth-century art was formidable. The freedom of an artist to choose his subject matter and the treatment of it was forced to disappear. The paintings of its members were limited to classical myths, and color was subordinated to draftsmanship.

* * *

Obtaining a likeness of Lucy Brooke (pl. 33) was a matter of recording her characteristic, straight, short hair; the burgeoning structure of her face as suggested by the formation of her chin and jaw; her beautiful, blue eyes; and the interesting shapes and planes of her lips.

Sittings were no problem, as her parents lived not far from my studio. Lucy was a good friend of my grandchildren, and I had often been in her house and enjoyed the beautiful view across the marshes and a large pond.

Plate 33. GORDON C. AYMAR. *Lucy Brooke.* 1961. Water
    color. Collection of Mr. and Mrs. Joel Brooke

Together we selected an attractive dress (this is one of my favorites) and a chair which was in harmony with the curves of her head, skirt, and collar. Opposing these curves are the straight lines of the braid across her dress and those of the chair arm, landscape, and book. Her partly opened mouth suggests a relaxed frame of mind, due, perhaps, to working with a friend.

When I showed her the finished painting, she asked me to turn it upside down, which I did, wondering whether she was instinctively an artist and wanted to examine it as an abstract design. No, she wanted to see the illustrations in the book!

* * *

Some paintings are likenesses of types rather than of individuals. While "L'Artiste" (pl. 34) may have been painted of one of Daumier's friends (it is not believed to be a self-portrait), it is more of an impression of an artist at work than a likeness of a particular person.

Through his gift of caricature Honoré Daumier (1808-1879) was able to capture that moment when the artist is pausing to examine what he has done. His mood is one of self-criticism. There is an overtone of energy in the manner in which the figure and clothing are rendered. This man is no meticulous miniature painter. When the brush touches the canvas, his intentions are forcefully expressed. The scrubby clothing and tousled hair are indicative of the person who is totally absorbed in his craft.

Daumier did not wish to use the common practice of posing his model in full light. What had to be expressed was revealed in broad forms and shadow. The figure comes alive with the sharp touches of light on the head and jacket. The wiggly line on the edge of the coat, painted in a matter of seconds, is characteristic of Daumier, and similar lines appear in many of his other pictures.

This is not a large painting (13⅞" x 10⅝"), and obviously it had no pretensions of being an imposing work of art. Daumier was captivated by the effect of light and shadow, and merely wished to record this evanescent moment.

A word-portrait of Daumier might be a "tossed salad" of the many adjectives which have been used to describe him—original, fertile, abnormally violent, immoderate, ardent, lavish, satirical, witty, cynical, brutal.

An etched portrait of him by Delteil shows the hard, penetrating look of his eyes, the determined lines and forms of his forehead, the tightly pursed mouth.

Daumier's ability as a caricaturist was inborn. At the age of seven he began to draw pictures of people, emphasizing their personal peculiarities. The Louvre soon became his study hall, with emphasis first on the antique

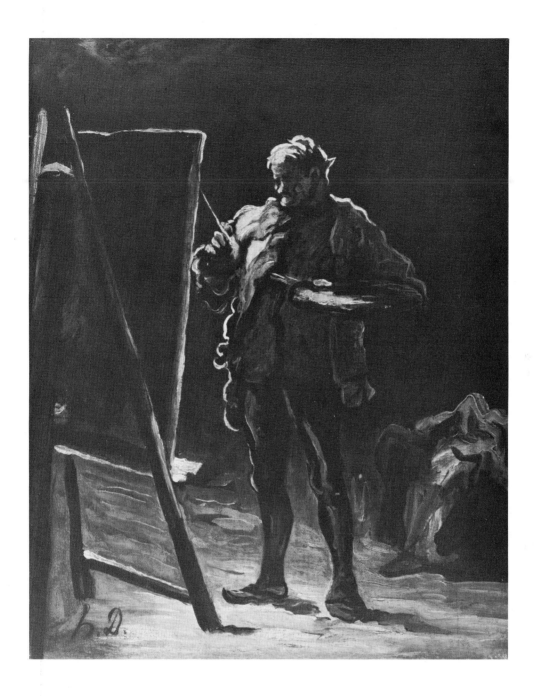

Plate 34. HONORÉ DAUMIER. *L'Artiste.* Courtesy, Sterling and Francine Clark Art Institute, Williamstown, Massachusetts

and later on Flemish and Dutch painting. At Boudin's Academy he specialized in anatomy, a proclivity which was to serve him throughout his career.

If it had not been for the flourishing medium of lithography, he would probably not have been able to survive. When this artist was twenty-four, "Gargantua," which ridiculed Louis Philippe and his regime, caused such a stir that Daumier was imprisoned for six months. According to a letter written to a friend, he did four times as much work in prison as when he had been living at home.

The method he used to execute lithographed portraits showed an unusually conscientious approach to commercial work. The figures were first modeled in clay *from memory*, and then the lithograph was drawn from this sculptured form.

In Delteil's book on Daumier are reproduced 3,958 of his lithographs, a remarkable record of productivity. In 1860 he left *Le Charivari*, the journal for which he had done so many illustrations, in order to devote more time to painting; but four years later he returned, apparently convinced that lithography was not only a means of earning a living, but his prime métier as well.

Toward the end of his life destitution descended upon him. Corot tactfully gave him a little cottage in Valmondois, and there he lived in peace, on congenial terms with the country people, whom he loved and respected. Total blindness finally overtook him, the greatest burden which an artist can have.

* * *

Is the portrait of "Madame Boreau" (pl. 35) a physical likeness or is it not? Who can say? Gustave Courbet (1819 - 1877) was certainly an outstanding realist, completely involved in nature. But there is something masquelike in his rendering of this subject's face. It has become an assemblage of features, rather than a portrayal of a particular person. This impression apparently was conveyed also to a grandson of mine who, upon seeing Courbet's painting, spontaneously remarked, "He hasn't said much about the face."

This effect could not have been the result of the artist's boredom at having to paint the lady's portrait. As a matter of fact, he painted four quite different pictures of her.

The color scheme he has used is typical of the dark harmonies of the period. The color is mainly confined to her yellowish complexion and the touches of pink and yellow in the sunset and the flowers. A mild, subdued contrast is added in the dull green of the leaves. One important part of the design is the orangey tone of her shoulder as seen through the black lace, which is repeated by the color of her glove. This shoulder triangle points to the bouquet, as do her arm and hand and the lines at the top of her dress.

78

Plate 35. GUSTAVE COURBET. *Madame Boreau.* 1863.
Cleveland Museum of Art, Cleveland, Ohio,
Leonard C. Hanna Jr. Collection

Courbet was self-taught and despised the academies. He refused to paint in the approved style of his day, which dealt with the visionary, the romantic, and the ideal. His forthright declaration that it was better to paint a dunghill than to ignore nature appealed to the younger artists, as did his statements that he could not paint an angel because he had never seen one, and that an *abstract* object, which did not exist, did not belong in painting.

When his pictures were rejected at the Paris Exposition of 1855, he showed them in an old wooden shed and circulated pamphlets containing his belief in naturalism.

He was a bold and bitter Socialist, and his paintings of peasants were done as much to protest against the intellectuals and dilettantes as they were to give himself artistically stimulating subject matter.

These political convictions caused him to join the Commune of 1871, and he was assigned to oversee the destruction of Napoleon's column in the Place Vendôme. A few years after this, he suffered imprisonment and was heavily fined. Upon his release from solitary confinement in a cell crawling with vermin, he retreated to Switzerland and died there seven years later.

His influence on many of the painters of his day was notable, and Thomas Eakins during his trip to Paris was much impressed with Courbet's earthy approach. An international respect for his painting and for his reversion to the simple, the unaffected, and the natural increased toward the end of his life.

* * *

The "Portrait of the Artist" (pl. 36) by John La Farge (1835 - 1910) shows this artist's complete understanding that a likeness is not necessarily a matter of recording each feature in detail. He knew that the full-length silhouette revealed many individual characteristics—the person's height, as charted by the relation of the size of the head to the total body; his weight, by the thickness of the figure; the normal attitude of his feet, knees, pelvis, shoulders, head, and hands.

La Farge, in painting this picture, was primarily interested in the submergence of the figure in shadow. He had become absorbed in the effects of light through his designs for stained-glass windows, and this may have influenced him. Having established the treatment of the figure, he then designed the curvilinear landscape in which the path swings gracefully around, ending behind the subject's head. The rock on the left side is related to the curve of his back; the line of the hill follows the angle of his hat and, by passing in line with his head, helps to draw one's eye to this focal point.

The reproduction of this picture gives the impression that it is of considerable size, due to the proportions of the figure, but it is actually only $16'' \times 11\frac{1}{2}''$. From the inscription at the bottom we learn that it was painted in a matter of two days, October 26 and 27, 1859.

Plate 36. JOHN LA FARGE. *Portrait of the Artist.* 1859.
Oil on wood. Metropolitan Museum of Art, New
York, Samuel D. Lee Fund

La Farge was practically self-taught except for a few weeks in the studio of Couture in Paris and a short time working with William Morris Hunt on his return to the United States. He soon devoted his energies to the complicated and difficult vocation of mural painting, and in this field he became what might be considered the first outstanding artist in this country. He was a born intellectual, and he studied, wrote, and lectured. His respect for the work of the great masters of the past guided him in the style with which his wall decorations were painted. During his long, active life he painted murals for churches in Boston and New York, and for public buildings such as the Library of Congress, the capitol building in St. Paul, and Bowdoin College.

* * *

It is possible also to suggest the likeness of young children in a full-length figure. It is the characteristic pose, the relation of the size of the head to the body, which determines this.

John Irwin III (pl. 37) was standing on rough ground looking across the valley toward a ridge. The sketch which I made for this portrait indicates that the figure and the likeness were well advanced at this point, but the foliage and the clouds were completely redesigned in the final version.

* * *

Nothing could be farther apart as far as "likeness" is concerned than Eakins' "Portrait of Mrs. Edith Mahon" (pl. 39) and the Renoir "Mother and Children" (pl. 38). Mrs. Mahon is a living human being; she is an individual and there is no one else like her on earth. Renoir's "Mother and Children" are types, symbols, idealizations; they are an artist's dreamlike impression of what these types might appear to be.

This does not imply that the Eakins is superior to the Renoir, and it may seem unfair to make this comparison. The fact that Renoir gave his picture the all-inclusive title of "Mother and Children" would suggest that he was aiming at a symbol and was not interested in being specific about each one's individual differences.

What method does Renoir use for achieving his goal? First of all, form is completely subordinated to vibrant color. There is an almost total absence of light and shade. His interest is in the "prettiness" of the costumes and the gentle, innocent mood of his subjects. This somewhat sentimental and romantic feeling may have been an unconscious reflection of his early enthusiasm for Boucher and Watteau, not in their artistic execution, but in their concern for the ideal, the fanciful.

The colors are rather cool—the cool pink of the doll's skirt, the pink cheeks, ears, and lips of all three models. The mother's dark-blue coat is the only thing that holds the pale tones together. In this painting in particular,

82

Plate 37. GORDON C. AYMAR. *John Irwin III*. 1959.
Water color. Collection of Mr. and Mrs. John N.
Irwin II

Plate 38. AUGUSTE RENOIR. *Mother and Children.* ©
Frick Collection, New York

and in several others, the artist uses his own favorite cliche of the pale auburn-blond hair and the dark, dark eyes. This apparently was his ideal of feminine beauty. Fortunately, in this painting he was not influenced by his admiration for the distressingly overbuxom bodies which dominated some of his later paintings.

As early as 1868 he had begun to paint landscapes with his friend Monet. In that year he succeeded in showing a portrait at the Salon. The first exhibition of the impressionists took place in 1874. It was about this time that Renoir, whose work had not been widely accepted and who was living in poverty, painted the "Mother and Children." Before this he had been influenced by the stronger, darker, more traditional style of Monet and Courbet. Applying the luminous palettes of his fellow artists Pissarro, Monet, and Sisley to the rendering of the figure, he began a new trend which, in his case, was to last for about seven years. Then, in the fall of 1881, he went to Naples and, strangely enough, became a great admirer of Raphael. Perhaps it was this master's idealizing and "beautifying" of his characters which appealed to him, because Raphael's composition, color, draftsmanship, and formality were directly the opposite of Renoir's.

* * *

Everything that Thomas Eakins (1844-1916) painted conveyed his genuine belief that the world around him was the proper source from which to draw his subject matter—cello players, actresses, prize fighters, singers, hunters, oarsmen, wrestlers, surgeons, chess players. Nature provided all that he wanted, and nothing that was contrived appealed to him.

His portraits are uniformly impressive in two respects—their preoccupation with the dramatic quality of light and shadow and an almost alarming revelation of an unselfconscious mood in his sitters. These people whom he paints are themselves, relaxed, thinking their own thoughts. None of them reflects the customary awareness of the slightly embarrassing situation of having to pose.

In the "Portrait of Mrs. Edith Mahon" (pl. 39), the English pianist, Eakins has shown his straightforward, uncompromising, psychologically penetrating study of personality. She was a friend of the Eakins and the portrait was apparently a gift to her, according to the inscription on the back of the canvas. Mrs. Eakins described her as dignified, short, and possessed of a pleasant appearance. She also says that, although Mrs. Mahon never discussed it, she had experienced much sorrow. This is evident in her expression.

Eakins was mainly concerned with writing the biography of her face. The picture has none of the elaborate composition of a pretentious portrait. The head is about life-size, so that we can see clearly that he was trying to

Plate 39. THOMAS EAKINS. *Portrait of Mrs. Edith Mahon.*
Smith College Museum of Art, Northampton,
Massachusetts

Plate 40. GORDON C. AYMAR. *Raymond Rubicam*. 1959.
Oil on canvas. Collection of Raymond Rubicam

make each feature speak for itself—the relic of a frown, the slightly distracted left eye, the sad mouth. The strong light and shade serve to define every plane in her face. The bright high lights in her eyes even suggest the presence of moisture. The fact that certain strokes of the brush are visible in her dress and on parts of her face does not mean that he painted her likeness in a broad, free manner. Actually, the painting of her eyes and other details of her features required extreme precision.

While an Eakins painting is realistic, he cannot be called a traditional classicist. His whole point of view is earthy, direct, strictly American. He graduated with honors from high school in Philadelphia, and then attended the Pennsylvania Academy Of The Fine Arts. As a young student at the École des Beaux-Arts in Paris, he worked under Gérôme, whom he admired for his carefully rendered paintings. Leaving for Spain after three meaningful years, he devoted his time to studying such masters as Ribera, Rembrandt, and Velázquez.

Due to his unswerving desire to tell the truth in his portraits, many of them were rejected and left in his studio. His well-known picture of the Gross Clinic was refused by the jury of the Centennial Exposition, but it was finally acquired by Jefferson Medical College, who had commissioned it. Throughout Eakins' life he remained true to his artistic beliefs, and never gave in to current criticism. His stature has grown perceptibly since his death, and today he is represented in museums abroad as well as in those throughout the United States.

*   *   *

Raymond Rubicam (pl. 40) has an intense, penetrating mind, and his vigor and determination are expressed in the sharp lines in his face and the over-all sculptured form of it. To make his likeness come alive, it was necessary for me to accent certain points: his dark eyes are slightly tilted, and are the center of attraction; a single, strong high light was reserved to emphasize them. His nose is clearly defined, and his firmly modeled chin reveals his strength. The wrinkles between his eyebrows are the result of concentration over the years.

When I asked Mr. Rubicam what his main interests were, he answered without a moment's hestitation, "Books." There are many ways in which a sitter can be related to books in a picture—he can read them, hold them, or sit in front of them. The idea came to me that, while the ordinary bookshelf is rather dull and monotonous, it should be possible to treat the book covers as a somewhat modern color pattern, which would, presumably, look well in his contemporary house in Arizona. The varying reds, blues, golds, and browns act as a strong background without detracting from the focus on his head. The colors of his skin and hair are also in harmony with these colors, as are the blues of his shirt and tie. The horizontals and verticals of the books and shelves are a foil for the curves of his head, and the straight lines of his coat carry the verticals of the books into the lower part of the picture.

*　*　*

George Grosz (1893-1959) was a talented caricaturist in his early years, and it was this characteristic which enabled him to produce the kind of likeness which is so apparent in "The Poet Max Hermann-Neisse" (pl. 41). Grosz denied that he ever wanted to be a caricaturist, stating that it was the life he had seen and suffered in Germany that forced him to think in these terms.

His tight observation of the structure of the poet's head—the form of the skull, the shape of each feature, including the ear—has created an image that is so telling that it transcends the physical and becomes spiritual. He has represented a man whose life has been one of suffering. His body is disintegrating and his mind is tortured. The look of crippled age in his posture fulfills this impression. In spite of the clutter of objects, there is a feeling of barrenness—the lone bottle, glass, and cigarette.

The angles of chair and canvas stretchers, if such they be, bear a reminiscent overtone of cubism. Grosz was one of the leaders of the Dada movement in Berlin. He had gone through World War I in the German infantry, and his caustic, burning, cartoonlike satire on the military is some of his most powerful work. He was trained at the Royal Saxon Academy of the Fine Arts in Dresden, the Royal Arts and Crafts School in Berlin, and the Académie Colarossi in Paris. Coming to New York in 1932, he worked with Maurice Sterne in running an art school, and later taught at the Art Students League and the Columbia School of Fine Arts. He had become an American citizen in 1938, and died in Berlin in 1959.

*　*　*

The importance of a likeness of the physical body in a portrait cannot be overestimated. Portraits never have been, nor ever will be, commissioned unless the sitter is confident that a reasonable likeness will appear in the finished painting. Dr. Samuel Johnson, when asked whether he felt that a portrait was more important as a likeness or as a work of art, declared that in portraits "their chief excellence is being like."

If an artist intends to make portrait painting his profession, he must be able to qualify in this category of producing a physical resemblance.

Plate 41. GEORGE GROSZ. *The Poet Max Hermann-Neisse.* 1927. Collection, Museum of Modern Art, New York, Purchase

REVEALING THE INNER MAN

THE SECOND aspect of a likeness is the interpretation of the sitter's personality. This is not simply a superficial matter of portraying a person with a pleasing look or a harsh one. It involves lifelong study. It is an understanding of how all the basic emotions are recorded on the face momentarily, and what impression their constant repetition leaves as ineradicable marks.

One of the contributions to a study of this facet of the problem of painting a portrait has come from what newspaper photographers have recorded with their candid cameras. Over the years I have been examining these photographs, which have held me spellbound because of their power of revealing what is taking place in the inner man.

I have watched the changes in the faces of Hindenburg and Hitler, as one went down in power and the other went up. I have followed the demeanor of McCarthy in his meteoric passage through the news columns and out the other side. I have studied the granitelike mask of Stalin, and the relatively open countenances of the Americans who negotiated with him. I have marveled at the laughter and anger of Khrushchev. I have been fascinated with reading between the lines those attitudes and intentions which only a flash bulb can uncover.

And photographed indelibly on my memory are the pictures of the nameless ones—the aging mother looking up into the face of her uniformed son who has just returned from a Communist prison; the old Parisian down whose cheeks run passionate tears as he watches the Germans enter the city.

The news columns have their own way of reporting events, but for millions of readers these events are colored immeasureably and made to come alive by the photographs of the people involved. Their expressive faces reveal deep human secrets, and lasting impressions are made and inflexible conclusions drawn from the intuitive interpretation of these faces.

For the face *is* a book. An Indonesian can read the face of a Latvian; a man from the mountains can read the face of a man from the plains; an ignorant man, the face of a man with university degrees; a poor man, the face of a rich man; a Moslem, the face of a Christian. A baby can read a face, and he instantly expresses his reaction to it.

Here, within an area of roughly six by eight inches, is the most comprehensive, the most diverse, and the most subtle means of communication on earth. "Your face, my thane, is as a book where men may read strange matters."

Yet we take it for granted.

Hand in hand with the voice, the features of the face assist in interpreting the most abstract philosophical thought, the most intricate mathematical formula, the most trivial turn of thought, and the most basic animal emotion.

Yet we never once pause to marvel.

So I am proposing that we turn completely objective and examine this remarkable instrument as though we had never seen it before. We are a Man-from-Mars, where a face is not a face as we know it, and we are making a scientific report on it. Let no one think for a moment that by being objective we are failing to sympathize with the situation portrayed, particularly if it is accompanied by pain or grief or a similar emotion. We are thoughtfully examining the God-given instrument in humility and wonder.

Let us take up the features briefly, one by one. The mouth is the most mobile feature, accommodating itself both to admitting food and drink and to molding sounds of speech and song. Its flexibility and elusive structure give a portrait painter more trouble than all the other features put together. It delineates in an unmistakable way such things as a smile, a laugh, a pout, a shout, a gasp, dismay, joy, disgust, and anger. It runs the gamut of the emotions and interprets each with equal clarity.

A smile, for instance, may actually *begin* with the raising of the cheeks. This tends to raise the lower eyelid, and a very engaging look may consist of this alone, without any marked widening of the mouth. This is the basis of the "secret" of the smile of the Mona Lisa (La Gioconda). An artificial smile is generally the widening of the mouth *without* the raising of the cheeks.

The chin is the least mobile, the least descriptive feature, but goes along with the jaw and mouth to assist them with their various functions.

The forehead is inextricably associated with the eyebrows, whose facile powers can register, almost single-handedly, wonder, pity, fright, pain, cynicism, concentration, wistfulness, displeasure, and expectation, in infinite variations and combinations. According to Pliny: "Other animals have eyebrows, but only man's express grief and joy, mercy and severity by moving together or singly to signal from his soul. They show our agreement and disagreement, and supremely our contempt. Haughtiness enthrones herself in them, and though conceived in the heart, rises to the eyebrows and there hangs in the loftiest and steepest part of the body which it can occupy alone."

The nose, outside of its function in breathing, is chiefly expressive in sneering and in registering the effect of good and bad odors.

But the eyes—the eyes are the place one looks for the most complete, reliable, and pertinent information. It is true that our ears are bent on learning what is being said (which may or may not express what is going on in the mind), but our eyes, unless we are forced to read lips, are focused on eyes. Emerson appreciated this when he wrote: "Eyes are bold as lions—roving, running, leaping here and there, far and near. They speak all languages. They wait for no introduction; ask no leave of age or rank; they respect neither poverty nor riches, neither learning nor power nor virtue nor sex; but intrude, and come again and go through and through you in a moment of time. What inundation of life and thought is discharged from one soul into another through them!"

A shrewd look is generally accompanied by a contraction of the eyelids, presumably to conceal what goes on behind the eyes. The same device of half closing the eyes is also used in moments of concentration.

Paradoxically, a stare, which may indicate that the mind is not attending to things present, is wide-eyed, while terror opens the eyes wider than ever in order to give its utmost attention to things at hand. Or could it be that there is something of the stare in terror, since the mind may be placing more emphasis on imagined, impending disaster than on the problem of how to avoid this disaster?

The sparkling eye and the flashing smile (which, of course, involves the eye) owe something, oddly enough, to the tear ducts. "I laughed till I cried" carries this to an extreme, and is concerned exclusively with laughter. Tears of joy, on the other hand, are the result of mixed emotions.

One of the amazing things about the eye is that a noticeable change of expression is registered by an alteration in the lids which could only be measured microscopically.

These are crude and abbreviated comments on a subject as vast as life itself. They are intended only to suggest that there is such a thing as an alphabet of the face, which spells out words of meaning for all mankind.

Great painters throughout the centuries have rendered the human face with an understanding that is actually uncanny. There is the penetration of Daumier; the lusty human touch of Hals; the sense of drama of Goya; the minute touch of Memling, which creates the illusion of utter reality; the sensitivity of Velázquez—all the great who have opened their hearts and minds, and their art, to the human side of life as well as the aesthetic.

The picture of himself painted by Vincent van Gogh shortly before he committed suicide is a talented revelation of the inner man, not alone in the distorted features—the terrified eye, the agonized frown, the beaten mouth, but also in the designed confusion of swirling forms, the singing music of color. Color, for Van Gogh, *was* music. This portrait, based on reds and greens with slight undertones of violet, is comparable to the striking of a frightening, dissonant chord, the swirls being the passionate vibrato. He actually referred once to reds and greens as "those terrible things—man's passions." Here art transcends the literal representation. It employs the complete visual vocabulary—form, texture, and, to a lesser degree, light and shade, and, above all, the emphasis on color.

While the newspaper photographer provides us with a miraculous document recording the *fleeting* expression, the great portrait painters give us a talented interpretation of the *permanent* person, a biography of a life condensed into one image. Through their knowledge of what each feature contributes they are able to *create* the inner personality, emphasizing a characteristic which may be instantaneously revealed and supplying the impression of one that is not momentarily present.

I shall never forget the comment of a lady whose husband's portrait I had just painted. She studied the portrait and said, "I see you are not only interested in his outside, but also what churns up inside." After all, the body is only an envelope of flesh; it is the spirit that counts.

Edward Burne-Jones observed, "The only expression allowable in great portraiture is the expression of character and moral quality, not anything temporary, fleeting or accidental."

An actor studies the personality of the person he is portraying. He then *becomes* that person and through gesture, facial expression, intonation, and accent brings him to life. I believe that it is a distinct advantage for a portrait painter to have acting ability. He can then "become" the sitter, and, through the feeling in his bones, reproduce him. When I am painting alone, at times I even act the sitter in front of a mirror in order to observe what happens to the face and the body under these circumstances.

The big problem is not only to be able to record the personality, but to sense it as well and to create a mood in the sitter which will allow it to come forth. A very pertinent question which applies to the portraitist appears in Job 41:14: "Who can open the doors of his face?"

94

* * *

No one can "reveal the inner man" better than Jan van Eyck (1385 - 1441). First of all, he understood man; secondly, he developed a technique which is well-nigh incomparable. While the Italians of his period were modeling the faces in their paintings by adding black to the flesh color in the shadows and even in the halftones, van Eyck was using darker values of the same flesh colors with very subtle gradations. The people of Flanders respected precision—in thinking, in planning, in executing, even in dreaming, as we see in the writing of some of their philosophers.

Chancellor Rolin (pl. 42) as a donor was a major part in the painting "The Virgin with Chancellor Rolin." He is shown here as a detail from the left side of the picture. He was a veritable power in the state, and was instrumental in helping to establish the distinguished house of Burgundy, which, under Philip the Good, became the most influential and wealthy sovereignty in all of Europe.

Vigor and determination are shown in the chancellor's jaw and mouth, together with the penetrating, questioning look of a man bound to make critical decisions. The intensity of his look is achieved partly by the frown and partly by the raising of the lower lids.

It is interesting that the light is falling on his face (which is such an important part of the picture), with only a small area reserved for shadow to model it. If his head had been moved only slightly to the left, it would have had the simple, dark plane of the shadowed stone behind it. I can only assume that van Eyck wished to subdue his head in relation to that of the Virgin by making his profile blend in with the light stripe formed by the edge of the stone wall.

The rendering of the marble column is typical of van Eyck's meticulous craftsmanship. He signed some of his pictures with the motto "Als ikh kan," which may be freely translated, "As well as I can." His utter devotion to his art has made him an example to all artists of all time. The creation of nature was a religion for him. The manner in which he inscribed the portrait of Giovanni Arnolfini and his wife is a testimonial to this attitude. It reads, "Johannes de Eyck was here 1434." This means that he existed in this environment with these two people, and the painting is his evidence. It *is* the place; these *are* the people.

Van Eyck was among the leaders of the discovery of atmospheric perspective, and in the picture shown here this element is suggested in the pale mountains of the landscape. The foreground of the landscape, reveling in details, has all the characteristics of a tapestry of the period.

Rolin's sumptuous robe is an indication of the luxurious clothing worn at this time by the wealthy in Flanders.

Van Eyck's career was extremely successful. He was made court painter when he was thirty-five and served the duke during his entire life. He was

Plate 42. JAN VAN EYCK. *The Virgin with Chancellor Rolin* (detail). Louvre, Paris. Phot. Réunion Musées Nationaux

not only an artist; he was a much respected diplomat. He went with the Flemish ambassadors to Portugal to arrange for the marriage of the duke to the Infanta Isabella. Upon his death his family was granted a substantial pension.

* * *

The "Portrait of a Gentleman of Florence" (pl. 43) represents a condensed image of the city during its years of strife from the middle of the fifteenth to the middle of the sixteenth century. This subject's expression is the essence of disillusion, suspicion born of experience, weary determination. His hand is about to require submission or receive a substantial bribe. He is discouraged, morose.

Ridolfo Ghirlandajo (1483-1561), son of the artist Domenico Ghirlandajo, has understood all this and has been able to create it on canvas. This is not simply an assemblage of features. It is a story told by the activity of each feature—the drooping eyelids, the chiseled frown, the raised left eyebrow, the pouches under the eyes, the gaunt shape of the cheeks, the cynical sneer of the nose, the droop and pout of the lower lip. The side glance of the eyes helps to register a certain slyness, although this position may also be found in looks of shyness and timidity.

The color scheme in this portrait is somber and simple—a dull, dark-red coat, with a flash of light red on the top of the black cloak, a black headdress, and the charming greens, browns, and blues of the small landscape. The slope of the hill points toward the man's eyes, and the tall tree serves to soften the otherwise harsh line of the window as it meets the light sky. For a gentleman of Florence to be shown with a farm scene and distant country is not surprising. The cities of Italy were tight units with walls around them to prevent attacks. The open country began at the very walls.

During this period Charles VIII of France had entered Florence with his troops; Savonarola had dominated it for a while; Spanish mercenaries had sacked Prato; Machiavelli's astute, devious, and bold tactics had prevailed; the Medici had come and gone; and the city had surrendered to Emperor Charles V. It is a miracle that in these disturbed times art could have flourished, but it produced such men as Botticelli, Filippo Lippi, Domenico Ghirlandajo, Gozzoli, Lorenzo di Credi, Piero di Cosimo, Pollaiuolo, and Verrocchio.

Ridolfo was fortunate to have been trained by such an outstanding master as his father, whose portraits were some of his most distinguished works. Two very familiar ones by the father are "An Old Man and His Grandson," in which a tender, blond-haired boy is looking up at his wart-nosed grandfather. The other is the exquisite and beautifully designed profile of Giovanna Tornabuoni.

* * *

Plate 43. RIDOLFO GHIRLANDAJO. *Portrait of a Gentleman of Florence.* c. 1550. Courtesy, Art Institute
of Chicago, Collection of Mr. and Mrs. Martin A.
Ryerson

With a candor which must have been somewhat startling at the time, Anthony More (1512? - 1576) painted "Mary Tudor, Queen of England" (pl. 44), the determined, ruthless, cruel "Bloody Mary." She is posing with the stiff authority of a queen, encrusted with jewels. Her sharp jaw, tight mouth, the furrow in her cheek, the vicious eyes are painted with scrupulous frankness.

More, known in Spain as Antonio Moro, was in the service of Philip II when he painted this picture for the king just before the king was about to marry her. Mary had already begun to persecute the Protestants. Dozens of leaders were burned at the stake, and the bodies of the poor were hanging from gibbets throughout London. Seventy-three citizens of Colchester were tied to a rope and hauled through the streets to their death. Never had England suffered so from defeat, bloodshed, and unjust government.

More was Van Scorel's most famous pupil. He moved to Antwerp, where he qualified as a "free master." He was a devoted disciple of Titian, whose influence appears in most of his work. He became immediately successful in painting royalty and members of the court, and traveled to Italy, Spain, Portugal, and England, where he was knighted. Seldom have we had such a telling record of the artist's times as we have from More. His clarity of vision and brave psychological interpretation have made him outstanding in the field of portraiture.

* * *

Anyone capable of inventing such imaginative, expressive, and original religious paintings as El Greco (Domenico Teotocopulo, 1548? - 1614) would have a creative background which would not fail to show in his portrait painting. He has dissected "Cardinal Don Fernando Niño de Guevara" (pl. 45) for all time in this representation of him. He has made him the heartless, unsure, cruel Grand Inquisitor of Spain, a title which was bestowed upon him as an honor, but which today is an incrimination. Guevara casts a penetrating, sidelong glance at the artist. The stiff back and rigid arms reflect his domineering mood. His mouth appears to be on the point of opening to pronounce a death sentence. The mustache, drooping down over the corners of the mouth, increases the lugubrious expression.

The color scheme is dominated by the cold red of the robe and biretta. The wall is a brownish yellow and the door, a warm brown. The edge of the door, which almost divides the picture in half, leads the eye directly toward his head. The piece of paper on the floor, containing the artist's signature, is an accent employed to balance the light areas of the head and hands.

El Greco (the Greek) was a nickname which was given him when he left Crete and went to Venice to study painting. Titian, Tintoretto, Michel-

Plate 44. ANTHONY MORE. *Mary Tudor, Queen of England*. Isabella Stewart Gardner Museum, Boston

Plate 45. EL GRECO. *Cardinal Don Fernando Niño de
Guevara*. Metropolitan Museum of Art, New
York, Bequest of Mrs. H. O. Havemeyer, 1929,
H. O. Havemeyer Collection

angelo, and the Bassani were the guiding influences in his work. He left about 1575 for Toledo, and spent the rest of his life in Spain. Though he continued with the color of Titian and the violent bodily gestures of Tintoretto, he was entirely himself in his elongated distortions of the human figure. It was from Tintoretto that he learned to make clay or wax models as preliminary studies for his religious paintings, rather than the customary oil sketches.

* * *

It was an interesting experience for me to paint the picture "John Carton" (pl. 46). Often children of his age tend to be the opposite of the serious, thoughtful personality which is so much a part of this boy. Incidentally, he assumed the pose himself. He is looking out over the land which is so characteristic of certain areas in Illinois. The tall grass (turkeyfoot) growing around him is indigenous to this part of the country. Treating the grass as pure design, quite apart from making a literal representation of it, gives a realistic painter all the challenge and satisfactions which are assumed to belong solely to the abstract artist.

* * *

The personal character and firm convictions about right and wrong, the evil and the good, dominated Hogarth's artistic life. He was dissatisfied with the quality of taste which existed in England at the time; jealous of the invasion of foreign artists who, he claimed, were charlatans without conscience, who wove their way into fashionable society. He maligned them, jibed at their pretentions, and soon had these "phizmongers," as he called them, attacking him to his face and behind his back. He finally abandoned portrait painting, and today there are only about twelve of his portraits in public collections.

For these reasons it is worth while to examine the picture "Miss Mary Edwards" (pl. 47). With all the skill which he exhibited in his series of paintings and engravings of "The Rake's Progress," here he has "illustrated" a lady of fashion with poise, dignity, an air of pride and self-satisfaction. She almost conveys a feeling of condescension as she strokes the dog's head. There is a whimsical overtone in her facial expression which is produced by the slightly raised left eyebrow. The luxury and elegance of her elaborate dress and jewelry is in keeping with the social pride of the period. Hogarth has even been perceptive enough to have the dog stare upward (and not at his mistress) as he concentrates on the feeling of her hand upon his head. Without the artist's understanding of the underlying nature of *all* types of human beings, he could not have portrayed this subject's personality so clearly.

102

Plate 46. GORDON C. AYMAR. *John Carton.* 1962. Water
color. Collection of Mr. and Mrs. Laurence Carton

Plate 47. WILLIAM HOGARTH. *Miss Mary Edwards.* ©
Frick Collection, New York

The color scheme is simple and rich—the warm red of the dress, which is the dominating feature, the brownish-whites of the lace and scroll, the dark browns of the background and the dog's fur, and the muted greens of the curtain and globe.

William Hogarth (1697-1764) was the son of a schoolmaster who had little of this world's goods. At an early age he became the apprentice of an engraver who specialized in gold and silver. This training was an indispensable aid to Hogarth in producing the many engravings of "The Rake's Progress," and it was these that earned him his living. His paintings for this series were giddy sermons on the ultimate disaster which is the conclusion of a bawdy life. He himself admitted that he was more concerned with contributing his talents to abolishing brutality than he was with painting pictures as great as Raphael's, and he demonstrated this to a degree in "The Four Stages of Cruelty," in which he traces the development of cruelty from a boy who teases a cat through various harassments to ultimate murder.

* * *

The portrait of "Elizabeth Armstrong" (pl. 48) is an illustration of an attempt to suggest a personality not only by the pose and facial expression, but by putting the subject in an unreal background. The wood-panel opening in the wall shows the full moon and pine tree—an almost Oriental touch.

In the finished sketch for this painting I left the landscape blank and made twelve different color sketches as overlays, to see which idea would be most appropriate. These included distant mountains and water, fairy characters, and a tiny knight on horseback, followed by his running spear bearer. The one finally selected seemed to be less diverting and suggested more of a mood.

At the final sitting, when the background had been completed, this imaginative, pensive, fanciful little lady exclaimed, "Look what Elizabeth is thinking!"

* * *

I have included Romney's drawing of "Anger, Fear and Envy" (pl. 49) primarily to illustrate the fact that a suave, sophisticated painter of fashion, who was chiefly concerned with making resemblances of beautiful, cultivated masks, was also concerned with the basic emotions. He undoubtedly believed that unless he understood the total human being, he would be unable to suggest the undertones which sometimes appeared in their faces.

In this drawing there are the violence, the shout, the wide-open eyes of Anger; the twisted, shoulder-to-cheek pose, the explosive eye, the distorted mouth, and the raised eyebrow of Fear; and the stealthy, sidelong glance, the frown, and the pursed mouth of Envy.

* * *

Plate 48. GORDON C. AYMAR. *Elizabeth Armstrong.*
1961. Water color

Plate 49. GEORGE ROMNEY. *Anger, Fear and Envy*. Yale
University Art Gallery, New Haven, Connecticut,
Gift of Mr. and Mrs. J. Richardson Dilworth

I have shown so many grim examples of the portrayal of lugubrious personalities because it is somewhat surprising to see how the great of those days apparently accepted this interpretation of themselves. Now, as a relief, we have the portrait of "Princesa de la Paz" (pl. 50) by Goya.

Goya's breadth and depth of human understanding enabled him to paint not only the domineering characters, but also this enchanting, innocent, timid young lady. Goya is like the great musician who can impress with his boisterous fortissimos and, a moment later, charm with his sensitive pianissimo.

The princess is posing obediently just as Goya has requested. Her wide-open eyes stare at the spot she has been instructed to watch. Her dress is simple and unpretentious compared with the elaborate costumes of the period, and this has enabled the artist to focus attention on her head. Goya has painted her bonnet with the skill of his quick facture. It suggests rather than depicts details. He has, however, felt it worth while to concentrate on the portrait of the man who appears on her ring. The familiar flat, dark background serves to define her glowing head and figure.

Many artists are limited in their ability to interpret different types of personalities. Goya's "Princess" is a testimonial not only to his appreciation of the total human being, but also to his technical skill in being able to state what he has sensed.

Louis Thiers, the famous nineteenth-century historian, journalist, and statesman, was well equipped to appreciate the function of the features of the face; Goya must have agreed with him when he said, "Le visage est le théâtre de la pensée" ("The face is the theater of the thought").

* * *

In the portrait of "Gamaliel Painter" by William Jennys (pl. 51), who was active in the latter part of the eighteenth century and the beginning of the nineteenth century, we have an outstanding example of the work of one of our best limners. He was an itinerant artist who traveled all over Connecticut, Massachusetts, Vermont, and New Hampshire painting portraits.

In this picture he has rendered his subject with almost brutal frankness. Storrs Lee, formerly of Middlebury College, Vermont, has described Painter as ". . . a man of all trades: a farmer, a miller, soldier, woodsman, politician, real estate agent, surveyor, churchman, educator, legislator and judge—an exceedingly clever man who could develop an interest in a job that needed to be done. During the early days of the Revolution, he even became a self-appointed intelligence officer, and, disguised as an idiot salesman of wildflowers and tarts among the British, picked up information on enemy war plans which undoubtedly shortened the war in northern New

Plate 50. Francisco de Goya y Lucientes. *Princesa de
la Paz*. Courtesy, Shelburne Museum, Shelburne,
Vermont

Plate 51. WILLIAM JENNYS. *Gamaliel Painter*. Middlebury College, Middlebury, Vermont

England."[3] Men were like that in those days. They learned about life the hard way. In a direct, firm style Jennys has recorded his subject's determination, his vigor, his puritanical severity, his penetrating look. This man could not be fooled or cajoled, nor would he give an inch.

It is our good fortune today to have some idea of the rewards received by itinerant painters of that day. In an account book dated 1801 it appears that Jennys painted the portrait of Dr. and Mrs. William Stoddard Williams for the sum of $24, which did not include the frame. Dr. Williams paid Jennys $2 for that item.

* * *

In the portrait of the actress Elizabeth Farren (pl. 52) Sir Thomas Lawrence (1769-1830) has exhibited a very subtle and skillful ability to interpret human character. In examining what he has done to suggest her personality, let us admit at the start that the "Queen of Comedy" would have been able to act the part of anyone she wished to resemble. A contemporary critic said that Lawrence had placed both her mind and character on canvas. He described her as "arch, careless, spirited, elegant and engaging."

Elizabeth Farren's career began at the age of fifteen, when she appeared in *She Stoops to Conquer.* It ended twenty years later when she retired and married the Earl of Derby.

Lawrence painted this picture when he was twenty. It was exhibited in the Royal Academy, and Sir Joshua Reynolds, the president—and Lawrence's former teacher—said that he considered it a masterpiece. Miss Farren, however, had been continually teased about the slimness of her figure, and she asked him to make it a bit fatter. With a diplomatic skill which must have been a valuable gift in the fashionable circles of his day, he persuaded her to leave it untouched.

When still a boy, Lawrence entertained the guests in his father's inn by making sketches of them. At the age of twelve in the fashionable resort of Bath he was idolized by his many sitters. At that time he charged one guinea for a portrait. Originally, he hoped to become an actor, a proclivity which undoubtedly helped him in his interpretation of people. His steps up the ladder of fame are spectacular. At eighteen he was studying at the school of the Royal Academy; four years later he was made an associate member. At the age of twenty-three he was appointed Painter in Ordinary to the king. Ten years later he became a full member of the Academy, and eventually was elected its president. In the meantime he had been knighted for his distinguished contribution to the art of England.

[3] W. Storrs Lee, quoted in Arthur K. D. Healy, *The Painter of the Painter Portraits?* (Middlebury, Vt.: Middlebury College, n.d.).

Plate 52. THOMAS LAWRENCE. *Elizabeth Farren, Count-ess of Derby*. 1790. Metropolitan Museum of Art, New York, Bequest of Edward S. Harkness, 1940

He belonged completely to his period and expressed it with ease, flair, and sympathy. Could anything have been more appropriate as a decoration for the tall-ceilinged, ornate rooms of the manor houses than this painting, which is nearly eight feet tall? The duke finally persuaded Lawrence to part with it for the sum of one hundred guineas.

The color scheme is handsome—the warm white of her dress and cloak, her powdered hair, the light brown of the fur, the dark reddish-brown of her gloves, which is repeated in the brown of the foreground, the warm green of the landscape and the dark blue of the sky, changing, as it descends, to greenish-grays. The blue of the sky is repeated in the ribbon near her right hand and in the muff.

Obviously, Lawrence's aim was to please. Let us not assume, however, that he tossed these pictures off with a careless facility. He is reported to have worked two days and two nights consecutively on one painting. He would spend a full day making a life-size chalk drawing of the head, and one sitter said that he sat forty times for the painting of the head alone.

*   *   *

Amedeo Modigliani (1884 - 1920) had no interest whatever in "revealing the inner man." He himself stated that the figures he painted had no desire to express anything, unless it were the mute acceptance of life. They are the very essence of melancholy. He was involved only with using them as elongated shapes which satisfied his eyes. Of the several portraits he painted of Jeanne Hébuterne ("Portrait of a Young Woman," pl. 53), her hair appears red in some and black in others. Her eyes are sometimes a dark blue, and in others a pale blue throughout, with a scarcely definable pupil. This was a perfectly legitimate approach for an artist who used the human figure as a source from which to create his own beauty. His use of color is most perceptive and satisfying, and generally employs large areas carefully designed to sing together in harmony.

In the portrait herewith reproduced the subject's hair is red, the background is ocherish with touches of warm and cool color, and the dress is a warm blue. The artist has used this blue in a more neutral tone to define the profile. As a likeness we can assume it to be a caricature, and it is far more alive in his rendering of the very dark-brown eyes than most of his other paintings, which tend to be masks rather than personalities.

Modigliani rejected still lifes and landscapes, which is rather surprising since they offer great opportunities to treat nature with complete freedom. Apparently there was something about the human form which intrigued him, and when he was intrigued, nothing would stop him.

Regardless of his lack of concern with probing into a person's character, it is interesting to study Jeanne's face as that of a person who was willing to

Plate 53. AMEDEO MODIGLIANI. *Portrait of a Young Woman*. C. 1918. Yale University Art Gallery, New Haven, Connecticut, Bequest of Mrs. Kate Lancaster Brewster

live with Modigliani as his mistress, to be disowned by her parents, to bear him a daughter, and, upon his death, to commit suicide by jumping out of the window in her father's house.

Modigliani was born in Leghorn, Italy, and at the age of fourteen studied with Micheli. He visited Rome, Florence, and Venice, lived in the museums and art galleries, and was influenced largely by the works of Murillo, Dürer, Titian, and, above all, Cezanne. In 1906 he moved to Paris and had the opportunity of meeting such artists as Utrillo, Picasso, Soutine, Kisling, and Lipchitz. He became absorbed in sculpture, and responded immediately to the current interest in primitive African art and that of Brancusi. In many of his paintings there is a reflection of this awareness of sculptured form. He was in bad health most of his short life, but in spite of this he threw himself wildly into his painting. His portraits were often completed in two days, sometimes in two hours. At one point he worked for a dealer at the modest rate of forty francs and a bottle of brandy per painting. He exhibited in the Salon des Independants in 1910 and 1912, and five years later had a one-man show at the Berthe Weill Gallery. He died from tuberculosis, use of hashish, alcoholism, and riotous living, content despite all his ills, apparently, if he could express himself on canvas.

* * *

Augustus Edwin John (1878 - 1961) painted the "Portrait of the German Foreign Minister, Dr. Gustav Stresemann" (pl. 54) about 1924. Personally, I am at a loss to know why he selected this expression to pass on to posterity. If a psychoanalyst were observing the picture for the first time, he might be tempted to assign certain attributes to the sitter which would seem contrary to his career. Here is the face of a man who seems to be the epitome of cynicism, shrewd calculation, belligerency. The portrait might well be entitled "The Sneer." But we must not forget that, from among the many worthy candidates from countries all over the world, this man was chosen as the recipient of the Nobel Peace Prize.

The position of the head, thrust back, thus emphasizing the double chin, contributes to the hostile expression. The large nostril seems to be inhaling a not-too-pleasant odor. The sneer is conveyed by the raising of the cheek above the nostril. The shrewd look is the result of the raising of the left, lower eyelid. The right eye is looking surreptitiously around the corner at the artist.

The portrait appears to have been painted rather quickly, if one can judge from the free, sketchy treatment of the body and hands. It suggests that the artist wanted to capture an informal pose. The left hand, especially, seems to have been a matter of accident rather than arrangement. He un-

Plate 54. AUGUSTUS EDWIN JOHN. *Portrait of the German
Prime Minister, Dr. Gustav Stresemann.* c. **1924.**
Albright-Knox Art Gallery, Buffalo, New York,
Fellows for Life Fund

doubtedly wished to stress the diagonal lines of the arms and the coat, even to the point where he has omitted any indication of the right arm of the chair, which, under normal conditions, would have been shown. After this free rendering of the major portion of the painting, he then concentrated on the head, in which there is much more detail.

When John was sixteen, he attended the Slade School. At the age of fifty he was made a member of the Royal Academy, and, some years later, a retrospective exhibition of his work was held at the Tate Gallery and, in 1954, a similar one at the Academy.

* * *

To one of Picasso's less pretentious and more agreeable periods belongs the "Head of the Acrobat's Wife" (pl. 55). In the language of realism he has been able to convey the impression of the sort of person she is today and was yesterday. It is the face of one who has suffered, is discouraged, and is almost deranged. Her mouth droops in sadness; her eyes are distorted. They might suggest excessive fatigue, a mental problem, disillusion, dogged endurance. It is a tragic expression.

The picture is also called "Woman with a Helmet of Hair." It is painted in *gouache*, and is mainly black and white on a blue ground (the Blue Period, 1904). There are slight variations in the blues, with overtones of pink (in the lips), purple, and yellow-green.

Would it have been more worth while for a man with such talent and insight to have stayed with this more sensitive manner of expressing himself?

* * *

At one point in Picasso's frantic journey through the sanctuaries of art, he painted the portrait "Gertrude Stein" (pl. 56), during a recess between the perceptive Blue and Pink Periods and the advent of cubism. She said that she devoted ninety sittings to this painting. Then, apparently in a state of complete frustration, Picasso painted the head from memory in the course of one day. Forty years later, with personal courage that few people would have had, she gave it to the Metropolitan Museum.

It is not often that one has the opportunity of seeing a photograph of the model of a well-known artist and his painting as well. Fortunately, we have the photograph of Gertrude Stein (pl. 57) taken in 1906, the same year in which this portrait was painted. Since Picasso's intention, obviously, was not to obtain a photographic likeness, we might consider it rather as an interpretation of character. Certainly nothing could be farther apart than the photographic image of the gentle, peaceful, contented, warmly glowing

117

Plate 55. PABLO PICASSO. *Head of the Acrobat's Wife.*
1904. Gouache. Courtesy, Art Institute of Chicago, Gift of Kate L. Brewster

Gertrude Stein and the morose, hard, distracted, calculating person in the painting. Picasso was a caricaturist; so we can assume that he could have captured the pleasant side of her, even from memory, if he had wanted to.

Is this head intended to suggest a mask? There are overtones and implications in all of Picasso's paintings. Gertrude Stein herself once told Picasso that at last she realized that one of his still lifes was actually a picture of three musicians!

He often said that there was only one thing he wanted his pictures to express—emotion. He declared that what really interested him was the drama of the inner man and that everything else was false.

* * *

When the familiar phrase "a speaking likeness" is used, it implies that the painter has endowed his sitter with life, that the subject seems to be on the verge of speaking. Speech may reveal (or conceal) thought *and* feelings. The most complimentary thing that a sitter can say about a finished portrait is, "That's the way I *feel!*"

It is this ability of revelation that a portrait painter cultivates over the years. He is learning a basic language—the language of the face.

Aristotle has phrased it in the following words: "The aim of Art is to represent not the outward appearance of things, but their inner significance; for this, and not the external manner and detail, constitutes true reality."

Plate 56. PABLO PICASSO. *Gertrude Stein.* 1906. Metropolitan Museum of Art, New York, Bequest of Gertrude Stein, 1946

Plate 57. *Gertrude Stein.* 1906. Yale University, New
Haven, Connecticut, Gertrude Stein Collection

FROM SKETCH TO FINISH

 KETCHES made for portraits are revealing in many ways. In the first place, they record the artist's original impression of his sitter, uninfluenced by later attention to detail or by revised judgments as to personality and by alterations usual in executing a finished painting. The sketch often captures a mood which may disappear with future sittings. At times this is noticeable in the lively look of the sitter in the sketch compared with the boredom which is caused by subsequent sittings for the finished painting.

The sketch is often a witness to the artist's ability to *draw*. And, at times, there will be evidence in the finished painting of improvements in pose and design which did not exist in the sketch.

A sketch may be executed in almost any medium, from the silverpoint employed during the fifteenth century to water color, oil, pencil, charcoal, or pen and ink. All media are available, and which one will be chosen depends on the artist's instinctive preference. Some fine paintings have undoubtedly been made without a preliminary sketch. These, generally, are oil paintings, as it is relatively easy to make changes in this medium as the picture develops.

A sketch gives the impression of a man speaking off the record, completely unaware of, and not concerned with, spectators. Sketches were, and are, a vital part of the artist's craftsmanship, particularly when

122

they are all that the artist has to work from, because of a sitter's inability to devote the necessary time. This is a situation with which the painters of royalty were acquainted, and to which the artists of today must adjust themselves in painting distinguished or busy patrons.

Many of the sketches of the great artists have notes written on them, indicating what colors to emphasize. For example, on Van Eyck's drawing for the portrait of Cardinal Albergati he has written, "Color of eyes, yellow-brown, lips whitish, patches on nose and around eyebrows, sanguine."

One of the devices which I, personally, use to refresh my memory on the colors of the face is to make a quick water-color sketch of one half of a full face (the right or left side). It is generally about six inches high. I make only half of the face, since it is merely for color notes, and I do not wish to become involved in this sketch with the full sculptural likeness. I then write notes beside it, calling attention to the individual peculiarities in form as well as color, and to those points which time has not allowed me to develop properly in the sketch.

It is not unusual to find that a freshness and spontaneity of handling which existed in the sketch have disappeared in the final painting, and that perhaps even the likeness is not so telling. The old adage still holds true that it takes two people to paint a portrait—one to paint it; the other to make him stop before he ruins it. De la Tour mentions the problems in which he became involved when he tried to "improve" a portrait he had already given to the Academy. After a hundred changes his friends said he had spoiled the likeness; the Academy regretted that he had altered it. He then tried, without much success, to restore it to its original state.

* * *

The "Portrait of a Young Man" (pl. 58) is reproduced near actual size. It is drawn in silverpoint on paper which is treated with a special ground. This accounts for the crackled appearance, particularly on the left-hand margin. Pretend that you yourself are drawing this sketch. The details of the features would be difficult for the average artist to execute in this size. Some artists—and this is true especially of the fifteenth-century Flemish school—have this individual propensity, just as others feel at home standing before an easel and making broad strokes with a large brush. There is no one best or greatest manner, regardless of which one may prefer. Each has its own place in the wide-open door of art.

This sketch was presumably done by Dierik Bouts (1410?-1475), although various authorities over the years have disagreed as to whether it was by Bouts, one of his followers, or someone in the workshop of Memling. If it is a Bouts, it is the only drawing by this artist which has been preserved. All seem to agree that, whoever drew it, it is an original and not a copy.

Plate 58. DIERIK BOUTS. *Portrait of a Young Man*. Silverpoint. Smith College Museum of Art, Northampton, Massachusetts

It is obviously a preliminary study and is not intended to be a finished work of art, such as the drawing by Ingres (pl. 113). The lines of the coat in the left-hand corner, where Bouts subsequently indicated what may have been a table on which the subject is resting his arm, is testimony that this was not intended to be a final drawing as such. Also, any artist of that period, if this had been a final work, would have adjusted and redesigned the sitter's two collars, which, with their present casual look, must have been represented as they actually were.

One interesting observation is that the artist has suggested the folds in the sleeves in the sharp, hard, designed manner in which the final painting would be executed. The cloth would have been much more rounded and soft.

The face is the place where the artist has concentrated his interest, and there are many points about it that show his effort to record the *individual* characteristics, such as the angular lines over the upper eyelids, the structure of the nose (both bone and cartilage), the carefully shaped chin, the almost feminine mouth. From the thickness of the line which forms the shape of the right cheek, it would seem that the artist drew this several times to make an accurate record of its subtle curves.

Bouts was born in Haarlem, West Netherlands, and about the middle of the century went to Louvain with many other artists who were attracted by the vast reconstruction that was going on in the town. The university, founded in 1426, was growing rapidly, and a century later consisted of forty-three colleges with over four thousand students.

Bouts's religious paintings show an unostentatious gentleness and serenity compared with those of his contemporaries. His art has been somewhat underestimated through the years, but fortunately today we have enough examples of it to establish him as one of the great interpreters of the spiritual world.

*   *   *

Sir Peter Paul Rubens (1577 - 1640) was known to have been more interested in his huge, flamboyant, religious, mythological, and historical paintings than in the art of portraiture. Being a man of diplomacy, however, he found it advisable to paint the portraits of some of his patrons. Thomas Howard, Earl of Arundel and Earl Marshal of England, was one of these distinguished men. Arundel is best known for his collection of the Arundel marbles, which he eventually gave to Oxford University.

The sketch (pl. 59) is done with a brush and brown and black ink. A brown and gray wash has been added and touches of bluish-red were used to heighten the general color effect. Rubens, even in the sketches for his large and complicated religious paintings, began with a suggestion of color.

By examining such parts as the hair and the hands, it is easy to see how spontaneously and directly he drew this. The commanding pose is typical

Plate 59. PETER PAUL RUBENS. *Sir Thomas Howard, Earl of Arundel.* Brush sketch in ink and wash. Courtesy, Sterling and Francine Clark Art Institute, Williamstown, Massachusetts

Plate 60. PETER PAUL RUBENS. *Portrait of Sir Thomas
Howard, Earl of Arundel.* Oil. Isabella Stewart
Gardner Museum, Boston

of the important characters of the period. Each was accustomed to put his hand upon his hip and thrust his elbow sharply forward. The helmet is indicated with a minimum of effort, merely to put it in position.

In the finished painting (pl. 60), executed in 1629/30, the pose is almost identical with that of the sketch. Undoubtedly, a model was substituted for the sitter in order to paint the figure, as it must have taken considerable time to record all these details. Notice the unconventional, angular form of the light shape over his head. This counteracts, to a certain extent, the sharp angle of his left arm. The lines of the arch oppose the backward swing of his head. These small matters of composition were no problem to an artist who created the most complicated, turbulent compositions.

The sketch of the head and the head in the finished painting are worth comparing. In the sketch Arundel has a more tense and almost worried look. His eyes go past the spectator. In the painting he looks directly out, and his expression is calm and more composed. His face shows great character, and he is the epitome of forceful English aristocracy. Every aspect of his head is done to perfection. His eyes have been painted, not as a witness to the artist's concern with detailed precision, but in order to give every indication of his model's appearance and mood. In the painting there can be seen even the high light on the moisture in his eye just above the lower eyelid. The hair is represented as a soft mass, but, where it seemed necessary, Rubens has painted each separate hair. The whole head is that masterful combination of a general impression and also of detail painted *con amore*, an expression which Rubens used in describing one of his paintings.

Rubens was not interested in devising a meticulous design in which shapes were carefully related. He demanded the quick impression, the handsome, buoyant handling. Nature was painted with gusto, and he was satisfied with a reasonable representation of it. The total effect of the picture is very quiet and restrained, when we take into account the fact that it is the work of the baroque period's most ebullient representative.

Rubens spent his youth in the prosperous town of Antwerp. After a period of training under Vaenius, he went to Italy in 1600 and spent eight years there, during which time his style was deeply influenced. The freely emotional spirit of the Italians was sympathetically received by Rubens, and his paintings show a forceful energy which almost exceeds theirs. When he returned to Antwerp, his fame was established and he was flooded with commissions. Being an executive as well as a brilliant painter, he developed a method of production which included a workshop of nearly two hundred assistants. They enlarged his sketches and applied coats of thin color as the beginning of the final painting. He carried the sketches for his large pictures to a relatively high degree of finish, so that the assistants had substantial material from which to work. When they were through, he added strong touches of opaque color to make the picture conform to his own ideas. Inci-

128

dentally, he charged less for pictures in which assistants had played a part than for those he had painted entirely himself. About 1620 Van Dyck became one of his major helpers.

How a man who was of such stature as an artist could devote so much time to the field of diplomacy is difficult to understand, but Rubens had an influence on the relationships between Flanders, Spain, Holland, and England. At the age of twenty-six he was sent by the duke of Mantua to Spain, where he spent a year studying the great masters who were his favorites, especially Titian and Tintoretto. The Archduchess Isabella appointed him to be her ambassador in 1623 and he served her for ten years, being knighted by the king at the end of this period.

Helena Fourment became Rubens' second wife when she was only sixteen. Eventually, he bought the handsome Castle of Steen and lived there in relative peace until he died.

* * *

Isabella Brant was Rubens' first wife. During the course of her life Rubens must have made many sketches of her. The drawing reproduced herewith (pl. 61) was probably done about the time he painted her portrait (pl. 62). This was somewhere between 1620 and 1625. She died in 1626 at the early age of thirty-five.

The sketch is remarkable for the strength with which Rubens has given us the veritable form of every feature. He selected an almost full light, but, by the skillful handling of the shadows, the well-related halftones, and the strong high lights, her face has become three-dimensional.

In the painting he has retained all the facial characteristics of the sketch, but, by turning her face to one side, the artist has made her gaze less direct and more coy, and, by flattening out the light, which now comes from a different angle, he has reduced the sculptured effect. The final result is rather insipid in treatment.

The drawing gives us an interesting study in the structure of a smile. Dickens once said, "There are only two styles of portrait painting: the serious and the smirk." Perhaps he would have put this in the latter category. The line ripples from the center of her lips outward to the corners, where it begins to emphasize the indentations in the cheeks. There is no raising of the lower eyelids, which is often so much a part of a smile. The eyes are rather naïvely wide open, and in both pictures the artist has indicated the charming tilt of her right eye.

The most handsome picture Rubens painted of Isabella was done soon after they were married, and he included a self-portrait. They are both dressed in clothes that must have been the height of fashion. This painting is in the Alte Pinakothek in Munich.

* * *

Plate 61. PETER PAUL RUBENS. *Isabella Brant.* Sketch.
Courtesy, trustees of the British Museum, London

Plate 62. PETER PAUL RUBENS. *Portrait of Isabella Brant.*
c. 1620-25. Oil on panel. Cleveland Museum of
Art, Cleveland, Ohio, Mr. and Mrs. William H.
Marlatt Fund

"The Painter's Daughters Teasing a Cat" (pl. 63), a traditional but highly inappropriate title, was painted when Thomas Gainsborough (1727-1788) was about thirty-two years old. The family was then living in Bath, which, as an exceedingly fashionable resort, enabled the artist to be near his subjects.

From this unfinished painting we can learn facts about Gainsborough's technique which we would not otherwise have known. The girl's arms are roughly outlined, as is the body of the cat. From this stage he seems to have proceeded to an equally sketchy modeling, as in the hands, forearms, and dresses. He then finished the girls' heads, and carefully worked out the colors and tones of the background around their heads. So often we think that the great painters developed a picture as a whole, stage by stage. Here we have an illustration which shows that from the very rough indication of shapes this artist proceeded directly to finish the faces down to the most meticulous detail. We find this method also in some of the unfinished religious paintings of the Renaissance. These paintings must have been preceded by carefully rendered sketches, but in the final picture the figures were finished one by one.

The color scheme of Gainsborough's painting is soft and pleasant, with the flesh tones subtle but positive, the pink lips and cheeks being the strongest color in a rather sober plan. The dresses are ocherish and the background, dull colors of brown, purple, and yellow.

Another painting of these children, done somewhat earlier, is also unfinished. Why were these two paintings, which must have meant much to him, not completed? Did he feel that he had captured all he wished at this point? Was he bored with having to refine all the details in his fashionable portraits? Did he realize how everything was now focused satisfactorily on their faces, due to the sketchy treatment of the rest of the pictures? Or did he simply not have the time to finish them because of his many commissions?

Gainsborough's sketchy method was castigated by William Blake, who referred to it as "the blot and blur method of imitation." By "imitation" he was scornfully referring to representing nature as she is. Gainsborough was known to have used at times a brush attached to a rod nearly six feet long. How he managed to control this is beyond my comprehension. His purpose was to be able to view his model and his painting at the same distance. Sir Joshua Reynolds, his lifelong rival, was keenly aware of this sketchy method. He wrote, "This chaos, this uncouth and shapeless appearance, by a kind of magic, at a certain distance assumes form, and all the parts seem to drop into their proper places." He also wrote that if there were ever sufficient genius in the country to produce an English school, Gainsborough would be handed down to posterity as one of its leaders.

Incidentally, Gainsborough was one of the few portrait painters of his time who did not have the draperies painted by assistants. He always completed the entire painting himself. Hayman was his teacher for a brief period,
132

Plate 63. THOMAS GAINSBOROUGH. *The Painter's Daughters Teasing a Cat.* Courtesy, trustees of the National Gallery, London

but he was almost entirely self-taught. Van Dyck was his idol. He had a natural, inborn appreciation of good breeding and the accouterments of gracious living.

Toward the end of his life he did not even show at the Academy, of which he had been a founding member. After six months of illness he wrote Sir Joshua a touching letter, saying that he had always admired his work and loved him, and asked that Reynolds come to his studio just to look at his paintings, so that he might have the honor of talking with him.

I always think of Gainsborough as Walpole wrote about him upon seeing the portrait he had painted of one of his friends:

> That pleasing aspect, and that front serene,
> That comely stature and the graceful mien,
> Shall, taught to live by Gainsbro's wondrous hand,
> In bloom perennial, on the canvas stand!

* * *

The primary purpose for including the "Study for Murat in the 'Battle of Aboukir'" (pl. 64) is to show the degree to which preliminary sketches were carried in this period. This study is only twenty-one inches high, and was painted by Baron Antoine Jean Gros (1771-1835). A larger, signed sketch for the entire painting is in the collection of the Detroit Institute of Arts. The final painting is of considerable size, and was ordered by Joachim Murat, who became one of Napoleon's leading generals and was finally made king of Naples.

The study was made around 1805/06, and is typical of the chaotic compositions of these war scenes. There are definite points in the design, however, which show an attempt to weave a sense of order into the confused shapes. Some of these suggest a triangular or pyramidal understructure.

Gros has given Murat an expression in his eyes of a tension that would have been natural at that moment, but the over-all impression is one of almost unnatural poise. In his "Napoleon at Arcole" Gros has used the same facial expression.

Portrait painters have problems at times with sitters who fail to hold the pose. This is not always confined to working with young children. When Gros painted the portrait of Napoleon, the general was so restless that his wife finally had to hold him firmly on her lap. This has been testified to by an eyewitness.

When Gros was fifteen, he began to study with Jacques Louis David. Some years later Napoleon assigned him the duty of advising him on the selection of paintings which he planned to remove from Italy. In the difficult times following the domination by Napoleon, he finally committed suicide.

134

* * *

Plate 64. After ANTOINE JEAN GROS. *Study for Murat
in the "Battle of Aboukir."* Oil on canvas. Smith
College Museum of Art, Northampton, Massa-
chusetts

It is a meaningful experience for an artist to be able to study Copley's sketch for the portrait of "Adam Viscount Duncan, Admiral of the White" (pl. 65). It is painted in oil on canvas, and is nearly two feet high. The finished picture is in the Dundee Museum in Scotland.

The first impression is that of a completely finished painting. The head is modeled with strength and sureness. Nothing in it has been left unsaid. We are so accustomed to seeing hair rendered in this free manner that we accept it as the final treatment. It is only when we examine the coat and the epaulets that we notice the sketchy treatment.

Through this sketch we now are privileged to study the degree to which Copley felt it necessary to work, in order to provide himself with adequate information for his finished painting. The rendering of form by light and shade is what primarily concerned him. The strong shadows are painted with careful attention to their soft and hard edges. This is particularly evident in the hard edges of the nostril and upper lip, and the softening of the shadows on the upper lip and right cheek. Secondly, he has studied the overall relationship of the halftones which form the forehead, cheeks, and jaw. And, finally, he has completed the modeling by carefully applying the high lights. The manner in which the ear is painted suggests what the treatment of the other features may have been before he completed the sketch. He has taken a small but practical liberty in outlining the nose on the shadow side to make a stenographic rather than a totally realistic record of its shape. The varying degrees with which the far side of the face blends into the dark background are rendered with perception.

The color scheme is simple, and it is interesting to note that Copley has practically mixed his colors on the canvas: the background is a combination of red-brown and yellow-brown; blues and greens are mixed together on the coat. The entire sketch is executed with thin coats of oil paint; in the epaulet one can even see the texture of the canvas. His next step was to apply thicker paint in finishing the head.

The admiral shows all the strength of a determined character. His frown is not that of a momentary expression, but is the result of concentration over the years. The stare suggests self-discipline in posing for the long periods which Copley required and also the fact that the admiral may have been using this time to examine some of his own problems.

The whole picture is a witness to the extraordinary ability of this great painter to transfer three dimensions to two. It will serve as a lesson to artists for generations to come.

* * *

The drawing of Jane Avril (pl. 66) by Henri de Toulouse-Lautrec (1864-1901) is, of course, not the final sketch for her portrait (pl. 67). It probably was done during a preliminary sitting leading up to the final treat-

Plate 65. JOHN SINGLETON COPLEY. *Adam Viscount
Duncan, Admiral of the White.* Oil sketch on
canvas. Yale University Art Gallery, New Haven,
Connecticut, John Hill Morgan Fund

Plate 66. HENRI DE TOULOUSE-LAUTREC. *Jane Avril.*
Sketch. Fogg Museum of Art, Harvard University,
Cambridge, Massachusetts, Bequest of Grenville
L. Winthrop

Plate 67. HENRI DE TOULOUSE-LAUTREC. *Portrait of Jane
Avril.* 1892. Oil on paper-board. Courtesy, Sterling and Francine Clark Art Institute, Williamstown, Massachusetts

ment. It is worth studying, however, to see what characteristics the artist continued to observe. In both pictures he has the tightly pursed mouth, the upturned nose, the partially closed eyes, and the angular jaw and chin. In the sketch he was more concerned with an accurate record of the subject's features. The study of the eyes is much more factual, and there is an intensity in her gaze which does not appear in the rather dissipated look in the painting. The proportions are far more meticulously drawn in the sketch.

When Toulouse-Lautrec executed the painting, he was primarily absorbed with the color patterns as a whole—the pallid face, the fantastic hat and cloak, the "nervous" background, the subject's red hair, and the focal point of her lips. The general proportions of the face are broadly exaggerated, and become a part of the freely rendered figure. While he has retained and even strengthened the modeling of the head, it has been reduced to simpler, flatter shapes in the finished portrait.

This artist was a gifted caricaturist from his early youth, and it is this facet of his work which is most clearly associated with his paintings and posters. Even when he was studying with Fernand Cormon at the age of twenty-two, and making every effort to produce an exact copy of the model, he instinctively exaggerated those details which made each model different.

This tendency may have sprung from two tragic accidents which occurred when he was fourteen and fifteen. His legs were broken and never grew again. Even in maturity he was only four and a half feet high. Coming from one of the two oldest families in France, he was rejected by his eccentric father, the count, for his failure to conform to family standards and, perhaps, for his embarrassing physical appearance. He lived a typically Bohemian life, and cafes, inebriates, and brothels became subject matter.

When he was twenty-six, he was put in a sanitarium, suffering from a nervous breakdown. He painted fifty pictures during the first three months he was there to prove to his father that he should be released. His father even refused to answer the letter containing this request.

It was probably this mixture of tradition and nonconformity and family maladjustment which added to the artist's natural ironic wit and biting sarcasm. People had become targets on which he enjoyed venting his spleen; this is startlingly evident in all his work.

When Toulouse-Lautrec died, the contents of his studio were offered to the Louvre as a gift, but the gift was refused. It was then given to the town of Albi, and in 1922 a beautiful medieval palace was reconditioned and made into a museum which bears his name.

* * *

The "Study for the Portrait of Mme Hertel" (pl. 68) by Hilaire Germain Edgar Degas (1834-1917) is obviously the sketch for the "Woman with Chrysanthemums" (pl. 69).

In certain aspects the sketch seems to be a more factual image of the lady. Instinctively, the artist has used line to define her features and hand. This is the quick, effective way of rendering a sketch. The modeling is a matter of fine lines as distinguished from the flat tones produced by a paper stump. In the finished painting he has modified what probably were individual characteristics, such as the long, pointed nose and the ear which protrudes at a slight angle. He has also given her right shoulder a more pleasing position than the rather hunched look in the sketch. Only one physical peculiarity appears in the painting which is not especially noticeable in the sketch—the left eye points outward more than the right eye. The casual, the informal, the unassuming is further suggested by the pair of gloves carelessly tossed upon the table.

The "Woman with Chrysanthemums" was painted in 1865 when Degas was just beginning to free himself from the classic and the traditional. He was genuinely independent, and here he has broken all the rules of composition by placing the woman on the margin of the picture, and has dared to have her looking out rather than in, which had always been an accepted practice. The accent is certainly on the flowers. (It almost suggests the title "Chrysanthemums with Woman.") The lightest lights and the darkest darks are reserved for the still life. On most of the flowers each petal has been indicated, whereas the ruffle on the front of the lady's dress is merely suggested by a few hastily applied lines. Her face has been given a rather smooth treatment, which contrasts with the flecky handling of the flowers. Degas painted this in oil on canvas, and it is slightly over three feet wide.

Degas studied briefly with Barrias and Lamothe, and entered the École des Beaux-Arts when he was twenty-one. After what appears to have been a brief stay, he went to Rome to study the work of the great masters, particularly those of the fifteenth century. One of the most important influences in his painting was Ingres, who had been a teacher of Lamothe. Degas was an unusual combination of an artist who believed in the influence of the old masters and at the same time turned to original experimentation, unwilling to be bound by the fetters of classicism. He was fully aware that many of these great men who appear so conservative today were actually radicals.

While he made the acquaintance of such artists as Monet, Pissaro, Renoir, and Manet, he had no really close friends. He never married, and was a bitter, self-centered member of the wealthy aristocracy, whose wit was typically Shavian. Pissaro once remarked that he was a dreadful man, but also forthright and loyal.

Perhaps this is an appropriate place to call attention to the fact that the name Degas is pronounced Duh-gáh, and not Day-gah, as is frequently heard. His brother René actually spelled it "de Gas."

* * *

Plate 68. EDGAR DEGAS. *Study for the Portrait of Mme Hertel*. Fogg Museum of Art, Harvard University, Cambridge, Massachusetts, Meta and Paul J. Sachs Collection

Plate 69. EDGAR DEGAS. *Woman with Chrysanthemums.*
Oil on canvas. Metropolitan Museum of Art, New
York, Bequest of Mrs. H. O. Havemeyer, 1929,
H. O. Havemeyer Collection

Degas' handling of crayon and charcoal is effective and direct. This is clearly evident in his "Study for the Portrait of Diego Martelli" (pl. 70). Whether or not this particular one was done from memory is a matter of speculation. He recommended this practice but, as he was somewhat reticent about his procedures, it is not possible to know when he used this method and when he drew from nature. His next step was to make innumerable tracings of the preliminary sketch, and in these he developed the picture, with attention given more to matters of composition and line than to perfecting a likeness.

This study is 17¾" high and, in the finished painting, now in the National Gallery of Scotland in Edinburgh, the figure is twice the size. It is surprising how little difference there is between the study and the final painting. The pose is identical in every respect; the only noticeable change is that he has simplified the folds in the lower left trouser. The right arm of the chair has been made more perpendicular, undoubtedly to help in the over-all design.

The Fogg Museum also has a more detailed sketch for this same painting. In it Degas has drawn the upper half of the figure and has concentrated on the head.

In the study reproduced herewith, the horizontal and vertical lines are a traditional method of enlarging a sketch. The squares are doubled in size on the canvas, which makes it possible to draw a more or less accurate replica of the smaller study by enlarging the material contained in each square.

The final portrait was painted in 1879, and shows the subject at one side of the canvas looking outward. He forms the left half of the picture, the right being devoted to a table cluttered with papers. (Incidentally, Martelli was not an engraver, as has been so frequently stated.) Degas has chosen to look down upon him from above, which tends to emphasize Martelli's obese body and small stature. The free approach to perspective was one of this artist's devoted interests.

*   *   *

In 1902 John Singer Sargent (1856 - 1925), while on a holiday in Spain, painted the water color entitled "In the Generalife" (pl. 71). It represents his sister, Emily, at her easel in the garden of the Generalife Palace in Granada. She is accompanied by Jane de Glehn and Dolores, a Spanish woman.

This example is particularly interesting because of the varying degrees of finish throughout the painting. His sister's head is roughly sketched in, with a focus only on general form. The face of the lady with the hat is rather clearly defined, and the Spanish woman's head has been carefully rendered. Perhaps the artist treated the heads in this way because his sister was more often available to him as a model, whereas he might not have had an oppor-

144

Plate 70. EDGAR DEGAS. *Study for the Portrait of Diego Martelli*. Fogg Museum of Art, Harvard University, Cambridge, Massachusetts, Meta and Paul J. Sachs Collection

Plate 71. JOHN SINGER SARGENT. *In the Generalife.*
Drawing. Metropolitan Museum of Art, New
York, Purchase, 1915, Joseph Pulitzer Bequest

tunity to work with the Spanish lady again. He has certainly captured the ladies' sober absorption as they watch Emily at work.

At about this time Sargent began to make water-color sketches during his travels. Some of the best of them were done in Italy, Spain, and Florida. They were immediately recognized as outstanding and, while he was still in Florida, he was commissioned by the Worcester Art Museum to execute several paintings in this medium.

It is not surprising that Sargent, whose handling is so direct and confident, should have been able to conquer the many problems inherent in water color. He has created this composition with all the verve which was so much a part of his nature. The execution of a sketch of this kind is so revealing that it is almost equivalent to being present while the artist is at work. Each brush stroke suggests the motion of the artist's hand. Which strokes are wet and which are dry are equally obvious.

Sargent was born of American parents in Florence, Italy, and began his studies at the Academy, due to the encouragement of his mother, who was an amateur painter. His family traveled constantly, and he was exposed to the art of Italy, Germany, France, and Spain. He entered the Paris studio of Carolus Duran when he was eighteen, and three years later a portrait of his master which he had painted was accepted by the Salon. Within a few years he had painted the famous "Madame X." He then moved to London, and eventually established himself as the much-sought-after portraitist of society in both London and Boston.

His fame will undoubtedly rest on his portraits rather than on the murals done for the Boston Public Library and for the Museum of Fine Arts in Boston. He had a definite gift for portraiture, and not only appreciated the look of the patrician but was able to record it. He was never cruel in his analysis of his sitter, but was truthful and honest. This last characteristic has been heartily agreed upon by his intimate artist friends.

During his lifetime he was widely honored and became a member of the Royal Academy, the National Academy, an officer of the Légion d'Honneur, and received the Order Pour le Mérite and the Order of Leopold of Belgium. Cambridge University conferred an LL.D. upon him.

Regardless of his current position in the field of art, it is quite clear that Sargent's work will not be forgotten.

RENDERING THE HUMAN FORM

THERE are as many ways to depict the face of man as there are artists. Each artist has his own particular manner. A child draws a head in outline. An art student, taught in the academic tradition, begins his drawing with a light outline; adds the varying soft and hard edges of the shadow; fills in the shadow as a flat area; modifies this with whatever light is reflected in the shadow. He then models the light area, beginning with the shadow edge, and ends with the high lights.

Some of today's painters make their forms with hard, geometric planes. The artists of the Orient use a delicate outline filled in with soft, flat tones. There has been a style throughout the years which sedulously omitted outline, based on the feeling that nature offers us form without any indication of line. This is a perfectly valid point of view and is a basic approach.

There are infinite variations in the way form is revealed by light—the harsh, sparkling effect of full, direct sunlight (pl. 164); the cool, quiet north light of a studio window (pl. 73); the glow of candlelight (pl. 74); the mysterious luminosity of a Rembrandt (pl. 78); the flat effect of a flashlight built into a camera; the strong contrasts due to lighting from the side (pl. 75); and the overhead light from the sky, casting shadows across the eye sockets. These are a few of the myriad effects which may occur on a single face. Nature, thanks be to God, will always provide this infinite variety.

And there is a quality about the human face and body which is unique. Gilbert Stuart, with the true appreciation of the great artist, once said that "flesh is like no other substance under heaven. It has all the gaiety of the silk-mercer's shop without its gaudiness of gloss, and all the softness of old mahogany, without its sadness."

* * *

It will be interesting to examine van Eyck's rendering of a detail (pl. 72) from his "The Virgin with Chancellor Rolin" (pl. 42). The actual length of the hands in the original painting is about 1¾", which will give us some idea of the size of the brush strokes and the degree of finish.

The hands take form through outline and flat modeling rather than by means of light and shade. This is particularly noticeable in the line that defines the right side of the right hand. There is an awareness of *design* in the straight lines of the fingers, especially in the continuation of the line of the index finger as it is extended over the thumb. The textures of the fur cuff and robe are treated with as much care as that of the flesh of the hand.

Examine the minute details of the buildings, streets, and human figures in the town. It is remarkable that any painter should be able to reproduce such a multitude of tiny shapes, and still have the various elements of the entire picture in proper relation to one another.

* * *

Many changes had taken place in the social order and in the artist's concept of portraiture from the time and locale of van Eyck to the productive years of Agnolo Bronzino (1502? - 1572). In Italy the harsh, relentless, honest treatment of a sitter's likeness and personality had been changed to the socially proper mask. This mask was partially the result of intrigue in the courts of the nobility. No one dared to allow his thoughts to be reflected in his face for fear of what might happen to him. In the social world the mask had become a matter of prestige, haughtiness, and pride.

Even in the young this artificial manner had been indoctrinated, as is evident in the portrait of "Lodovico Capponi" (pl. 73). With a complete absence of expression the subject has frozen into a suitable pose. While Bronzino has retained certain personal characteristics, such as the raised left eyebrow and the slight distortion of the eyes, on the whole the face has been idealized, the hands have an added and almost feminine delicacy. The artist's treatment of form is largely a matter of light and shade, with a very substantial use of reflected light, not only on the flesh, but on the left sleeve as well. Bronzino's modeling tends to be exceptionally soft — a fact which results in a smoothness which today's artist might consider overdone.

Plate 72. JAN VAN EYCK. *The Virgin with the Chancellor Rolin* (detail). Louvre, Paris. Phot. Réunion Musées Nationaux

Plate 73. Agnolo Bronzino. *Lodovico Capponi*. Panel.
© Frick Collection, New York

The color scheme of Capponi's portrait is as simple as the rendering of details is complicated. His jacket is a purplish-black; the curtain, a simple green; the flesh color of head and hands is skillfully placed from the point of view of design; and his reddish-brown hair is repeated in the color of the objects he is holding in his hands. The portrait is of substantial size (45⅞" x 33¾"), undoubtedly to fit in with the magnificence of the sixteenth-century architecture and furnishings of the room in which it was to hang.

Bronzino was the pupil and devoted friend of Pontormo, who was only eight or nine years his senior. A portrait by his master of a young man, Ugolino Martelli, shows almost identical lighting and the same effeminate hands. Florence, where they both worked, was undergoing drastic changes in the arts, and the magnificent masculinity of Michelangelo was gradually giving way to the more effete and social school of mannerism. Artists such as Bronzino flourished under the patronage of the aristocracy. When he was twenty-seven, he entered the service of the duke of Urbino. Ten years later he had become court painter to the duke of Como. The ideal of human beauty which Raphael had emphasized in his religious paintings undoubtedly affected Bronzino's point of view. His portraits may have given his sitters a certain general likeness, but his tendency to idealize is certainly apparent, and this tendency was probably not discouraged by his proud subjects.

* * *

In the latter part of the sixteenth century and the beginning of the seventeenth the effects of candlelight were absorbing the attention of various artists. In France, La Tour was painting his stylized but realistic pictures, in which the element that unified the design was light rather than color pattern. In northern Italy, Caravaggio, born about twenty-eight years earlier, demonstrated his belief in rendering form by intense light in a manner which may have influenced La Tour.

Hendrick Terbrugghen (c. 1588-1629) painted the "Old Man Writing by Candlelight" (pl. 74) shortly before he died. It again represents the discovery of indoor light. The color scheme is not a reflection of de La Tour's dominating cinnabar red. The man's robe is an ocherish-orange; the white turban he is wearing has been changed to a soft yellow by the candle flame; the background is gray. There are fascinating touches, such as the upper part of the cheek, where the eyeglass has intensified the light. The folds of the old man's coat sleeves are a bold design of beautifully related shapes. The detail in the shadow area of the hands has been executed with great judgment. It is easy to commit the error of introducing too much detail, or to choose the simple way of painting the shadows too flat and without the proper amount of form. The composition of this picture is compact, and the sub-

Plate 74. HENDRICK TERBRUGGHEN. *Old Man Writing by Candlelight.* Oil on canvas. Smith College Museum of Art, Northampton, Massachusetts

ject's head is suitably related to his hands by the oval design of the collar. For me this has always been one of the outstanding examples of the candlelight era. It also indicates the fact that the paths of art are limitless. The painters of this period were not copying one another's paintings in a literal sense. They were comrades, working side by side, with a stimulating objective—the investigation of the effect of light on form. Rembrandt created light; whereas, for the candlelight school, nature was their goal.

Terbrugghen was born in Deventer and studied with Bloemart. He spent ten years in Rome and Naples, and was declared by Rubens to be "one of the ablest painters in his country."

*   *   *

Now we have come to the period when the artist had a complete understanding and control of physical appearance. The outstanding painter in Spain was Diego Rodríguez de Silva y Velázquez (1599 - 1660). His stature never diminished to the extent of that of many of the great artists of the past. From the time of his appointment as painter to King Philip IV at the age of twenty-three until his death, he was an unworldly as well as a worldly success.

His "Portrait of the Poet Góngora" (pl. 75) is an excellent example of rendering form by light and shade. He did not always select such a sharp contrast between the two, but in his early years he was influenced by Caravaggio's preoccupation with strong chiaroscuro. The sharp, hard, sculptural quality of Góngora's head must have guided the artist in selecting the light in which to paint him. Velázquez did not tend to elaborate upon a sitter's costume. He must have welcomed the simple, severe type of coat which the poet was wearing. He treated it as a completely flat area, devoid of any light and shade. This makes it a perfect foil for the vigorous modeling of the head. The background is unobtrusive also, and the left half is kept dark to contrast with the light side of the face, while the other side is made lighter to emphasize to a lesser degree the shadow side.

After dividing the head into a strong light and a strong shadow, he probably brought these two areas together by a careful execution of the edges of the shadow, from the softest effect on the upper forehead to the hard lines formed near the eyelid, at the top of the nose, on the ear, on the side of the upper lip, on the mouth, and finally on the chin.

Part of Velázquez' great talent was in painting the light areas in such a way that they were not uninteresting, unmodeled shapes. He has recorded the simplest, strongest light on the forehead, and this diminishes as it descends to the chin. The various small planes are indicated with a brush handling which has seldom been excelled. It appears to be directly applied without subsequent retouching. It is the slightly hard edges of these brush strokes

154

Plate 75. DIEGO DE SILVA Y VELÁZQUEZ. *Portrait of the Poet Góngora.* Courtesy, Museum of Fine Arts, Boston

which give genuine character to the modeling. He may have found it necessary occasionally to modify these strokes by softening an edge with his finger.

While the general effect is bold and simple, we should not be misled into thinking that the artist was not concerned with detail. The painting of the shape of the lower eyelid and the light line defining the lower lip as it touches the upper lip are indications of the necessity for this technique.

If Góngora's head had actually been measured mathematically, it might have been less elongated, but this slight and justifiable exaggeration must have given emphasis to one of his more noticeable characteristics.

The poet seems to be of a morose nature, disgruntled with life, perhaps somewhat bitter about its problems. He was one of Spain's great writers and founded a style which was highly sophisticated. He was born in Córdoba in 1561 and died in 1627. The portrait is now known to have been commissioned by the painter Pacheco, to whom Velázquez was apprenticed when he was very young. It was painted in 1622.

Velázquez' career was extraordinary. He served in the king's palace for thirty-seven years in a studio connected with the king's apartment by a passageway. During his service he painted at least thirty-four portraits of Philip IV. Being of noble blood, he was not allowed to accept money for his work, except in executing paintings for his master, the king. To give us an idea of his unusual facility we have only to remember that while Philip was on his way to war Velázquez painted a three-quarter-length portrait of him in three short sittings. He was one of the painters whose work may be studied and analyzed, but which ultimately will be found to be impenetrable.

* * *

When Carol Park Armstrong (pl. 76), a granddaughter, appeared in her dressing gown to say good night, the idea for her portrait came into being. Her temperament was sensitive, intelligent, and fanciful. The expression on her face often suggested that she was on the margin of the real and the unreal. The placid mouth, the wide-open eyes, the slightly raised eyebrows contributed to this mystical feeling. She is looking out with a sense of wonder. When her cousin, who was two years younger, saw the finished painting, he stood in front of it for some time and then said, "What does she want?" No adult could have made a more perceptive comment.

It would have been the height of crudity to paint Carol in strong light and shade. The general effect of the picture had to be soft, ethereal. In order to obtain this, all the values were kept pale—the pink background, the white robe, and the beige rug. In treating these it was essential to render them with just sufficient modeling to suggest a third dimension. Consequently, the
156

Plate 76. GORDON C. AYMAR. *Carol Park Armstrong.*
1955. Water color

shadows are reduced to a minimum. The simple, vertical shape of her body placed in the center of the picture and the horizontal baseboard and rug add an overtone of inaction and peace.

* * *

L. Howell LaMotte (pl. 77) was a good friend of mine with whom I had a feeling of warm understanding, so that it was not difficult to obtain an appropriate expression which would encompass his strength, purpose, and genial nature.

He is wearing a dark, reddish-brown sport jacket; his tie is dark with a slight overtone of green; his face color is strong; the trees, a characteristic part of his home in Florida, carry out a darker, duller brown than that of the coat; the sky is a soft, warm green, with darker tones repeated in the leaves.

Because of the interesting sculptural shape of his head, I was able to place the emphasis on *form*. To obtain this effect, the main light is coming from the side. In applying the paint, the brush strokes were made rather sharp and direct, in an attempt to suggest the masculine qualities of his face.

* * *

Rembrandt Harmensz van Rijn (1606 - 1669) painted the "Portrait of a Young Student" (pl. 78) about 1657. It shows his continuing preoccupation with the effects of light. His passion for a particular type of light is characteristic of nearly all of his well-known paintings. Rembrandt did not merely reproduce an impression which he was observing. He translated what the camera might have recorded into his own concept. He created this light himself; it was his own and belonged to no one else.

In this painting a rather high studio-window light is falling across the subject's face. Rembrandt preferred to paint a considerable number of his subjects wearing hats. This made the light and shade on the features more interesting, and gave the artist an opportunity to introduce reflected light into the shadow.

Most of this painting is rendered in a sketchy manner. He has even left the outline of the right shoulder unchanged. This makes it possible for us to see what the picture must have looked like at a certain stage.

The strong light on the boy's face is not allowed to affect his coat, nor does his cap indicate a literal use of this light. Actually, to cast as strong a shadow as is on his face, the light would have shown the left-hand side of the cap with a definitely lighter area. A reflected light as sharp as that in the shadow on his face would have appeared also on his coat; yet there is none.

158

Plate 77. GORDON C. AYMAR. *L. Howell LaMotte.* 1959.
     Oil on canvas

Plate 78. REMBRANT VAN RIJN. *Portrait of a Young
Student.* c. 1657. Cleveland Museum of Art, Cleveland, Ohio, Gift of Hanna Fund

The glow of light on the background comes mainly near the left side of the face. This device was often used by Rembrandt. It almost seems as though it emanated from the face itself. It is the opposite of the usual placing of the head with the light side against a dark background and the shadow side against a lighter tone, as in Velázquez' "Portrait of the Poet Góngora" (pl. 75).

Rembrandt's luminous effects are achieved partly by the relation of the hard and the soft. Notice how he has reserved the sharp edges for the nose, cheek, and lips, while the hands are simply suggested without contrasts, lines, or edges. Everything is relative, and this manner of handling caused him to write to a friend to whom he had given óne of his paintings, saying that the picture should be hung in a strong light and should be viewed from a distance. Nothing could be farther from the point of view of the school of Memling, where every detail is painted with sharp accuracy and the spectator tends to view it from a short distance.

Rembrandt's warm, dark, subdued color does not compete with this emphasis on light. It is subservient to it, and fortifies the impression of radiant light. A century later, when color had become a more important element, an artist referred to Rembrandt's color as "brown sauce."

The young student in this illustration is painted in a ruminative mood, with the human perception and curiosity about personality which made Rembrandt so outstanding in the field of portraiture. During the four years from 1627 to 1631 he painted 41 portraits; during the next four-year period he painted 102. He continually examined his own inner self in his self-portraits, of which there are known to be over 60.

So much has been written of Rembrandt's life that there is little need to mention the details. His early works, executed in Leyden, where he was born, were surprisingly small in size (one of his best religious paintings is less than 16" x 12"), and they bore a careful, detailed realism which later ceased to interest him. His self-portrait, painted the year before he died, shows this different approach. The paint is built up in patches with palette knife and fingers. It had become almost a matter of sculpture. The color is reduced almost to a monochrome.

Rembrandt's life was filled with tragedy—the death of his beautiful young wife Saskia, that of their first three children, his mistress Hendrickje, and finally his son Titus. From a situation of great wealth acquired during his life in Amsterdam, where he settled in 1631, he sank into bankruptcy, due to a general mismanagement of his affairs. During these latter years, however, he produced some of his greatest paintings. His art had proved itself to have more meaning for him than possessions.

* * *

A year before Velázquez died, Hyacinthe François Honorat Mathias Pierre-le-Martyr André Jean Rigaud was born (1659 - 1743). His "Portrait of a Man" (pl. 79) shows the same use of strong light and shade as in Velázquez' (pl. 75), but here the shadow is considerably darker, and the light areas do not have such interesting modeling. The edges of the shadows are all softer, resulting in a smoothness and refinement which is associated with much of Rigaud's painting. It was considered a treatment suitable for the elegance of the aristocracy. The oval shape of the picture was a matter of fashion, and the frames of the Louis XIV period were an integral part of the whole effect.

Rigaud has treated the man's robe with flair. He always painted these accessories himself without depending on assistants. With an imagination which has no connection with the dull, factual representation of clothing, he has invented folds and ornamented them with light. This free treatment of draperies was one of Rigaud's very successful characteristics. It is creative music as distinguished from literal, descriptive prose.

Rigaud was born in Perpignan, in southern France. He inherited his talent from his father and grandfather, both of whom were artists. At the early age of fourteen he began his studies at Montpellier, where he continued working for four years. In Paris he studied at the Academy, and his work was largely influenced by the paintings of Van Dyck. When he was twenty-nine, he had reached a point of proficiency which persuaded the brother of Louis XIV to sit for him. In 1702 he became an assistant professor at the Academy, and later a full professor. His carefully kept records show that during his sixty-two years of practice he produced an average of thirty to forty portraits a year. When he died, he had painted five kings and all the French princes of the blood.

* * *

To render a man's head it is not always essential to employ strong light and shade. When I painted the portrait of Raymond Ingersoll (pl. 80), who gave the Ingersoll wing to the Brooklyn Public Library, it was necessary to work from many photographs, since he had died a number of years before. As the picture was to hang in the library, it was natural for me to paint him reading. The nearly full light on his face gave an opportunity to describe him, not in bold planes, but rather by *drawing*. Consequently, the planes are painted with light and dark shapes which, in value, are not far removed one from another. They are resolved roughly into three values. The dark consists of the shadows on his neck, behind his nose, on the far side of his forehead and lower lip. The middle tones are reserved for the general skin tone. The light planes are the high lights on his forehead, upper cheek, and

162

Plate 79. HYACINTHE RIGAUD. *Portrait of a Man*. Oil on
canvas. Courtesy, Sterling and Francine Clark Art
Institute, Williamstown, Massachusetts

Plate 80. GORDON C. AYMAR. *Raymond Ingersoll.* 1963.
Oil on canvas. Collection, Brooklyn Public Library, Gift of Mrs. Raymond Ingersoll

nose. His expression of gentleness and distinction is a matter of draftsman-ship. The dog under his arm was an informal touch which supplemented the impression of relaxation.

The color scheme is restrained—a soft green for the chair; a greenish-ocher for the curtain, which is repeated in his necktie; greenish-tan wood-work; and the small area of dark greenish-black marble of the corner of the fireplace. His suit is a warm, dark gray.

In instances such as this it is important to have the help of loving rela-tives to interpret the personality. Without such assistance the final result would be cold and meaningless.

*　*　*

The treatment of the "Peasant of the Camargue" (pl. 81) by Vincent van Gogh (1853 - 1890) is typical of Van Gogh's intensity and violence in executing all his work. In this picture he used quill and reed pen-and-ink over soft graphite pencil on white paper. The original (which is 19½" x 15") gives a much bolder impression than the reproduction. The background is full of shimmering light and movement. The planes of his face are indicated by lines which follow the direction of a plane. This is particularly evident in the subject's chin. The texture and color of his cheeks called for a different handling.

This pen-and-ink drawing is almost the equivalent of a diagram of Van Gogh's brush-stroke method in painting—the swerving lines of the face and the pointillist handling of the background.

The failure of the nineteenth-century public, art dealers, and critics to express any concrete or helpful interest in Van Gogh's work is a testimo-nial to the fact that the enduring value of contemporary art is extremely difficult to estimate. During this artist's entire lifetime he managed to sell only one of his paintings, "The Red Vine."

Strangely enough, Van Gogh began as an artist with a concentration on drawing, to which he devoted his time exclusively for a number of years. He studied the laws of proportion, anatomy, chiaroscuro, and perspective, and maintained that they were essential if an artist were to do genuinely creative work. When he was twenty-eight, he began to give his full time to painting in oils, a technique about which he knew little or nothing. He developed his own method, and stated that form was the element which interested him most. Four years later he had become completely immersed in color.

He painted eight hundred and sixty-two pictures in the brief span of his active painting life, fourteen of which were self-portraits. A large por-tion of these were executed during the three years before he died.

Plate 81. VINCENT VAN GOGH. *Peasant of the Camargue.*
Fogg Museum of Art, Harvard University, Cam-
bridge, Massachusetts, Bequest of Grenville L.
Winthrop

Much has been written about the tragic side of Van Gogh's life, ending in suicide at the age of thirty-seven. One detail, however, I have always found particularly touching. Just before his suicide he walked out into the fields with his easel in his arms and leaned it against a haystack. This was his last act, and it represented a consecration of the thing that meant most to him—the symbol of his painting.

* * *

The "Portrait of Mrs. Frederick Mead" (pl. 82) by Sargent is a splendid example of this artist's forthright rendering, his firm drawing, and his use of the hard edge of a brush stroke to define the planes of a head.

He has well understood the pattern of light and shade on Mrs. Mead's head—the darkest shadows being saved for the eye socket, the end of the nose, the neck, and the lips; the medium shadow for the cheek, jaw, nose, and nostril. He has painted her hair in an equally simple manner—the dark shadow relieved slightly by reflected light; the light areas by a general tone; and the high lights with appropriate simplicity.

Sargent's purpose in painting in his characteristic manner was to produce a picture which would *carry*. At a slight distance the hard edges of various planes tend to soften, yet they still maintain a strength which prevents the modeling from becoming unpleasantly soft. The white area of this subject's dress has been painted freely, wet on wet.

He has represented a very distinguished lady without pomp and circumstance. Her expression is relaxed and sympathetic. She is not acting. There is an overtone of sadness in her eyes, particularly in the left one. Her slight smile is in no sense artificial. To understand how this has been achieved, hold your finger over the right half of her mouth (right from your point of view). Her expression is rather empty. Now cover the other side, and her smile at once comes alive.

The artist's penetrating rendering of the features once enabled a physician, so the story goes, to diagnose a disease which until then had not been identified.

Sargent's handling of his brush in painting the human form has been termed "wizardry," and this is a good description of it. His skill in this respect is unsurpassed. I have given considerable thought to this aspect of his work, since my own approach is the exact opposite. The apparently swift, spontaneous handling would suggest that the entire painting process was executed with little difficulty and with considerable speed. I cannot believe that this was the case. In order to succeed with the subtleties of modeling a head and giving it correct sculptural form it would be a prerequisite to devote a great deal of time and concentration to mixing the paint to produce the exact value, hue, and degree of neutrality. Then it may be

167

Plate 82. JOHN SINGER SARGENT. *Portrait of Mrs. Frederick Mead.* 1893. Oil on canvas. Yale University Art Gallery, New Haven, Connecticut, Edwin Austin Abbey Collection

assumed that the brush stroke could be made with confidence and, presumably, without the need of fussy alteration. Prior to the exact mixing of the proper brushful of color there would be the clearly imagined concept of what the painting was intended to look like when finished.

The inscription over Mrs. Mead's head records the fact that this was a gift to his friend Mrs. Abbey. It does not appear to represent a struggle to create a distinguished "work of art." It is a painting done without stress or pressure in recording the personality of this charming lady.

* * *

At one point in his varied career André Derain (1880-1954) returned to classical realism. Having started painting with the Fauvists at the beginning of the century, he passed through the styles of cubism and expressionism, but in each phase he maintained a poise and a restraint which showed his devotion to the traditional. He had studied at the Académie Carrière and, later, at the Académie Julian. He respected the art of the old masters and spent days copying at the Louvre.

The "Portrait of a Girl (Young Girl with a Pear)" (pl. 83) shows his interest in form. The lines are hard and firm. One is conscious of an almost mathematical approach to the various details—two eyes, two eyebrows, a nose, a mouth, an ear. To model these he used a restrained light and sharpened the edges of the planes revealed by this light. In the jaw and the sides of her forearms he has used reflected light, more as an outline of form than as a study in light and shade. The girl's expression which he has captured (or invented) is the wide-eyed stare of youth. He has not blasphemed nature by abnormal distortion. The composition is a fresh and satisfying combination of the human figure and a still life.

At the beginning of his career Derain met Matisse and worked with Vlaminck at Châtou, where he had been born. On a trip to Spain when he was thirty he painted with Picasso, who was at the beginning of his cubist period. Apparently Derain withdrew from this point of view, for a few years later he restudied the French and Netherlandish painters of the fifteenth century. I was interested to learn that he was profoundly affected by the "Villeneuve-les-Avignon Pietà" in the Louvre. I can quite understand this, for on a recent trip to Europe this was the painting that most impressed me. After the war, in which he served as a truck driver, he designed sets for the Ballet Russe. This artist's last years were spent in southern France and Italy, and overtones of the impressionists appeared again in his painting.

* * *

Perhaps the two opposite ends of the pole in painting the human form are the "Claire de Lune" (pl. 84) by Suizan Miki (1887-1957) and Ivan

169

Plate 83. ANDRÉ DERAIN. *Portrait of a Girl (Jeune Fille à la Poire)*. Albright-Knox Art Gallery, Buffalo, New York. Collection of Mr. and Mrs. Seymour H. Knox

Albright's "Woman" (pl. 85). Miki's is unusual in that it is the twentieth-century epitome of the tradition of Utamaro and Harunobu. It is fortunate that this artist did not reject the traditional on the theory that there was nothing more to be said in this particular language. How restful to be able to dismiss light and shade and sculptured form, and limit oneself to line and undisturbed, pure flat pattern. Miki demonstrates how much freedom and latitude there is within these limits The sharply twisted pose of the lady contemplating the moon, the charming gesture of her hands, and the exquisite treatment of her hair, all combine to give us a painting which merits endless enjoyment. As a composition it is delightful, with her figure placed in one corner of the picture. The angle of the handle of the fan is repeated quietly by the wooden frame at the left. The angle of the small, straight ornament in her hair offsets these diagonals. Her features are indicated with the most sensitive lines. Nothing has ever been discovered that can equal silk as a surface for painting this type of picture. It adds an elegance all its own; but what skill it must take to apply these delicate tones! As a change from the shape of the average Western portrait, it is an interesting relief to select a square. (The picture is 33⅛" x 31⅞".)

Miki was born in Kyoto, and studied with Seiho Takeuchi, who was one of the most distinguished Japanese painters of the last century. At the age of seventeen Miki was so advanced in his profession that he won his first prize in an exhibition in which many prominent artists were showing their work. He then received a first prize from the Japan Art Association. When he was twenty, he won thirteen special awards for paintings he had exhibited for the Department of Education. He was later elected a member of their examining board. His paintings are in the collections of five Japanese princes, and are in museums and galleries in Asia, Europe, and America.

* * *

It is seldom that one can identify the work of an artist half a block away, but this is certainly true of Ivan Albright (1897 -   ). His pictures are his own and belong to no one else, not even to a school. The human form and its garments are seen by him in one aspect only. It is the busy flutter of detail which has always fascinated him. Whereas the Persians were interested in composing beautiful and intricate patterns in flat color in miniature size, Albright is bent on filling a canvas 33" x 22" (pl. 85) with tiny, boiling forms rendered in harsh light and shade. His use of color is limited to a dark, somber palette. No young child with a soft, smooth face would qualify as his subject. The disintegrating, gnarled, rough-textured flesh of the aged is where he wishes to devote his energies. And he must repeat these forms and textures in their clothing.

171

Plate 84. SUIZAN MIKI. *Claire de Lune*. Paint on silk.
Metropolitan Museum of Art, New York, Gift of
Suizan Miki, 1952

Plate 85. Ivan le Lorraine Albright. *Woman.* 1928.
Collection, Museum of Modern Art, New York

The picture entitled "Woman" (pl. 85) is the very essence of Albright. There she sits, resigned, worn out, the wreckage of life cast up on the beach of time. The old masters would have reduced the coat and imitation fur collar and cuffs to relatively flat, dark, simple patterns to emphasize the light and shadowed areas of her face and hands. Not Ivan Albright. These elements become a counterpoint to the face and hands. They sing the same song but with different timing.

After completing the seething forms, he has inserted the most minute details—the hairs in the fur, the hairs on her upper lip, each individual eyelash. Her left thumbnail is even shaped as she cut it the last time. But these forms are far from photographic. No sleeves on any coat ever looked like these. They are inventions—twisted, restless shapes which echo those of her hands and face. Even the background is smoldering. This is truly super-realism.

Albright's technique was nurtured in many schools—the École des Beaux-Arts at Nantes, the Art Institute of Chicago, the Pennsylvania Academy Of The Fine Arts in Philadelphia, and the National Academy of Design in New York. Before studying painting, he took courses in architecture, and became a medical draftsman in the army in World War I. This last experience undoubtedly contributed to his sharp examination of detail and his awareness of the disintegration of flesh.

His work has been widely acclaimed and he has held one-man shows in the Institute in Chicago and the Whitney Museum of American Art in New York.

THE SELF-PORTRAIT

IT WOULD BE interesting to know the circumstances under which a self-portrait is made. Why does an artist want to paint himself? Is it a matter of vanity? A desire to be preserved for posterity? A dearth of sitters and an urge to keep painting? A Christmas present for one's spouse? A stipulation of the Academy prior to election? A curiosity to find out just what one does look like? A chance to record the physical lineaments of a personality known so intimately and inescapably? Or is it the opportunity to make a striking and original painting without interference? It may be any one of these reasons or several of them combined.

When we study the many portraits Rembrandt did of himself (there are over one hundred paintings, drawings, and etchings), it seems clear that his primary motive was the irresistible desire for artistic exploration. He was his own convenient, manageable model. From this point on, he was able to study effects of light, composition, facial expression, and all the elements a painter spends his life trying to conquer.

In 1658 Rembrandt painted the rather imposing picture of himself now in the Frick Collection in New York; in 1659, the very roughly handled head and shoulders in the museum in Aix, in which he looks old and worried. The following year he painted the well-known one in the Louvre. Here he is Rembrandt the artist, with mahlstick, palette, and brushes. He has the tired, almost pathetic look of the painter who is discouraged with the endless search for perfection. One year later he depicted himself almost in caricature. He has the appearance of a local character, with a quizzical look and wrinkled forehead. His stare is that of the painter trying to eliminate detail and view his model as a whole. This picture is in Spiez in the J. de Bruijn Collection. (Incidentally, he signs his name here without the "t".)

In a book which I found many years ago there are reproductions of sixty-two self-portraits of Rembrandt. They depict him as young, old, questioning, mouth drawn, mouth half-open, laughing, sad, distinguished, sloppy, tired, observant, eyebrows raised in wonder, perplexed, majestic, naïve. There are many mannerisms which are evident, and, although Rembrandt did not depart too often from his "natural" point of view, there are certain variations in style. His portrait painted in 1655, which is in the National Museum in Stockholm, is particularly interesting. It is almost impressionistic in its treatment. In it his main interest apparently was the transient effect of light. The handling of the features is allowed to be really subservient to this rendering.

I have examined with care fourteen self-portraits by Vincent van Gogh. Here the motive was a continuing study of color and its handling. Many are portraits of head and shoulders with an almost identical pose and lighting. The difference lies in the varied uses of this artist's characteristic palette. One critic referred to it as his "frenzied passion for color."

In re-reading some condensed notes which I made while studying the self-portraits in the Uffizi Gallery in Florence, I find that one immediate, single impression is often received from such paintings. I have noted:

RAPHAEL: sweet, soft
VASARI: worried
TITIAN: old and noble
RUBENS: fine color
GIOVANNI CONTARINI: handsome
REMBRANDT: wider range of color than is generally associated with his work
VAN DYCK: aristocratic
SALOMON ADLER: smiling (Why is there an unwritten law that a portrait should not have a really hearty smile?)
SARGENT: man of distinction

At times quick, condensed judgments such as these may reveal things which even the artist may not be aware of, since he has many problems to solve.

176

There are many examples of self-portraits that illustrate the painter's desire to be free of his sitter's requirements, expressed or implied. Sir Joshua Reynolds, who certainly painted many portraits of severely conventional people, must have enjoyed painting the picture of himself which is in the National Portrait Gallery in London. Here he is shielding his eyes from the strong studio light in a gesture that is more than informal.

Carlo Dolci, with a weary, sorrowful look, holds a picture of himself painting. The expression of his eyes in this small picture is totally different from that in the full face. Now the eyes have the intent, almost glassy stare of the observing painter; his mouth is open as he makes one breath-taking stroke with his brush. This was obviously an interesting approach which he could not have used with a client.

Fra Filippo Lippi appropriately chose a sober, reverent look as he folds his hands in prayer at the "Coronation of the Virgin." There have been literally hundreds of similar instances in which artists of high standing have painted themselves into religious paintings.

Maerten van Heemskerck devised a really original composition for his self-portrait. The items which he introduced were not unusual at the time (1553)—the ancient ruins; the distant, small figure of the person whose portrait was painted in the foreground; the folded, pinned piece of paper bearing signature and date. The composition of these, however, and their relation one to another were distinctly fresh and different.

Another self-portrait which seems almost like a confession is that of Frans Hals in the Clowes Collection. Gone are the vibrant gaiety, the bawdy laughter, the joy of clowning. This is the morning after, the dissipated look, the drooping eyelids, the pouches under the eyes. There is no self-consciousness here, no acting. This is the truth; this is the man.

For me one of the great self-portraits is one of Rembrandt's, painted when he was forty-four years old. This is in the Widener Collection in Philadelphia. After a period of enjoying it ecstatically with the sense of sight, there comes a moment when an artist's inquiring mind wants to know *why* it is so wonderful. With a silent, reverent apology to the artist for leaving the meaningful area of enjoyment and entering the crass field of analysis, one discovers that it is the superlative achievement in *all* categories that makes it so enduring a work of art.

Many self-portraits register the look of absorption which dominates the face of an artist at work. In some cases it is a frown, in others a piercing eye, in still others a stare. Some have even captured that slightly fey expression that may indicate that the painter is making a totally objective observation of external forms, colors, and surfaces, without reference to any meaning which they might convey. This is a device whereby the artist bypasses what is sometimes referred to as his brain, in order that the sensory impression received from his eye may be transmitted directly down his arm to his paintbrush without interference or interpretation. As Goethe puts it, "Thinking is more interesting than knowing, but not so interesting as looking."

* * *

When Nicolas Poussin (1594 - 1665) painted his "Self-Portrait" (pl. 86) at the age of fifty-six, he applied the same rigid standards of classical perfection which he used in his historical, religious, and mythological pictures. He was by nature an intellectual, who accepted the art of ancient Greece and Rome as paramount.

The dominating part of his self-portrait is the head, which is, of course, the basis of most portraits. The strong light and shade provides this accent. The light values are repeated in his hand, and in the head of the goddess. What could be more appropriate than to use pictures, canvases, and frames as units of composition? These shapes form a perfect foil for the curves of the hair, face, and robe.

The color scheme is strong and simple—various dark browns in the background and in his hair; dark blues in the robe and in the sky of the painting with the goddess; warm, strong flesh color repeated in her crown, hair, and gown. There is a touch of red brocade behind his back.

Poussin has represented himself as a man of strength and dignity, with the air of a nobleman.

There is nothing fortuitous in the composition of the painting. Vertically, his head is directly in the center of the picture. The space above his head is exactly the height of his head. His eyes are on a line with the thin strip of blue sky in the painting behind him. A line drawn through the first three lines of the inscription would lead to the goddess' face.

This geometric approach is carried down to the smallest detail. There is a fleck of light on his cloak, directly below his face. A line drawn along the dark edge of the top of the chair back runs through this light, and a line through the edge of his robe at the lower right-hand corner of the picture also passes through it. The same is true of the line across the top of the dark landscape over the goddess' head.

Poussin was born in a family that had no regard for the calling of an artist. His father wanted him to become a lawyer, but when he was eighteen he had the opportunity of watching the artist Quentin Varin at work on a religious painting. This excited him to the point where he realized that he wanted painting for his career. Knowing that he would not be able to change his father's opinion, he ran away from home. A friend of his referred to him as a young man with the furious determination of the devil.

When he went to Rome in 1624, he had acquired a sufficient reputation to receive, four years after his arrival, a commission to paint a picture for

178

Plate 86. Nicolas Poussin. *Self-Portrait*. Louvre, Paris.
Phot. Réunion Musées Nationaux

St. Peter's. By 1640 his reputation had become international, and he received an invitation from Louis XIII to decorate the palace of the Louvre, which was being fully restored. The king gave him a little palace in the garden of the Tuilleries, where he worked on the project for two years but finally gave up his commission, due to the frustrations caused by his French fellow artists who were jealous of his being awarded so important an assignment. He returned to Rome and spent the rest of his life there.

*   *   *

Camille Pissarro (1830-1903) painted his "Portrait of the Artist" (pl. 87) when he was seventy-three years old. This was one of his last paintings; he died in the fall of that same year.

He is looking at himself in a mirror, and his head and body are turned away from the light and are in full shadow. This is what makes the portrait rather unusual. For Pissarro it was a challenge to observe the effects of light and shade and color. Bold, hard depiction of the features did not interest him. It was the general impression which he wished to paint. The streets of Paris, seen through the window, give depth to the picture, and form an interesting pattern of color to offset the simple vertical shapes of the rest of the background. Pissarro has not attempted to emphasize any of his personal characteristics; he is simply looking at his reflection.

In a letter to his son Lucien he wrote: "Remember that I have the temperament of a peasant, I am melancholy, harsh and savage in my works. . . . It takes me hours of reflection to decide on the slightest detail."

Born on the beautiful island of St. Thomas in the Caribbean in the days when it was completely unspoiled, he must have been absorbed from early youth with the interaction of light and color. He studied in Paris, and among his friends were Corot, Monet, and Manet. He exhibited with the impressionists in 1874, and some years later Gauguin and Seurat led him in the direction of the neoimpressionists.

*   *   *

The "Self-Portrait" of Degas (pl. 88) is very revealing. It was painted when he was twenty-three or twenty-four. It is, first of all, the sensitive face of an artist. He has the melancholy look of one who is somewhat withdrawn from the world and friends. His features are refined, and suggest his aristocratic background. (His aunt married her cousin, the Marquis of Cicerale, and his sister became the Duchess of Morbilli.)

In the portrait there is a slight indication of determination in his chin. He has chosen a beautiful light in which to pose, with the strongest source coming from above, supplemented by a minor light from his left side.

180

Plate 87. CAMILLE PISSARRO. *Portrait of the Artist.* 1903.
    Reproduced by courtesy of the trustees of Tate
    Gallery, London

Plate 88. EDGAR DEGAS. *Self-Portrait*. 1857/58. Oil on
canvas. Courtesy, Sterling and Francine Clark Art
Institute, Williamstown, Massachusetts

When Degas was forty years old, his eyesight started to fail and gradually became worse. He died at the age of eighty-three, totally blind. To be sure, he had spent his life in what he referred to as "memorizing" nature, and presumably he could still visualize beauty, even without sight. But creatively he could not paint, whereas Beethoven could write a great symphony after he had finally become totally deaf.

Degas said that his art was far from spontaneous, that it was due to reflection and to studying the great masters of the past. In his witty way he referred to those who copied nature as "brazen impostors."

* * *

Jean Edouard Vuillard (1867-1940) was about twenty-two years old when he painted his "Self-Portrait with His Friend, Varoquez" (pl. 89). It is a clear indication of a period of his work which was not yet concerned with shimmering color and pattern. It has the overtone of the conventional, academic painting of the late 1880's. It is obviously unfinished, but in this condition we are able to study the various stages which might have led to the more finished state. The execution of the body of his friend is merely a matter of covering the canvas with an unobjectionable tone. It is remarkable how much of a "likeness" can be suggested in the rough indication of Varoquez' face. Vuillard has studied carefully the effects of light on his own head and hand, and we can assume that this would have been the treatment of the rest of the picture if he had decided to finish it. Did he not like the picture at this stage? Did he feel that the composition was unsatisfactory for a two-figure portrait? He was beginning to suggest diagonals, such as the one formed by the bottle, his hand, and the picture on the wall. The angle of Varoquez' right shoulder aims toward Vuillard's brushes, and this implied diagonal is immediately offset by the line of the palette. Regardless of how the artist intended the picture to look eventually, it is very pleasing in its present state.

Vuillard was born in Cuiseaux, Saône-et-Loire. His mother was twenty-seven years younger than his father, and when his father died, she became a dressmaker, having inherited an interest in textile design from her father. Perhaps this is one of the reasons one is so conscious of the patterns of material in Vuillard's later paintings. He never married and lived with his mother until she died. This undoubtedly had a profound effect upon his life. He was diffident, timid, shy—characteristics which he has recorded in his self-portrait. He was a listener rather than a speaker at the lively meetings held by the Nabis (the Prophets) to discuss art. The quality of his painting declined during the latter part of his life. He was probably confused by the various violent movements in art at that period, and lost confidence in his ability to express himself in his own particular manner.

* * *

183

Plate 89. ÉDOUARD VUILLARD. *Self-Portrait with His Friend, Varoquez.* 1888/90. Oil on canvas. Metropolitan Museum of Art, New York, Gift of Alex M. Lewyt, 1955

The self-portrait of Sir William Newenham Montague Orpen (1878-1931), entitled "Leading the Life in the West" (pl. 90), is an example of how free a painter feels from any restrictions when he is painting a picture of himself. Instead of the formal, socially correct environment, this artist has used a cluttered foreground and an equally complicated background. The items around the mirror, filling in the borders of the picture, are a daring element of composition, breaking all the classical laws. They are beautifully designed, in addition to their illustrative quality. In order to place a slight emphasis on the critical area of the head, the artist has reserved the lightest light to isolate the dark face, and the line of the shade runs directly to his eyes. The derby, which is one of the darkest spots, helps to direct the eye to his head.

Orpen is pausing to submit himself to self-examination. His glance is quiet but searching, and his pose suggests that he was moving about when he happened to see himself in the mirror. There is also a tone of defiance in the widespread feet. It is refreshing to see an unconventional approach of this kind. At first glance it is merely an entertaining idea, but actually it becomes more profound, the longer one studies it. This picture was painted in 1914, a time when there was an increasing respect for the growing art of photography. Just as Degas helped to upset the formality of composition through his interest in the random, hit-or-miss effects of the camera, so Orpen in this picture pays homage to the "candid" look by this informal setting.

Orpen was born in Stillorgan, County Dublin, and studied at the Dublin Metropolitan School of Art. He then moved to London and continued his work at the Slade School, becoming an associate of the Royal Academy in 1910 and, nine years later, an Academician. He was created a Knight of the British Empire in 1918. I am sure that his duties as an official artist in World War I affected his outlook on art and on life.

* * *

In studying the Max Beckmann "Self-Portrait in Tuxedo" (pl. 91) we are looking in the face of a most unusual man through his own eyes. It was painted in 1927. Color gives way to the strong black-and-white pattern. The stiff curtain and the wall are brown; the flesh is made of grays and browns, with touches of pink. The artist was primarily interested in interpreting himself and, secondarily, in using strong light and shade to achieve this. The two sources of light enabled him not only to render form, but also to design a pattern which is interesting per se. To understand how freely he used light, we have only to examine the shirt front with the strong shadow, where there would have been little indication of such an effect. The right

185

Plate 90. WILLIAM ORPEN. *Leading the Life in the West.*
Oil on canvas. Metropolitan Museum of Art, New
York, Gift of George F. Baker, 1914

Plate 91. Max Beckmann. *Self-Portrait in Tuxedo.* 1927.
   Oil. Busch-Reisinger Museum, Harvard University, Cambridge, Massachusetts

cuff, which actually must have been in dark shadow, is painted in one of the light tones to make it a telling part of the over-all design. In this role it balances the left cuff.

Beckmann's creed was to learn by heart and render the real in order to reveal the unreal. His attitude was that, by memorizing these forms, one could use them as a composer uses musical notes. He then was able to *create* nature. One of his fundamental beliefs which has always appealed to me is his statement that nature is a wonderful chaos from which it is our obligation to make order and, in so doing, to perfect it.

Beckmann's World War I army career as a medical aide, living among dugouts, corpses, graves, and bodies in agony, gave him a great social conscience, and he expressed this in many of his paintings.

He was born in Leipzig in 1884 and went to art school in Weimar when he was nineteen. In 1925 he taught at the Frankfurt Art School, but he was harassed by Hitler for being a "degenerate" painter and was dismissed after eight years of service. He spent the last three years of his life in the United States, teaching first at Washington University in St. Louis and then at the Brooklyn Museum.

In his one-man show at the Museum of Modern Art in New York in 1964, there were twenty-seven self-portraits, among which were the somewhat impressionistic one painted in 1907 and the crude, bold representation executed in 1950, the year in which he died.

Beckmann was constantly examining himself as a gateway to the invisible. The love of the existing, tangible world was combined with an insatiable desire to understand the secrets hidden within.

*   *   *

At the age of twenty-seven Oskar Kokoschka (1886 -   ) painted a memorable and revealing "Self-Portrait" (pl. 92). It is not only a picture of an artist; it is a symbol of hallucination and insecurity. His wide-open eyes are not seeing a visible object of fright; they are reflecting an inner ghost of fear. He is a lost soul, expressing his awe at the mysteries of the universe. His hand is painted in a gesture which may indicate an attempt to protect himself, or it may be saying, as Peter did, "Is it I, Lord?"

The ability to illustrate such overtones is most unusual. If a portrait by Holbein is prose, a portrait by Kokoschka is poetry, dedicated to the Tragic Muse. Actually, part of his artistic abilities do take the form of poetry and drama. Four years after this portrait was painted, he moved to Dresden, where he acquired the title "Mad Kokoschka."

Even the proportions of height to width in his self-portrait are suggestive of those of an attenuated human being. His elongated head and body
188

Plate 92. Oskar Kokoschka. *Self-Portrait*. 1913. Oil
on canvas. Collection, Museum of Modern Art,
New York, Purchase

are a revelation in themselves. The speed of execution of his brush strokes indicates a tense and nervous mood. However, in addition to the impulsive use of brush and paint, there is the well-understood treatment of every detail—the furrowed forehead, the timid, pursed mouth, and, above all, the exaggeration of the sad eyes.

The color scheme is somber, almost morbid. The background is a heavy, cool gray, with muted greens, blues, and browns giving it mild relief. The face and hand are grays and browns. The only real color is in the clothing, where the basic gray is relieved with violets, oranges, and greens.

Kokoschka was born in southern Austria. He studied at the School of Applied Art in Vienna, which undoubtedly aided him in his illustrative lithographs. After World War I, during which he was wounded on the Russian front, he went to Dresden and taught at the Academy. Four years later he left, to travel restlessly through Europe and the Near East. He fled to London in 1938 to escape the German army, and later became a British subject. After a brief stay in Italy he settled in Salzburg, where he teaches at the school he founded, which he has named the School for Seeing. What could be more perceptive? Kokoschka is convinced that it is vision which counts and not theories, and it is on this belief that he centers his teaching.

*   *   *

It is exciting to see an artist use all of his creative talents in a painting. Lucian Freud (1922-) gives evidence of this in his "Self-Portrait" (pl. 93), painted when he was twenty-four years old. Perhaps this is the result of German ancestry of high quality, for he is the son of Ernst Freud, the architect, and the grandson of the famous Sigmund Freud. This family background is combined with a training in art in the English tradition. I say this with great respect, for in my opinion the British, with their notable moderation, have been able to *absorb* the various trends in art without throwing everything traditional out of the window and counting only on the *trend* to fortify them. Freud has not rejected the "representational" (an adjective of scorn used by some of today's critics), yet he has added to it the imaginative and the symbolic in a manner that is undisturbing.

This picture is also called "The Man with a Thistle," an object which he may have used as an abstract to suggest his own personal characteristics. The thistle is a beautiful design in itself, but, while some contemporary artists might have been content to stop there, Freud has combined it with his own head and shoulders, painted in a firm, realistic manner. The ladder at the right also must have had a meaning for him beyond its role as an object. Is this the ladder he hopes to ascend?

The picture as a design is very handsome. The geometrical relationships are carefully adjusted. The bristly, active form in the foreground would

190

Plate 93. LUCIAN FREUD. *Self-Portrait*. Reproduced by
courtesy of the trustees of Tate Gallery, London

have been merely an uninteresting addition if it had not been made proportionately so large. The almost leatherlike texture of the material on which the thistle is lying is a welcome contrast to the smooth texture behind his figure. Light and shade are reduced to a minimum on the thistle, and its shadow is almost negligible. The light and shade on Freud's body are introduced with conviction, and give one the feeling that he was perfectly trained in this aspect of painting. However, he has taken necessary liberties with chiaroscuro. Where he needed boldness and strength of contrast, he has used them, and yet the shadow on his face is less severe. We seldom see such a combination of realistic lighting and sharply designed outline. The planes of his face have been simplified so that they become an element of design. His hair is a masterpiece, giving not only an impression of curly hair but of excellent decoration as well. It also repeats, to a degree, the shapes in the thistle.

His features have been discreetly exaggerated—the thinness of his face; his long, pointed jaw; his long, slim nose; and his small ear. His appearance is sensitive, his look concentrated and searching, as though he were observing himself not only as a natural object, but as a personality.

Freud was born in Berlin and came to England with his parents when he was ten years old. He became a British subject, and studied at the Central School. He then had part-time training at Goldsmiths' College. Freud won the Arts Council Prize in the 1951 Festival of Britain Exhibition, and at the Venice Biennale three years later several of his paintings were shown. He has taught at the Slade School and works in London and Paris.

APORTRAIT PAINTER is confronted with two basic problems in interpreting his sitter. One is the difficulty of giving a complete revelation of a person whom he has just met; the other, creating an image of a close friend or relative.

I have never had the privilege of painting royalty, but I can sympathize with the feelings Hans Holbein must have had as he walked in the palace door in Brussels where Christina of Denmark, Duchess of Milan, was living with her aunt, the Governess of the Netherlands. He had been sent there by Henry VIII's councilor, Thomas Cromwell, to paint her portrait so that the king could decide whether or not he wanted to marry this young girl of sixteen.

She could not have been too eager to pose, since her portrait had just been painted for Henry by an artist whose name is unrecorded. When the English chargé d'affaires learned that Holbein was coming, he sent an express courier to stop the messenger who was carrying this first portrait to London, saying that the portrait was "neither so good as the occasion required, nor as Master Hans would be able to do it."

In three hours, which was all he was allowed, Holbein made the decision to paint her full length in her widow's dress (her husband had died when she was thirteen), and made a crayon sketch of her from which he painted the final portrait. The chargé d'affaires wrote

193

that Holbein showed himself "a master of the art, for the likeness is perfect." This is an instance when getting to know the sitter is reduced to minutes.

I have always been fascinated by the challenge of painting someone I was to see for the first time. If it happened to be an adult, I would show Ektachromes of my portraits to discover which approach the sitter appeared to like. If it were a child, after an attempt to make him (or her) feel at ease and after I had shown my pictures, the parents would "excuse" the child and, in a matter of minutes, would launch on an absorbing interpretation of his character and personality, so that I might, hopefully, record it.

I remember receiving a delightful series of letters from the father of a little six-year-old girl whom I was about to paint. They were well expressed and genuinely helpful. One remark stays in my mind. He said that he had started to go into her room, but the floor was covered from wall to wall with everything from dolls to clothing. After a rather severe rebuke from him, she said, "I'm a bird, and I don't know where to light." I tried in painting her to catch some of this fey quality.

The grandfather of a ten-year-old girl took me aside as I was about to begin work on a painting of his granddaughter and said, "Gordon, when you paint C——, don't make the horns too red!"

With young children I try to make as few suggestions about their pose as possible. If they become self-conscious, they tend to tighten their lips. I never mention this, as it inevitably makes them more self-conscious. Eventually, they begin to think of something else, and it is often possible to talk to them about their "favorite things." When this happens, the mouth relaxes.

Making friends with the young in this way is an important matter. I walked into a charming house once to meet an eight-year-old girl for the first time. As I entered the living room, she was sitting on the floor reading a little book (in French, incidentally). When she saw me, she threw herself forward and covered her face with her hands, obviously overcome at the horrible thought of posing for her portrait. The afternoon was largely spent in "getting to know you, getting to know all about you." A week after I had left the house I received a letter from her: "Dear Uncle Gordon, when you are here again, please stay at our house."

While it is often difficult to paint a likeness of a stranger, the situation has certain advantages. Here is a human being about whom one can be completely objective. He is not surrounded by thousands of haunting memories or associations. He can be studied almost as though he were a still life. What he has become is accurately described in his features. This includes his ancestral background as shown in the structure of his head, and, naturally, the way in which his mind and emotions have left their marks.

Occasionally, the friends of a prospective portrait subject will write their interpretation of him. A lady who had been a lifelong friend of a dis-

194

tinguished gentleman whom I was to paint wrote to me: "I never saw him lose his patience or his sense of proportion. His judgments are always fair, well-considered, and kindly. He lives and works on a high plane of idealism and practical efficiency." Comments like this are extremely helpful to make one aware of the sitter's personality and to check with the final portrait.

Yet no close friend or relative will necessarily agree on every aspect of a painter's interpretation. I remember two instances when the grown son of a sitter stood in front of the finished painting and said, "He's not tough enough!" Would a psychologist say that this was because the fathers had so often demanded discipline of their sons?

But there are problems connected with painting relatives. How can one condense into so small an area as a face all the emotions and experiences of a lifetime? What mood should be selected? Can an artist say all he wishes about close friends? Fortunately, they tend to be far less self-conscious while posing, with the result that a natural expression will appear almost immediately. With the stranger this does not always happen. Thinking nervously about how the portrait will eventually make one look is a disturbing experience.

Another advantage in painting a friend or relative is that the artist is able to suggest suitable backgrounds. He has the opportunity of choosing from many familiar ones, whereas with a stranger he is not acquainted with the stranger's many interests.

Degas has made a rather pathetic comment about painting members of the family. He wrote to a friend that there was apt to be a disturbed environment and that, although everyone was full of affection, yet they were inclined to have a rather irresponsible attitude and the artist was not taken so seriously as would have been the case if they had been strangers. I, fortunately, have never had such problems.

*   *   *

Albrecht Dürer made several searching paintings of his father (pl. 94), whom he loved and respected. The third of eighteen children, Dürer must have had considerable competition from his brothers and sisters for attention from this busy man. He gained a place in his father's respect, however, because, even in his early youth, he was full of purpose and anxious to learn. In his journal, written many years later, he refers to his father as a skillful, pure man, who lived a life of hard, self-disciplined labor, patient in spirit, quiet, friendly to others, and grateful to God for his blessings. These characteristics are written indelibly in the portrait. The artist has not minced matters. The painting even suggests by the father's penetrating gaze a strictness of discipline which is being directed toward his son. He is obviously

195

Plate 94. ALBRECHT DÜRER. *The Painter's Father.* On wood. Courtesy, trustees of National Gallery, London

Plate 95. ALBRECHT DÜRER. *Susanna of Bavaria*. Fogg
Museum of Art, Harvard University, Cambridge,
Massachusetts, Meta and Paul J. Sachs Collection

a man of determination, which is revealed by the tight mouth, the slightly raised lower eyelids, the sturdy jaw, and the evidence of a frown. With a complete understanding of what each of these features stood for, Dürer was able to write it on his father's face with his brush, as a novelist would have done with his pen.

Dürer's emphasis on line is illustrated in the outline of the light side of the face, the robe, and the fingers. This artist was rather self-conscious about his success in engraving compared with his painting. In a letter written from Venice to a patron in Germany he says that a recently completed painting, "The Feast of the Rose Garlands," had changed the opinion of his fellow artists, who used to say that he was good at engraving but did not understand how to use color.

*   *   *

Three years before he died, Albrecht Dürer drew this sketch for a portrait of "Susanna of Bavaria" (pl. 95). While the aristocracy were certainly interested in having their portraits painted, they were too involved with affairs of state and social duties to grant the artist more than a minimum of time for a sitting. This drawing, done in zinc or silverpoint on a green-tinted paper, indicates how skillful and experienced Dürer was in this field. First of all, he determined the over-all pattern, the position of the arms and the dog, which are so well related to each other. Having settled this major issue, he promptly registered the details of the subject's hat and clothing. The hands are left in a rough, unfinished state, with almost a touch of caricature in the stumpy, plump fingers, since they would ultimately be painted from a model. The artist has concentrated on the face in a delicate and detailed manner. Susanna's expression is one of calm self-satisfaction. Personal peculiarities, such as the odd shape of her left eye, were carefully drawn. There are almost imperceptible touches of white which are used to heighten the modeling. One gets the impression from studying the entire face that the artist was recording each feature with great accuracy since he would have to begin his painting with only this sketch as a basis.

Dürer was not the type to flatter his subjects. A sketch of his outstanding patron, Wilibald Pirckheimer, shows him in profile with a heavy double chin and crushed-in nose, unfortunate characteristics which would not have been so prominent if seen from the front.

*   *   *

Yale University wished to have a portrait of C. Mahlon Kline (pl. 96) to hang in the Science Center which he had given. Mr. Kline is a man of many interests, and his days are filled with work and engagements. Consequently, it was necessary to have as few sittings as possible.

Plate 96. GORDON C. AYMAR. *C. Mahlon Kline*. 1964.
Oil on canvas. Yale University Art Gallery, New
Haven, Connecticut, Gift of Sidney J. Weinberg

As the picture was to be hung in one of the modern buildings designed by Philip Johnson, I went there at once to study the surroundings. The university wanted a portrait in the traditional, realistic style, yet I felt that it could be treated in such a way that there would be an overtone of design and that this would help it to be in harmony with the environment.

Before going to Mr. Kline's office in Philadelphia for a sitting, I had the good fortune to talk with several of his friends, who gave me clues as to certain characteristics which I should be aware of and record.

When I began working, Mr. Kline was seated at his desk, going over a folder full of correspondence. As he looked up for a moment in response to a question, the pose became a reality. Fortunately, he was sitting in a modern chair, and, with a very slight readjustment, this became a useful part of the pictorial design. The brown leather cover was changed to a suitable red, so that it would create a proper note in relation to the wood-panel background. The angle of the chair is repeated in his necktie, the line of the coat beside it, and in his right upper arm. To offset these diagonals, the paper in his hand is emphasized, and his cuff becomes a median between these two angles. The fingers of his left hand help to supplement the line of the paper. The background was an invention to suggest some of the verticals of modern interiors, and the darkest panel was placed behind his head to define it and to modify the dark of his coat. The width of each panel was carefully adjusted to the total design.

It is interesting to note how the average person unacquainted with the basic principles of art fails to recognize the relation between these considerations of design and abstract art. But for thousands of years realistic painting has used the principles of abstract art as a skeleton on which to place muscles, flesh, and skin. Without this armature the body is merely a flabby mass of flesh. The *isolated* skeleton of abstract art, however, sometimes lacks the enduring interest which the flesh and blood of realism add to it.

*   *   *

For a young man of twenty-five to have been able to paint a portrait which is not only a record of personality but an enduring work of art as well is remarkable, to say the least.

Rembrandt's portrait of "Harmen Gerritsz van Rijn" (?) (pl. 97) has all the indications of maturity. Even at this age, Rembrandt's use of light and shade is as characteristic of his style as in many of the portraits of his late period, although he has rendered such details as the beard and the wrinkles around the eyes in greater detail than in his subsequent paintings. The color scheme is typical—the warm brown background, with a limited

Plate 97. Rembrandt van Rijn. *Harmen Gerritsz van Rijn* (?). c. 1631. Courtesy, Art Institute of Chicago, Mr. and Mrs. W. W. Kimball Collection

palette used for the brown chain and medallion, the flesh color, and the reflection of flesh color in the metal neckpiece. The artist has shown an awareness of the rather small, pursed mouth and the meditative eyes. There is the same restraint in executing detail in the hat and cloak that he used in many of his later portraits.

Rembrandt's father was a successful miller who wanted his son to become a lawyer. The study of law, however, did not last, for Rembrandt soon became a pupil of the artists Van Swanenburkh and Lastman in Amsterdam, both of whom had studied in Rome.

If this is actually a portrait of his father, we may feel assured that he was willing to give his talented son understanding, encouragement, and time for sittings, which might not have occurred if Rembrandt had been painting a stranger.

* * *

The portrait of John Trumbull (pl. 98) by Gilbert Stuart (1755-1828) is interesting from several points of view. First, it is the picture of a friend whom he had known in London in 1780, when Trumbull joined him as a fellow student of Benjamin West. This portrait was painted thirty-eight years later, when Trumbull was sixty-two years old.

Secondly, it is interesting as an example of what kind of *picture* an artist would make of an old friend and fellow artist, quite apart from rendering a likeness.

So far as the first aspect is concerned, it is an interpretation of a man with an outstanding career as a soldier (he finally became an adjutant general with the rank of colonel in the American army) and a painter of great ability. This is an unusual combination. Stuart has succeeded in capturing the distinguished look of a gentleman of authority and determination and also the sensitive look of an artist. Could anything be more difficult? Trumbull was a man of dignity and appeared to be rather austere, but he was also gifted with a warm heart. Stuart has recorded the look of an understanding sitter who is interested in observing the manner in which his famous rival is painting. I say "rival" because in 1804 Trumbull went to Boston with the intention of painting portraits and making his home there. He left almost immediately, for, he said, Boston did not provide enough portrait commissions for "two rival artists," Stuart and himself.

There is an almost imperceptible indication of the fact that Stuart was aware that Trumbull's left eye was practically blind. He had fallen downstairs when he was a little boy and had damaged it. It shows a slightly sad, dull look in contrast to the more alert expression of his right eye. The typical Stuart high lights appear in his eyes and on the tip of his nose.

202

Plate 98. GILBERT STUART. *John Trumbull*. 1818. Oil on
wood. Yale University Art Gallery, New Haven,
Connecticut, Bequest of Herbert L. Pratt

As for the aspect of the painting as a picture, it would be characteristic of Stuart to devote the major portion of his time to a study of the face. His wife, Jane, wrote shortly after his death: "In his work there is no appearance of labor . . . so long as he kept to the head. When that was complete, his enthusiasm seems to have abated."

He did not become involved in rendering the details of Trumbull's clothing, but he did give thought to the emphasis on the diagonal lines suggested by his coat collar and neckpiece, which lines are vaguely repeated in the upper right-hand corner of the painting. These diagonals are somewhat offset by the firm, vertical edge of the light and dark areas over his head.

Gilbert Stuart was born a few miles north of Narragansett Pier in Rhode Island. He went to London in 1775 and struggled to live there for a year before applying to Benjamin West for assistance and instruction. He helped support himself by playing the organ in church, attended Sir Joshua Reynold's lectures, and was a student and assistant of West for five years. One of his portraits was accepted by the Royal Academy, and it was not long before he achieved considerable success in this field.

He led an extravagant life in Ireland and left for America with the ambition to make a living by painting portraits of George Washington. After several years he was able to persuade the President to sit for him. Eventually, he painted three portraits of Washington from life—the Vaughan Type, the Lansdowne Type, and the Athenaeum Head. Stuart made approximately one hundred and fourteen replicas of these. Over sixty of them were of the famous Athenaeum Head.

Stuart's method was to sketch the head and figure loosely with the brush. He then painted the main areas in simple terms, suggesting their form but with no emphasis on detail. The paint was applied in thin layers with a generous use of medium, and the canvas inevitably shows through. He then built up his broad lights on the forehead and in certain places on the costume.

Stuart instructed his pupils to observe the human figure as though it were in a hazy atmosphere, since too much light ruined color and too little concealed it.

* * *

After many years of friendship with Dr. Henry Sloane Coffin (pl. 99) I had the privilege of painting his portrait. With this background it was not surprising that the ritual of posing, which is so often irksome, became a congenial and pleasurable experience. It was therefore all the more possible to read in his face and transfer to canvas his distinguished look, gentleness, thoughtfulness, and humor.

204

Plate 99. GORDON C. AYMAR. *Dr. Henry Sloane Coffin.*
1952. Oil on canvas. Collection of Mrs. Henry
Sloane Coffin.

From the many hoods representing the various degrees which had been bestowed upon him we selected an orange-red one. The background is a dark, warm brownish-gray.

Designing the folds in a gown such as this, offsetting angles with curves, sharpening and defining planes is an absorbing experience, even to the point of relating the curves in his spectacles with the curves of his cuff. Nature is not exactly like this, but she has taught us how to see these possibilities.

* * *

Édouard Manet (1832-1883) first met Berthe Morisot quite by accident as she was copying a painting in the Louvre. From that moment they became close friends. She later married Manet's brother, Eugène. She had studied with Corot and now became Manet's pupil; her work was deeply influenced by him. At one point it was she who was able to persuade him to lighten his palette, which had become rather somber.

With complete understanding between them in matters of art, and with a friendship which enabled him to capture her personality, Manet painted this sketchy portrait of her (pl. 100).

Rough as it is, he has been able to suggest the wide-eyed stare of an artist, who, while posing, might either have been studying the color effects of light on the studio wall or have been listening to him talk about painting.

The picture is composed of a rather severe, simple, triangular shape. At this time (it was painted about 1869), Manet was interested in rendering flat forms. He rejected the sculptured look produced by carefully painted light and shade. Courbet, whose independence, incidentally, he had respected, once remarked that Manet's paintings were as flat as playing cards. Perhaps Manet was trying to lead in a direction away from photography, which was beginning to declare a reality all its own.

Manet was the son of a distinguished lawyer, who became the chief of staff of the Paris Ministry of Justice. He led a more or less conventional life that was not typical of the Bohemians on the left bank. He was among the few talented artists who were independent financially and artistically. He began his studying under Couture, who taught traditionally.

When his painting of the nude "Olympia" caused a scandal at the Salon, he retreated to Spain, where he devoted much of his time to studying the works of Velázquez, whom he called the painter of painters. While he admired the verve of Goya, he considered him much inferior to Velázquez.

When Émile Zola, who had bravely defended Manet when he exhibited in the Salon des Refusés, posed for his portrait, he commented to a friend that the artist was so intent on his painting that he had forgotten all about his sitter and that he was not even conscious of his presence.

206

Plate 100. ÉDOUARD MANET. *Portrait of Berthe Morisot.*
c. 1869. Oil on canvas. Cleveland Museum of Art,
Cleveland, Ohio, Leonard C. Hanna, Jr., Collection

Manet holds a definite place in the history of art as a man who took steps away from the strict academic school of his period, and, although he did not consider himself an impressionist and did not exhibit with them, he did affect their point of view to some extent.

* * *

It was not difficult to decide on the blue-walled living room as an appropriate setting for Samuel Dorrance (pl. 101), whose family I had known for many years. The entrance to the hallway behind him provided a series of verticals, horizontals, and a feeling of depth. The simple white chair repeated the white trim; the blues of his sweater, shorts, and socks emphasized his very blond hair, and repeated the deep blue of his eyes.

I saw him working in the garden with his grandfather, and asked him to bring in the basket filled with colorful tomatoes. Placing two of these on the floor prevented the red area from becoming too concentrated. The colors of the floor and Sam's shoes form a base for the design, and tend to draw the reds and blues together.

* * *

When Édouard Vuillard painted the portrait of "Missia and Thadée Natanson" (pl. 102), he was not only familiar with their personalities, their backgrounds, and their personal relationship, but had often been in their home and undoubtedly had enjoyed the splendor of their environment.

At some fortunate moment he must have observed Missia sitting in a relaxed pose amid the lively patterns of walls, furniture covers, and rugs. Thadée leans thoughtfully on the piano in the background. He had married Missia when she was fifteen. From her early youth, apparently she had been a beautiful subject to paint. Toulouse-Lautrec and Bonnard both painted her, and Renoir made seven portraits of her. Before she died, she had had three husbands. Did Vuillard have the courage to suggest an air of melancholy, of ennui, an overtone of sadness, when he painted this picture?

The Natansons were loyal patrons of the Nabis, of which Vuillard was a member, and in the *Revue Blanche*, which they founded, did everything possible to support the movement.

To me, this picture, painted about 1897, represents the most interesting phase of this artist's style. The color scheme is a satisfying, all-over harmony of warm browns, yellows, and soft reds, relieved somewhat by the dull blue of the lamp. The color is extremely subtle, particularly in Missia's flesh, with its warm lights and cool color in the reflected lights. Unlike so many of the artists who were preoccupied exclusively with flat shapes of color, Vuillard has made a pattern of the light and shade on her face and body.

208

* * *

Plate 101. GORDON C. AYMAR. *Samuel Dorrance*. 1953.
Water color. Collection of Mrs. Evans Dorrance

Plate 102. ÉDOUARD VUILLARD. *Missia and Thadée Natanson*. c. 1897. Oil on paper mounted on canvas. Collection of Museum of Modern Art, New York, Gift of Nate B. and Frances Spingold

It is a privilege to be able to paint one's grandchild. Not only is it a recess from the discipline of working for other people, but the problems of ferreting out the personal characteristics are settled before the painting is begun. It becomes a matter of selecting those which are essentially indicative of a particular personality. Costumes and backgrounds are all a part of expressing this mood.

Johnnie Earle (pl. 103), even at the age of four, was an outdoorsman. Nature instinctively appealed to him. He had always lived near the water, and slickers and sou'westers were a natural part of his wardrobe. It also provided an opportunity to paint the interesting yellow of the oilskin, with its many facets and planes. Johnnie is looking over the marshes with that searching gaze and budding sense of humor which I still associate with him twelve years later.

Since we had three elephant-folio Audubon prints in our pale-yellow dining room where the picture was to hang, the decorative handling of the reeds and rocks under his feet was treated in the Audubon manner. (Incidentally, having studied many of the original Audubon paintings and compared them with the final prints executed by Havell, I can say that much of the clean-cut, detailed design was contributed by Havell as he engraved the originals on copper.) The flat beige-color sky and water set off the complicated pattern of Johnnie's clothing and the ground below him. At first I hesitated to introduce the apple into the picture for fear of making it too illustrative, but the touch of red seemed to me more important than the illustrative aspect.

*   *   *

In order to learn something of the background of Leon Kroll's picture of "Leo Ornstein at the Piano" (pl. 104), I took the liberty of writing to the artist about it. I received the following helpful comments: "Ornstein had a studio on the same floor right next to mine, so we were in and out of each other's places rather frequently. I watched him while he played the piano. I organized shapes to make an interesting design of straight and round and triangular sub-divisions, irrespective of what happened to be there. The division of the blue wall calls attention to the hand, a secondary focus, and also gave me a progressive series of triangles. These ideas, as you know, form only one facet of a work of art, basic as they are."

Here again was an instance of the reward of painting a friend whom one knew intimately and could visit and observe. One of the really important points the artist makes is that the handsome, strong design was made "irrespective of what happened to be there." This attitude allows the realistic painter to use nature as a composer uses a scale—he does not merely play the scale; his harmonies are composed from its notes.

Plate 103. GORDON C. AYMAR. *John Earle.* 1954. Water
color

Plate 104. Leon Kroll. *Leo Ornstein at the Piano*. 1918.
Oil. Courtesy, Art Institute of Chicago, Friends
of American Art Collection

The color scheme in Ornstein's portrait is simple—the strong blue wall contrasting with the warm and varied browns of his hair, jacket, the piano, and the picture frame on the wall. The flesh color of his face combined with his white shirt is repeated in his hand and cuff.

Leon Kroll (1884 -   ) studied at the Art Students League, the National Academy of Design, and the Academie Julian in Paris. He exhibited at the Armory Show in 1913, and has had one-man shows at the National Academy and the Carnegie Institute. His murals hang in the Department of Justice in Washington and the War Memorial in Worcester, Massachusetts.

*   *   *

Who would know better than Alexander Brook (1898 -   ) how to paint a picture of "George Biddle Playing the Flute" (pl. 105)? He was a close friend and had undoubtedly seen him many times in this pose. So it was only natural that he would have mentally recorded the gay, random pattern of the sheets of music on the stand and scattered all over the floor. Notice how the artist has exaggerated the perspective of the music on the stand in order to make the lines converge toward Biddle's head. The white sleeves repeat these light areas, and their angular shapes are in keeping with the other restless forms. Brook has observed the way in which Biddle wound his foot around his ankle and the interesting effect this had on the design of his trousers. The straight lines of the legs of the music stand, the rungs of the chair, and the line of the flute are all in harmony with the other angular lines. Offsetting this orderly confusion are the verticals of the wall, chest, and chair legs. There is one sharp horizontal—the cover of the chest, which leads directly to Biddle's face.

When the time came to paint the picture, it was half underway, and I am sure that Biddle was content to pose *and* play at the same time.

We tend to think of pictures of this period as rather carelessly put together, with little concern for the tenets of classical art, but, either instinctively or with an awareness of tradition, the *line* structure of this picture has been ingeniously planned, particularly in the arrangement of the sheets of music. The edges of those on the floor either repeat other lines, such as the chair rung, or aim at significant points in the composition.

Biddle came from Philadelphia, and was educated at Groton and Harvard. He decided that art was his career and studied at the Pennsylvania Academy and in Paris and Munich. After a period in the army in World War II, he retreated to Tahiti and then to the West Indies. He was a man of many interests, and worked not only on easel and mural paintings, but also on ceramics and lithography. Apparently the flute was a release from these demanding occupations.

214

Plate 105. ALEXANDER BROOK. *George Biddle Playing
the Flute*. 1929. Oil on canvas. Collection of Museum of Modern Art, New York, Gift of Abby
Aldrich Rockefeller

Alexander Brook's parents were Russian; he was born in Brooklyn. He studied at Pratt Institute and at the Art Students League under Miller. He won a scholarship and many prizes as a young man, and became assistant director of the Whitney Studio Club, which was the beginning of the Whitney Museum of American Art. This enabled him to paint while holding a remunerative position. Among his awards were the Logan Medal, a prize at the Art Institute of Chicago, and the Carnegie Institute International First Prize. Brook never went abroad to study, and was convinced that an American artist should be himself and no one else.

*   *   *

While there may be difficulties in summing up all one knows about a friend in one facial expression, it is, nevertheless, a great advantage to be familiar with the background of his character and thus able to suggest certain familiar traits.

Phillips Wyman (pl. 106) and I had known each other for many years. When this drawing was completed, his wife wrote me a letter from which she has graciously given me permission to quote. In it she said: "You have depicted the true character of Phil. You have shown a sensitive, intuitive, and intelligent person. One can almost 'hear' him listening to what is being said. His moistened lips are ready to respond to the discussion, after having carefully weighed his unbiased opinion." This degree of understanding could only have been achieved through long companionship.

This drawing is done with a sienna brown pencil. Each stroke must be made with confidence, since it is not the type which lends itself to erasure. Only very small alterations can be made, and these should be done with a razor blade. The paper is French handmade and is buff in color. High lights are touched in with a white pastel color stick. This combination of materials should prove to be as enduring as anything in its field.

216

Plate 106. GORDON C. AYMAR. *Phillips Wyman*. 1963.
Sienna-brown crayon on beige paper. Collection
of Mrs. Phillips Wyman

THE GROUP PORTRAIT

PAINTING a group portrait inevitably involves many problems. First, there is the added complication of making a satisfactory composition. With one figure alone to deal with, the design may be arranged to focus on this individual. With two or more figures, the question arises, "Is it necessary to present each figure with equal emphasis, or can certain ones be subdued?"

Rembrandt, in trying to avoid a merely mechanical representation of the many figures in the painting popularly called "The Night Watch," had grave problems with his clients. While some are clearly and prominently defined, others are in shadow in order to form an interesting and natural relationship. Those who were treated in this manner either refused to pay their share, or submitted by having their names lettered on an escutcheon in the background.

Some of the primitive family portraits handled the problem of emphasis by employing a simple, naïve, decorative pattern. There was little realism in the three-dimensional sense. But with the treatment of figures *and* background in full light and shade the difficulties increased. However, when children appear with adults, their difference in size subordinates them and makes the composition easier.

There are practical as well as artistic difficulties in group portraits. Who will inherit the picture? Will relatives and friends feel that Margaret's is not nearly so good a likeness as David's? Perhaps it is just as well for an artist to point out this possibility before undertaking the commission to combine them in one picture, for in separate pictures the comparison is not so demanding.

* * *

In his "Sixtus IV and His Attendants" (pl. 107) Melozzo da Forli (1438 - 1494) has succeeded in using a group composition which is as satisfying today as it was five hundred years ago. The Pope, seated at the right, is welcoming Bartolommeo Platina as the new librarian of the Vatican. Platina, kneeling, points to the inscription below, which lauds the Pope's contribution in rebuilding parts of Rome. In the center is Sixtus' nephew, Cardinal Giuliano della Rovere, who later became Pope Julius II. The three other nephews, from left to right, enjoy the titles of count, prefect of Rome, and cardinal. These were the days when nepotism reigned supreme.

The placing of these six figures is done with great perception. The Pope is identified by the chair and white robe; Platina is separated from the others by his kneeling position; the nephews' heads form a curve leading from the Pope's head across the picture. The future Pope stands somewhat apart, and the profile position of all the bodies is relieved by nephew number one, who is in three-quarter position, and nephew number two, who faces toward the left. The rather irregular composition of the figures sets them off from the meticulously detailed architecture with its rigid perspective.

The color scheme is strong, with the robes in reds, blues, and purples, and a contrasting green marble behind the future Pope.

Melozzo has not minced matters in painting the likenesses. Each one is characterized with vigorous drawing and modeling, which gives the viewer a feeling of reality. Not only are their physical differences evident, but their personalities as well.

Piero della Francesca was the teacher of Melozzo. He was able to impart to his students his skill in drawing, perspective, and color. There is a quality about the work of Piero, however, which is inimitable, but Melozzo substituted his own talents to replace this.

* * *

As a composer of paintings, Raphael (Raffaello Sanzio, 1483 - 1520) was outstanding, and the detail from "The Mass of Bolsena," sometimes called "The Miracle of Bolsena" (pl. 108), gives every indication of this. What could be more difficult than to compose the five soldiers of the Swiss Guard, all kneeling and, of necessity, facing in the same direction? Yet this artist's role as a master illustrator, a title given him by Berenson, enabled him to

Plate 107. MELOZZO DA FORLI. *Sixtus IV and His Attendants*. Vatican Museums and Galleries, Rome

provide a solution. He has broken the pattern of the men's profiles by introducing one head which faces us, and he has made figure number two (from left to right) the prominent one, with nothing overlapping him. The handsome chair was placed beside him to break the monotony of the group, and his right arm rests naturally upon it. The remaining figures are varied in costume, and also in the degree in which the total body is allowed to show. Color forms a relief, and makes a lively pattern of reds, blues, gold, and light green. The color of the hair of each soldier ranges in carefully modulated order from the blond of number one to the dark brown of number four.

Further examination of this detail of the Bolsena Mass as an illustration makes us very conscious of the remarkable mood Raphael has given each soldier—the stiff absorption of number one as he looks up at the Pope, the effective pose of number two, the concern of number three for what may be happening in our direction, the tense, almost belligerent look of number four. Number five is subdued to the point where only an overtone of wide-eyed respect is visible. Each head is painted with directness and confident, bold handling of the brush.

Having paid tribute to these various qualities in the painting, I wish to record my admiration for Raphael as a portraitist. These soldiers are living, recognizable men. Like his great portraits of "Pope Leo X with Two Cardinals" and "Count Baldassare Castiglioni," they show Raphael's complete appreciation of the individual, which is the essence of portraiture. This painting, which is one of his finest, was executed when he was twenty-nine.

Nothing could be farther from this rare talent than his predilection for painting the figures in his religious pictures as ideal images, completely devoid of character. For me, these are idealized to the point of being weak, languid, and saccharine (which, according to the dictionary, is at least three hundred times sweeter than cane sugar). Not that I do not respect his ambition to paint the ideal; but in so doing he failed to understand the strength of personality that ought to be revealed in a religious character. The Greeks expressed this in their sculptured gods and goddesses, and yet lost nothing of the ideal. Perhaps Raphael's determination to paint them without models "from a certain ideal that exists in my mind" was what led him to this unconvincing summary of character. De Tocqueville expressed it by saying that he attempted to "embellish beauty" and searched for something "better than nature."

Raphael's life is a novel of the young genius of multiple gifts—gentle, devoted, gracious, lovable, hard-working, with executive ability sufficient to induce the Pope to appoint him as overseer of the building of St. Peter's, in place of Bramante, who had died while engaged on this project. He was born in Urbino and, when he was about seventeen, began to study under Perugino, who had a deep influence on his style. He went to Florence in 1504

221

Plate 108. RAPHAEL (RAFFAELLO SANZIO). *The Mass of
Bolsena*. Vatican Museums and Galleries, Rome

to study the paintings of Leonardo and Michelangelo, who were active at that time; he remained there for four years. He was then called to Rome through his friendship with Bramante, a former fellow townsman.

It is sad to realize that so great a genius in the art of painting should have been diverted from it by such time-consuming matters as architecture and building. Leo X also appointed him to serve as superintendent of the streets of Rome, and he became involved not only in their design but also in their maintenance. It is possible that he caught malarial fever, which resulted in his early death, by working in the excavations where he was commissioned to select and purchase the ancient stones and marbles with which St. Peter's was to be built.

* * *

It may not be fair to judge Hals's "Children with a Goat" (pl. 109) as a group picture, although it is remarkably successful in this respect. Originally, it was part of a much larger painting, "Portrait of a Family in a Garden." The remainder of the picture still exists in a private collection.

Here is a work of art, however, which can stand on its own merits. Emerging from an over-all dark tone come the heads and figures of the children. No one of them insists on attracting attention. The eye runs from face to face. The goat is properly subdued, and comes to life only through the light touches on its fur. There is a skillfully designed triangle composed of the children's heads, the boy's straight arm, and the whip. This isolates the most important part of the picture. The boy's straight leg adds another line which affects the total design. It is well known that Hals made no preliminary drawings, but started immediately sketching in his composition on the final canvas.

What painter could have captured so well the gay, carefree mood of young children? The boy's look is outgoing, happy, confident. He is in command and knows how to handle the goat. The young girl is full of joy over escorting her sister on her ride, and the little one's expression is compounded of pleasure and timid expectancy. How could Hals have painted these fleeting expressions, when the face does not register them for more than a fraction of a second? How could he have given such an impression of complete realism rendered in full light and shade, when a child is never still?

* * *

In the days when Arthur Devis (c. 1711 - 1787) painted the group portrait of "The James Family" (pl. 110), the aristocracy were leading an idyllic existence on vast estates cared for by servants who devoted their lives to this

Plate 109. FRANS HALS. *Children with a Goat.* Royal
Museum of Fine Arts of Belgium, Brussels

one purpose. The "equality of man" had not begun to pose its problems, and, while the lower classes were severely handicapped by being deprived of education, they must have had certain satisfactions in having their masters fully responsible for them and a pride in being so closely associated with the wealthy and the illustrious.

Devis has conveyed a typical atmosphere of formality and manners, which characterized English society in the eighteenth century. The James family are on what appears to be the terrace of their mansion, with a landscape behind them which is full of natural beauty and peace. Good taste has allowed nature to express herself without the rigid design of overformal gardens. The handsome clothing which they are wearing is not a matter of self-display, but is simply appropriate for the life they were accustomed to lead.

The artist has solved the problem of balancing the figures with uncanny skill and understanding. Every detail in the painting has been placed with geometrical precision. It may be well for us, with our emphasis on the spontaneous and the random, to examine the care with which the composition of such pictures was executed. First, the main door in the building across the pond is in the exact center of the picture. The most prominent figure of the four is the father, whose clothes form the darkest note in the entire painting. His wife in her pale satin dress with its sharp high lights offers a contrast to these darks. An imaginary line drawn through their heads leads to the small cloud in the sky, and this is repeated by the line formed by the tops of the trees on the right. The angle of these lines is offset by the imaginary line connecting the heads of the two girls, a continuation of which is formed by the tops of the large trees at the left. The line across the bottom of the lady's dress leads to the gentleman's left foot, as does the line across the bottom of the children's dresses. The angle of this last line is repeated by the section of the wall which joins the dress of the taller girl. The figures of the children, since they are smaller than those of the parents, are moved toward the side of the picture in order to achieve a proper balance. There are numerous other subtle points in the composition, but those we have mentioned are sufficient to indicate that there is nothing accidental in this arrangement.

Oddly enough, this sophisticated construction is almost the opposite approach from the rather naïvely rendered heads which, in certain ways, almost suggest the work of the "primitive" painters of the next century. The way in which the lady holds her flowers, and the gesture of her hand in presenting her children to the spectator, are as stiff and artificial as are the pictures of these journeymen painters.

Arthur Devis was born in Preston in Lancashire. He studied with Peter Tillemans and, when he was about fifty, exhibited in the Strand in London. In spite of his many excellent paintings, he never became a member of the

Plate 110. ARTHUR DEVIS. *The James Family*. Reproduced by courtesy of the trustees of Tate Gallery, London

Royal Academy. His son, Arthur William Devis, however, was awarded a silver medal by the Academy, and his paintings were respected by Sir Joshua Reynolds.

*   *   *

The portraits by Sir Joshua Reynolds (1723-1792) (pl. 111) and George Romney (1734-1802) (pl. 112) should be considered together. They are typical examples of the "idea" coming primarily from a school in current fashion. Here is a real opportunity to catalogue their similarities and degrees of divergence in executing a group portrait.

The school which existed at that time dictated that when an artist was painting the aristocracy, the sitter should be placed in a stately environment. This generally included great classical columns and large, hanging draperies, which appear to be invented rather than a representation of a particular spot connected with the manor house. A portion of the estate was often included in the background, which served to suggest their surroundings and added a graceful touch. The costumes were always of the highest quality, and implied the life of elegance in which the sitters lived.

The Reynolds is a portrait of Jane, Countess of Harrington, and her two sons, Viscount Petersham and the Honorable Lincoln Stanhope. It was painted in 1786/87. The viscount's dress and hat and long, curly hair could not be more effeminate; yet there is a masterful, determined expression in his pose and face that may explain why the countess is desperately pulling at his skirt—undoubtedly to insist upon his posing instead of playing. Lincoln has the innocent look of the young, and is grasping his mother's arm for reassurance in the presence of this odd character, the artist. The picture of the countess, I feel, gives the impression of being a very good likeness.

The handling of everything but the faces is bold and sketchy. The artist obviously was not concerned with rendering the exquisite texture of the clothing. As a matter of fact, he instructed his pupils not to paint specific materials, such as woolen, linen, and silk. This, he said, reduced clothing to nothing more than drapery. This may have been a rationalization on his part, for, being hard pressed with important commissions, he employed a drapery painter, Peter Toms, to take care of all of this for him.

Notice how spontaneously Reynolds has introduced the lights in the sky, and how well these compose in carrying the light tones of the clothing into the upper corner, which gives a sense of space. The total design is based on triangular lines. Lincoln's head is the point where the lines meet. The drapery ending in the clouds forms one line; the heads of all three form another. To offset these there is the line from Lincoln's head through his arm and that of the countess. This is continued by the ribbon on the front

Plate 111. Joshua Reynolds. *Jane, Countess of Harrington, Viscount Petersham, The Honorable Lincoln Stanhope.* 1786/87. Oil on canvas. Yale University Art Gallery, New Haven, Connecticut, Gift of Paul Moore, 1908

Plate 112. GEORGE ROMNEY. *Henrietta, Countess of Warwick and Her Children.* Canvas. © Frick Collection, New York

of her dress. The column with its strong perpendicular serves to steady the whole composition.

Romney has treated his sky even more casually. The column and drapery also appear. One has a feeling that he devoted a great deal of his time to the face of Henrietta, Countess of Warwick, and to those of her children. Again, there is the close relationship between one of the children and the mother. Romney's interest in the beauty of the countess' satin dress is very apparent. He has succeeded in giving the feeling of texture, and he has not accepted a photographic rendering of the folds; they are definitely the result of a feeling for design.

One thing should be taken into account in comparing the two paintings: Reynolds' is slightly over four and a half feet high; Romney's, nearly eight feet. This means that, when reduced to the same size, Romney's larger painting will seem to be more highly finished and Reynolds' painting will appear to be the sketchier of the two.

The painting of Reynolds reproduced herewith was done toward the end of his life. Two years later he was forced to abandon painting because of failing eyesight. At this point in his career he had been influenced by the work of Rubens, which he had studied during his trip to Holland and Flanders a few years before. While on a previous visit to Rome, where he stayed for two years, he tried to "probe the technical secrets of the masters." He analyzed the work of the various schools, particularly in regard to the proportion of light, dark, and halftone which they employed. He found, for example, that the Venetians devoted no more than one quarter of their paintings to light, one quarter to very dark areas, and the remaining half to halftone. Rubens used more than a quarter for light; Rembrandt, hardly an eighth. This is an example of Reynolds' intellectual approach to composing a picture. His preoccupation with values as distinct from colors is further indicated in the technique he used—beginning his painting with a monochrome base and later adding glazes of color.

Reynolds started studying at the age of seventeen when he went to London to the studio of the portrait painter Thomas Hudson. During a brilliant career he became one of the founders of the Royal Academy and its first president.

William Hazlitt commented on the many fashionable sitters Reynolds had: "Lords, ladies, generals, authors, opera singers, musicians, the learned and the polite, besieged his doors, and found an unfailing welcome. What a rustling of silks! What a fluttering of flounces and brocades! What a cloud of powder and perfumes! What a flow of periwigs! What an exchange of civilities and of titles! . . . It must, I think, be allowed that this is the only mode in which genius can form a legitimate union with wealth and fashion. There is a sufficient tie in interest and vanity."

230

This method of allowing one's work to be governed by the taste of a current school was later decried by William Blake, who wrote:

Thank God, I never was sent to school
To be Flog'd into following the Style of a Fool.

* * *

Jean Auguste Dominique Ingres (1780-1867), with a deep admiration for traditional painting, particularly that of Raphael, might be expected to devote much of his attention to composition. In his portrait of "The Guillon-Lethière Family" (pl. 113) he has placed the three heads in a most satisfying relation to one another. The dominating head of the father is balanced by those of the mother and child. The lines of the father's clothing and his arm lead directly to the baby's head. The mother's sleeve and gown swing in lines opposing those of the father's clothing, and the parents' bodies turn toward each other and enfold the baby.

In a drawing of this kind one can trace the various steps, from the original, very light straight lines which indicated the general position of the figures, through the next phase of strong, confident outlines of the garments, then the filling in of shadows and such details as the collar of the man's cloak. Finally, there is the intense, detailed, accurate modeling of the faces. The artist has not used strong light and shade from the side, but has posed them in a rather full, head-on light and relied on restrained modeling to give them form.

Ingres was preëminently a draftsman, and he was conscious of this to the point where he used to say that drawing was paramount and that color was simply a tinting of form. He refused to exhibit his drawings with his oil paintings, saying that people would ignore the paintings and look only at the drawings.

He defined drawing very clearly when he stated that it did not consist merely in recording the *outlines* of planes. It was the expression of underlying form, the actual plane, and the modeling.

He has certainly given us, through his draftsmanship, the clear, penetrating look of Monsieur Lethière, the gentle look of his pretty wife, and the family likeness in the baby's expression, even in such details as the mouth and the formation of the eyes.

As has been the case with many of the great artists of the past, Ingres was originally taught by his father, who was an artist. He attended art school in Toulouse, and then went to Paris to work in David's studio. He was trained first for a musical career, and had been taught to play the violin. During the period in which he studied painting he supported himself by playing in a theater orchestra. At twenty-one he was awarded the Prix de

Plate 113. JEAN AUGUSTE DOMINIQUE INGRES. *The Guillon-Lethière Family*. Courtesy, Museum of Fine Arts, Boston

Rome, and lived in Italy for a number of years. His success was not immediate. He lived for a long time in obscurity, and barely made a living by painting portraits at two guineas apiece. He spent four years in Florence and then returned to Paris. By that time his standing was such that he was appointed director of the École de Rome. He fought with the devotees of the school of Rubens, declaring that this master had ruined painting, and finally forbade his students to look at Rubens' work. He said that Rubens refused to be a part of his own century, which Rubens called "renegade." The creed which Ingres taught was founded on what he believed to be the secret of Raphael's success—a combination of grace and the proper proportion of strength and character.

When he was sixty-seven years old, he wrote to a friend, "That cruel tyrant [his painting] even prevents me from sleeping, so absolute is her demand that she alone shall rule. . . ."

* * *

The portrait of "Madame Charpentier and Her Children" (pl. 114) was painted by Renoir in 1878. It was the beginning of a successful career. Renoir was already involved in the impressionist movement, but he altered his free style considerably when he painted this picture. It is rendered in a rather conventional manner which apparently delighted Madame Charpentier. Renoir was not only flexible in pleasing his patroness, but had the technical ability to paint in this manner.

Accepting the real challenge of painting a group picture, he has made a striking and lively design out of this complicated material. The pose of each figure is relaxed and natural, with the mother gazing peacefully to the left, the older daughter looking reflectively up, and the younger one watching her sister. The main lines of the composition focus attention primarily on Madame Charpentier's head.

I can visualize Renoir deciding on the Oriental screen for the background, placing madame on the sofa in front of it, together with one daughter, and learning to his delight that the dog would suffer the other child to sit on him. Having placed the dog, he must then have arranged the lady's arms and pulled her dress out to the right to complete the triangular composition. From the available furniture he then balanced the figures by what amounts to a still life in the upper right-hand corner.

In coping with the black fur of the dog, he may have asked Madame Charpentier to put on a dark dress, or he may even have asked her permission to paint the dress she was wearing in a harmonizing color. The light-blue dresses of the girls stand out sharply against the gold and red of the screen and the yellow and violet of the rug. The red of the screen is repeated in the table mat.

233

Plate 114. AUGUSTE RENOIR. *Madame Charpentier and Her Children*. 1878. Oil on canvas. Metropolitan Museum of Art, New York, Wolfe Fund, 1907

Madame Charpentier became Renoir's most important patroness, and with what he earned from her portrait he was able to go to Italy to study the work of the old masters.

While his painting might be regarded as superficial compared with the more earnest and serious work of other masters, it is rather pleasant to think of him as a defender of the amiable, content to be himself, to love what seemed to him engaging, and with independence to adhere to this point of view through his entire life. A number of his sitters used to remark that he often sang while he painted. I like to think of him in this mood, enjoying the very act of creating a picture.

And he is to be respected as a human being for his courage in struggling, during the last fifteen years of his life, to paint incessantly while suffering from severe arthritis. Carried from a wheel chair into his studio, he would hold his brush in his crippled hand and produce some of his finest paintings.

*   *   *

I feel strongly that for all too many centuries we have limited the presentation of portraits to the head-and-shoulders or, at most, the full-length figure. For me, the ways of presenting the individual are endless. It may seem presumptuous to introduce "The Boating Party" (pl. 115) by Mary Cassatt (1845 - 1926) as a "portrait," but it illustrates my belief that there should be a wider approach to portraiture than now exists. After all, even a vehicle so factual and literal as a dictionary defines a portrait, figuratively, as a "vivid description of a person." This leaves the door wide open for the imagination.

Take, for example, Andrew Wyeth's "Christina's World." The poor, crippled girl is lying on the grass with her back toward us, looking up the bare hill at her desolate house. Not one feature of her face is visible; yet here is a profound revelation of a human being, expressed by the pose, the emaciated arm, and the environment.

The portrait does not have to be merely a document; it can be a complete novel. Let us call Mary Cassatt's picture a group portrait, or, if you prefer, "Mother and Child." The look on the mother's face is a genuine study of expression. The child is in a peaceful frame of mind, which allows the mother to relax and dream.

The composition is a masterpiece of originality. The yellow and white curve formed by the side of the boat leads directly to the mother and child; the oar and the man's arm point to the exact center of their figures. The foot of the sail follows the curves of the boat; the leech aims at the man's hand. Even the sheet connects the sail with the lady's body. The line of her hat echoes the curves of the bow. To offset all the curves Mary Cassatt has

Plate 115. MARY CASSATT. *The Boating Party*. National
Gallery of Art, Washington, D. C., Chester Dale
Collection

introduced the straight, horizontal lines of the shore and those of the thwarts. Depth is achieved through the large scale of the man's figure in relation to the smaller ones in the stern, the graduated diminution of the size of the thwarts, the boat's lines of perspective, and the distant shore. The colors are extremely satisfying because of their beautiful relationships. They are not literal in any sense. They are *art*.

I am glad to have this opportunity to express my admiration for the work of this artist. If she had painted only this picture and "The Bath" (a mother bathing her little daughter), which is in the Art Institute of Chicago, she would have established a timeless reputation.

Mary Cassatt was born in Allegheny City, Pennsylvania. Her father was a man of considerable wealth, but she chose to devote her life to art, rather than fritter it away in a social milieu. Her initial study was at the Pennsylvania Academy of Fine Arts and, later, with Raimondi at the Academy in Parma. By chance one day she happened to see a pastel by Degas in a shop window. This was the turning point in her art life. From that moment she became his disciple and endeavored to paint in his manner.

She never married. Her models were mainly women and children, and she never lived the left-bank life of the Bohemians of that day. She exhibited with the impressionists, but finally, along with Degas, refused to show at their Sixth Exhibition. In 1890 they visited the famous Japanese print show in Paris, which made an immediate and deep impression on their work. Finally, her eyesight began to fail, and for a number of years before her death she was totally blind.

THE PART PLAYED BY COSTUME

 HERE is a legend affectionately handed down from generation to generation that at midnight on Christmas Eve the ancestral portraits stir, breathe the breath of life again, and descend from their frames to hold carnival upon earth as flesh and blood until the first crowing of the cock.

In wondering what such a conglomeration of personalities would turn out to be, I cannot help visualizing the mad costume ball that would come into being, from the elaborate robes and accessories of the seventeenth century to the dreary men's clothing of the late nineteenth and early twentieth century.

Costume plays several important roles. Not only is it a record of its period and, in the early days, a witness to the status of the subject, but from the painter's point of view it is inevitably an essential element of the *design* of the picture. The intrinsic beauty of satin, lace, embroidery, and the color pattern of fabric can become a guiding factor in the over-all beauty of a painting. And the awareness of the dressmakers of old of the designed shapes of the ladies' necklines, sleeves, waistlines, and skirts reflected their essential part in contributing to the character of the pictures painted by competent artists.

However, a contemporary of Dubordieu's wrote, "When your posterity shall see our pictures, they shall think we were foolishly proud of apparel."

In the full-length figures of both ladies and gentlemen in England and Italy in the seventeenth century the head is mathematically only a fraction of the canvas, completely subordinated to lavish garments and romantic landscape backgrounds. But when Rembrandt and his Netherlandish confreres painted portraits, the human element began to replace the interest in costume. In many of them the accent of light is on the head alone (pl. 75), and the dark clothing is made to blend with the dark background in order to place the emphasis on the face.

There is a definite feeling today among many of those who can afford to have their portraits painted that they do not want to be associated with what they consider the pretentious desire of their ancestors to appear socially impressive. This is particularly true of men, many of whom can be persuaded to pose only if they are in casual clothing. For the painter this suggests the opportunity of placing them in suitable landscape backgrounds (pl. 127). I have enjoyed painting one man and two boys with fishing rods in their hands, and another man engaged in shooting partridge, each one in his own environment. A distinguished doctor appears in a red sport jacket. In another instance, the president of a large corporation agreed to pose in his yachting clothes with a Caribbean water-and-mountain seascape over his shoulders. Some of the young ladies I have painted are wearing riding clothes, and one girl is in her sailing rig with a jib and the lake behind her.

Each artist in his own generation must accept the current trend in fashion and cope with the problem of making an interesting and enduring painting. This is a challenge, and with unrestrained freedom in composition and use of light and shade and color there is no reason why, with adequate ability, he cannot achieve this goal. I have in one instance, however, taken the liberty of *inventing* a costume. A beautiful girl posed in a blouse which, when I studied my sketch, seemed uninteresting and inadequate. She had a classical profile, and I proceeded to paint her in a red dress similar to an Italian man's costume of the fifteenth century. The collar is high on her neck and there is a white edging on the top of it.

Perhaps it would not be irrelevant at this point to emphasize the importance of framing a picture properly. It is only natural for an artist to be so absorbed with painting the picture that framing may seem merely a burdensome necessity. But good framing can add immeasurably to the beauty of a picture; bad framing can ruin it. The frame is an inseparable part of the picture itself.

There have been as many solutions to this problem throughout the years as there were styles in painting. The framing of the mid-eighteenth-century painting was an event. A contemporary of that period once ecstatically described a frame he had seen as one of the finest in the world, consisting of seventy life-size cupids with laurels in their hands, replicas of the British,

Irish, and French crowns, and a shield with the profiles of the king and queen. Today we find many canvases with the frame reduced to a narrow, flat strip of wood nailed on the side of the stretcher. Each frame, however, may be equally appropriate.

If one is creating or selecting a frame, one must consider where the picture will hang and what the style of the room furnishings may be. Some people are more sensitive to this than others, and I have had several clients suggest that I could feel entirely free to paint the kind of picture I wished and that, if necessary, they would redecorate the room in which it was to hang.

*   *   *

Can you imagine this "Portrait of a Gentleman" (pl. 116) if the subject were dressed in today's charcoal-gray suit, a shirt with a button-down collar, and a stringy tie? Would posterity care to have it hanging on the living room wall, in spite of the undoubtedly fresh approach in which the artist shows his subject gesticulating in truly Italian fashion? Fortunately for Lorenzo Lotto (1480 - 1556), the costume of the period provided the lavish use of fur, brocade, velvet, and silk for a gentleman, and added such touches as a handsome sword, which was a work of art and craftsmanship in itself. Gold chains and buttons assisted in the over-all impression of luxury.

The color scheme is composed of a blue sky and tablecloth, dark warm blue in the jacket and cloak, maroon in the trousers, purplish brown in the sleeves, a touch of dull green in the leaves on the table.

What the significance of the gesture might be is hard to determine. Was he saying: "No! No! Stay away! I'm posing"? Or was he hailing a knowledgeable friend to assist him in identifying the wild flowers? Whatever it suggests, it is a distinct relief from the still, formal poses of men's portraits through the centuries.

Gesture is that God-given ability to express thought and emotion through every bone and muscle of the body, as well as through the medium of facial expression. Artists from time immemorial have appreciated it and used it. Sculptors discovered it of necessity long before the painters did. Uccello demonstrates it in his battle scenes; Martini, in his crucifixions. But not until the painters had learned the proper anatomy of the human body and perspective as applied to the human body did the complete liberation finally come. For me, its great exponent is Veronese and, in a less conspicuous degree, Titian. Tintoretto, for my own particular taste, exaggerates gesture to the point where it ceases at times to be plausible, even though it does add greatly to the drama and general movement of the work.

Lotto was born in Venice but spent most of his life in towns such as

Plate 116. LORENZO LOTTO. *Portrait of a Gentleman.*
1525. Oil on canvas. Cleveland Museum of Art,
Cleveland, Ohio, Gift of Hanna Fund

Treviso and Bergamo. He worked in Rome for four years and, when he was only twenty-nine years old, received one hundred ducats in advance for a fresco which was to be painted for the upper floor of the Vatican. He painted many religious pictures, among which is the altarpiece in San Bartolommeo at Bergamo. He returned to Venice periodically, and thus kept in touch with such masters as Titian and Giorgione. In 1532 he settled in Vienna, and later, tired, as he said, of wandering, he came to Loretto, where he died.

* * *

Ladies often contribute much to a picture by their perceptive choice of costume. Mrs. Henry P. Staats (pl. 117) selected the dark, plain dress ornamented with the decorative design of pearls—a particular treatment which I had never seen before. The soft, red scarf was the triumphal touch, whose color was repeated by her lips, the berries which were on the base of the Dorothy Doughty bird, and the tiny spot of the chair cushion. The background was untouched white water-color paper, until it was framed with a black glass mat, at which point it became an almost vibrating element, advancing rather than receding. It was necessary to tone it down, and, incidentally, this made the pearls come alive.

I hope that the reader who is not a practicing artist will realize what microscopic dimensions are involved in producing the desired expression in an eye. A brush stroke with a width of an infinitesimal fraction of an inch will bring out the right expression or will destroy it. This is particularly true in a small painting (in this case the head is only 3⅓" high). The problem of applying the brush is nothing compared with that of *understanding* what changes in the eye produce various expressions.

* * *

Even in miniatures the painters of the seventeenth century reproduced every detail in the lace which embellished the collars of gentlemen. The "Portrait of a Dutchman" (pl. 118) by David Baudringhien (c. 1581 - 1650) indicates how important the ruff is as a part of the design, setting the face off from the rest of the picture and providing lines that lead directly to the face.

It was not known who painted this miniature until the frame was removed in order to clean it. It was then discovered from an inscription found on it that it had been painted in 1627 by an artist presumed to be Baudringhien.

To have been able to make such a clear statement of the personality of his sitter with the head barely 1⅝" in height is a real achievement. The

Plate 117. GORDON C. AYMAR. *Mrs. Henry P. Staats.*
1954. Water color. Collection of Mr. and Mrs.
Henry P. Staats

Plate 118. DAVID BAUDRINGHIEN. *Portrait of a Dutchman.* Oil on copper. Metropolitan Museum of Art, New York, Collection of Giovanni P. Morosini, presented by his daughter, Giulia, 1932

subject is quiet, refined, and undoubtedly a gentleman. The Metropolitan Museum also has a miniature of a woman by the same artist, forming a pair.

How fortunate these painters were to live in a world of fluted, crimped, and plaited ruffs, ruches, frills, and furbelows!

*   *   *

While today we may not have regal costumes to embellish our paintings, the traditional riding habit still exists. It is not only distinctive; it is distinguished. This is what was finally chosen for the portrait of Pamela Erdmann (pl. 119).

The color scheme is simple—the black jacket, a golden yellow waistcoat, which is in harmony with her auburn hair. The sky is a warm gray, supplementing the weathered wood rail, and there is a touch of pale, soft blue in the pointed shape in the sky. The small landscape is restrained, with muted fall colors and slightly bluish-gray distant hills.

*   *   *

There was no problem in making a picture out of the "Portrait of a Lady in a Ruff" (pl. 120) by Frans Hals. When she arrived in his studio dressed in the familiar lace cap, ruff, cuffs, and handsome gown, the "picture" was already made. From then on it was a matter of painting it in Hals' inimitable manner of setting on canvas with a single stroke light, texture, and color.

The picture was painted in 1638, at which time he had enough money to buy the colors needed for a full palette. In his declining years he could afford only the basic black and white, red, yellow ocher, and blue.

This costume is one which would have given Memling or van Eyck a real opportunity for painting the most minute detail. Instead, they are rendered by Hals, the man with the rapierlike touch. The care with which he had to paint the edge of the ruff must have been annoying to a man of his temperament, but this was a commission, and he undoubtedly felt the obligation to concentrate on what must have meant much to the lady. When he treated clothing after his own fashion, it became the splashed-in collar and cuffs of his "Jolly Toper."

*   *   *

Among the various costumes which Geoffrey Thompson (pl. 121) brought with him was the dark-blue winter jacket and cap and turtle-neck sweater. Turning up the collar made an interesting design. Pushing his cap

Plate 119. GORDON C. AYMAR. *Pamela Erdmann*. 1956.
Water color. Collection of Mrs. Sturtevant
Erdmann

Plate 120. FRANS HALS. *Portrait of a Lady in a Ruff.*
1638. Oil on canvas. Cleveland Museum of Art,
Cleveland, Ohio, Purchase from the J. H. Wade
Fund

Plate 121. GORDON C. AYMAR. *Geoffrey Thompson.*
1949. Water color. Collection of Mr. and Mrs.
Fred D. Thompson

back gave a casual look, and showed more of his characteristic, very blond hair.

As I thought about possible backgrounds, it occurred to me that this was an opportunity to paint the typical Brueghel winter scene with the decorative trees and tiny skating figures. The painting is designed with a large area devoted to the figure, which is closely cropped, and suggests the old Flemish relation of figure to background.

Instead of the customary device of turning the figure toward the landscape, his body is swung in the opposite direction, with the sharp, triangular shape of the light sweater emphasizing this effect. The upper line of the collar curves quietly from the right to the sharp angle at the left, which helps to draw the eye toward the landscape side. The pose of his head is also important in this respect.

The color scheme is simple, with the dark-blue clothing and dull purple-blue sky also emphasizing his light hair. The jacket is painted very flat with almost no suggestion of modeling, in order that the light and shade on his face and sweater may register more effectively.

*   *   *

If one were asked to select a costume which best represented regal power and status, it would be a suit of armor. Charles II, King of England (pl. 122), has posed in one adorned with gold designs, wearing a lace neckpiece, a red scarf around his waist, and a bright-blue silk band across his chest. A belt of gold supports his scabbard. Behind him, within easy reach, is his helmet, topped by a crown of ostrich feathers. His left hand clutches the sword handle, and his right directs the mace in a gesture of command.

Philippe de Champaigne (1602-1674) has made a remarkable painting of the king, subduing the endless details where necessary, in order to focus attention on the face. The king at this point in his career was twenty-three years old. He was in exile in France, as he had escaped from defeat by Cromwell two years prior to this. Four years before this picture was painted, his father, Charles I, had been tried for treason and executed. Champaigne has conveyed an air of melancholy determination. The subject's eyelids are drooping, probably with emotional fatigue. His lower lip has the fullness of a sensuous personality. He was described during his lifetime as cold but generous and courageous.

As a composition the picture shows great skill. The angle of the arms, sword belt, and mace form a compact design. The sword belt continues the line of the curtain. Verticals are made by the rope and tassel, the column, and the rear of the scarf; horizontals appear in the belt part of the scarf, the landscape, clouds, and table. His cuffs repeat the white of his collar.

249

Plate 122. PHILIPPE DE CHAMPAIGNE. *Charles II, King of England*. 1653. Oil on canvas. Cleveland Museum of Art, Cleveland, Ohio, Elizabeth Severance Prentiss Fund

Champaigne was born in Brussels and studied with Michel de Bordeau, Bouillon, and Fouquières. When he was nineteen he moved to Paris, continued his painting with Lallemand, and worked on the decoration of the Luxembourg. After a brief but busy period he was appointed painter to the king at the age of twenty-six and attained an outstanding position in seventeenth-century art.

* * *

Lorenzo Villaseñor (pl. 123) arrived in my studio with his red jacket on and a cloak over his arm which had been made for him during a visit to Madrid. The tailor had wanted to make the lining red, but Lorenzo had told him that, in his opinion, this would not be in the best taste. He had brought with him a half dozen neckties, striped, polka-dotted, plain. After going over them carefully, he pointed to the dark-blue knitted one and said that this would be his choice. He was right, and in no time at all we were launched on the portrait.

The arch over his head is an invention, but it seemed to suggest the environment and fit in with the landscape which is seen from his father's estate in Mexico.

Could anything be more enjoyable than to have such a perfect combination to work with—the essence of a cultivated young gentleman (he was thirteen years old at the time) and a costume whose beauty and character exceeded that of any male clothing I had ever painted?

* * *

It is a long distance from today's informal fashions to that of the flowing rhapsody of the costume in "Portrait of a Lady of the Earle Family" (pl. 124). The dressmakers of the seventeenth century had a genuine appreciation of the qualities of satins and silks and of their vast potential in expressing the poetry of drapery to adorn a lady's figure.

Sir Peter Lely (1618-1680) has taken advantage of the glossy sheen of his subject's cloak, and its shimmering light is further emphasized by the contrast of the soft velvet dress and the dark curtain behind her. The folds swirl around in forms that bring the eye back to her figure.

The gesture of her left hand would seem to indicate that she is directing our attention to the beauty of her landscape. Seldom has a lady's hand been painted with more grace than the hand that holds her cloak.

Lely was born Pieter Van der Faes at Soest in Westphalia, where his father was serving a term as an infantry captain. Upon their return to Holland, when Peter was of the proper age he studied for two years with

Plate 123. GORDON C. AYMAR. *Lorenzo Villaseñor.*
1960. Water color. Collection of Laura Wells de
Villaseñor

Plate 124. PETER LELY. *Portrait of a Lady of the Earle
Family.* c. 1658. Oil on canvas. Cleveland Museum
of Art, Cleveland, Ohio, Gift of Mrs. Otto Miller

Pieter Franz de Grebber. He moved to London at the age of twenty-nine, adopted the style of Van Dyck, who was some years his senior, and succeeded in painting the portraits of Charles I and the duke of York. He also painted a picture of Cromwell and, during the Restoration, portraits of Charles II and his court. In 1661 he was appointed the king's "Principal Painter," and was made a baronet shortly before his death. He was eminently successful, and left a collection of art which sold for £26,000, a very substantial sum in those days.

*　*　*

A simple sweater has many advantages as part of a costume. It defines the figure in a natural way, and its curves are a good supplement, in the turtle-neck version, to the curves of the head. In the case of Nancy Rich (pl. 125) it provides a pleasant color to contrast with the color of her hair.

A sweater is also relatively timeless and, may I add, there are hair styles which are as transitory as Pop art and those like Miss Rich's, which are so basic that they will endure for years.

Two things were particularly interesting to work on in this painting. The first was to transfer to paper her lovely face and her quiet poise; the second was to design and render the scene of hunters, horses, and dogs.

*　*　*

Oddly enough, one of the paintings which I have selected as an example of costume as the main interest was painted by Gilbert Stuart. It is the portrait of "John, Lord Fitz-Gibbon, First Earl of Clare" (pl. 126). Stuart was often criticized for his negligence and sketchy treatment in painting garments. He once defended himself by saying, "I copy the works of God, and leave clothes to the tailors and mantua-makers."

Yet here, in a portrait eight feet high, the head is only an infinitesimal portion of the painting, the remainder being devoted entirely to trappings, robes, draperies, and objects.

Perhaps one of the reasons for the gaudiness of the pretentious costumes which were worn at that period was to impress the simple man. Contact between the public and the important men in government was confined to limited glimpses through the windows of magnificent coaches or during brief, scattered, and infrequent addresses. The extremely limited audience of those who were able to read apparently made it seem necessary to impress ordinary people with lavish apparel and handsomely costumed servants.

There are certain touches in the handling of the details in this painting which would suggest that Stuart may have employed assistants to paint

254

Plate 125. GORDON C. AYMAR. *Nancy Rich.* 1958.
Water color. Collection of Mr. and Mrs. Joseph
Rich

Plate 126. GILBERT STUART. *John, Lord Fitz-Gibbon, First Earl of Clare.* 1788. Oil on canvas. Cleveland Museum of Art, Cleveland, Ohio, Purchase, General Income Fund

them. This is particularly noticeable in the ceremonial mace on the table. The harsh, crude outlines of the crown are not typical of Stuart's far more subtle handling and of his interest in the general effect rather than in forcing the form of each detail.

Lord Fitz-Gibbon had a distinguished career. Born in Ireland, he attended Trinity College in Dublin and, later, Christ Church at Oxford. After being attorney general he became chancellor, and within a span of but a few years was made a baron, then a viscount, and finally an earl. At first glance his face, as painted by Stuart, would appear to be weak, with no structure which would express masculine strength and courage. One might be inclined to classify him as a jackdaw strutting in peacocks' feathers. His pose is pompous, forbidding, and his expression is irritable. Actually, he was a man of energy and action and, although he was heartily disliked by many, was an outstanding representative of the government at a time when Ireland was infiltrated with treason.

Stuart has not minced matters in portraying this man. He often stated his belief that one should be "ever jealous about truth in painting."

* * *

The portrait of Huger King (pl. 127) was planned in this unconventional manner because he wanted to be painted at his beloved home in North Carolina, where relaxing in country clothes was part of the pleasure of being away from the city.

We spent a day walking over the land bounded by the Inland Waterway, looking for an appropriate setting. The dock near the house proved to be the best from the point of view of design. The angles of the weathered boards and pile draw the eye to the figure. The mooring line points to his head, and the lower part of it adds a curved shape which is repeated in the branches of the dead tree behind him. The forms of the clouds at the left serve to oppose the strong slope of the pattern of trees, which extends across the picture.

The color scheme is simple—the warm gray of the wood, the green of the trees, the green-blue sky and water, the yellow reeds. He is wearing a white jacket with a green shirt and khaki trousers.

Actually, there is no reason why the folds of sport clothes cannot be painted with as much feeling for design as the costumes of old. What they do lack is the handsome texture of satin and velvet and the luxurious detail of lace.

When the picture was completed, Mr. King, knowing of my interest in birds, said: "You really didn't care about painting me. You just wanted to paint the American egret in the background!"

* * *   257

Plate 127. GORDON C. AYMAR. *Huger King*. 1965. Water
color. Collection of Mr. and Mrs. Huger King

It is not necessary today to paint children solely in sport clothes. There are beautifully designed dresses for young girls which have a timeless quality and an intrinsic beauty which it is a pleasure to paint.

Deirdre Wheeler (pl. 128) wore a dress which immediately suggested the circular shape for her portrait. The white collar provides a design in itself, and its folds point toward her head. The gold lettering against a blue-green background was introduced to form a stable line within the circle, and the Dutch initial was used to repeat the elegance of the lace.

* * *

The appreciation of writers of the last century for the part played by costume is well expressed in a poem called "The Petition," which hangs on the wall of my studio. Unfortunately, the author did not sign his name.

THE PETITION

Artful Painter, by this Plan
Draw a Female if you can.
Paint her Features bold and gay.
Casting modesty away;
Let her art the mode express,
And fantastick be her Dress;
Cock her up a little Hat
Of various Colours, this and that;
Make her Cap the Fashion new,
An Inch of Gauze or Lace will do;
Cut her Hair the shortest Dock;
Nicely braid her Forehead Lock;
Put her on a Negligee,
A short Sack of Sherperdee
Ruffled up to keep her warm,
Eight or ten upon an Arm;
Let her Hoop extending wide
Shew her Garters and her Pride,
Her Stockings must be pure and white,
For they are seldom out of Sight,
Let her have a high heel'd Shoe,
And a glittering Buckle too;
Other Trifles that you find,
Make quite Careless as her Mind,
Thus equipp'd she's charming Ware
For the Races or the Fair.

Plate 128. GORDON C. AYMAR. *Deirdre Wheeler*. 1964.
Water color. Collection of Mrs. Murray Wheeler

PERSONAL PROBLEMS AND SATISFACTIONS

I AM SURE that it will not be a surprise to anyone to learn that there are problems connected with painting a portrait that have little or nothing to do with "the art."

From the first portrait ever painted to those that will be painted in the dim future, there has been, and always will be, the sitter who has no artistic perception whatever, no flexibility in departing from a fixed idea of what the portrait should look like or the pattern to which he believes it should conform.

In addition to the sitter's opinion of what the portrait should be as a painting, there is his desire to be portrayed as the person he hoped to be, rather than the true image of what he has finally become.

All this is entirely natural. Why should anyone want to be recorded in such a way that, every time he passes through the living room and looks at his portrait, he is revolted by some overtone revealing a characteristic which he had been struggling all his life to overcome? If portrait painters could only put themselves in their subjects' situation, their irritability would subside and their sympathy would be reflected in their painting.

The matter of flattery inevitably comes up in connection with portrait painting. It is not difficult to detect the portraits in which this has been a venal fault. One of Hoppner's friends said that it was his

261

practice, when he was painting a lady, to make as beautiful a face as possible, then to begin to work gently toward a likeness. If a bystander happened to exclaim, "Ah, now I see a likeness in the offing!" he would stop and, as far as he was concerned, the picture was finished.

This is certainly a crude treatment of the problem, but one which seems to have been accepted by many of the artists who received commissions from the wealthy and socially distinguished. The period in which Reynolds painted was marked both in England and France by this submissiveness to flattery. If Reynolds had stood for the honest, almost brutal beliefs of Rodin, he would certainly not have been chosen to paint the more than two thousand portraits attributed to him.

Sargent once wrote to a friend, explaining one of the reasons for his intention to give up portrait painting. He said he felt sorry for his lady sitters because, while they didn't actually ask him to make them beautiful, he had the impression during every sitting that this is what they hoped for.

Madame Vigée-Lebrun remarked, in her "Advice to the Portrait-Painter," that it was necessary to flatter women, to tell them that they were beautiful and compliment them on their complexion. This, she said, puts them in a good humor, and "they have more pleasure in posing."

On the other hand, there are examples, like Oliver Cromwell, who represent the opposite attitude. He said to Sir Peter Lely, "I desire you would use all your skill to paint my picture truly like me, and not flatter me at all; but remark all these roughnesses, pimples, warts, and everything as you see me, otherwise I will never pay a farthing for it."

My own personal stand in the matter of flattery is very simple. I am not a misogynist; I do not hate people. I believe in making them look their best, *but not one jot or tittle better.* If a girl has a runaway chin, is it necessary to paint her in profile? I feel sympathetic toward those whose faces are malformed in one way or another. If I were a Daumier, I would draw caricatures and not paint portraits. If I were a Grünewald, I would render them cruelly. Regardless of the sculptural formations of the face, which may not be attractive, there is the personality to interpret through facial expression, and this is a very rewarding factor.

What the sitter's family and friends have to say about the portrait is, very naturally, of real concern to the client. Perhaps a portrait is half finished, and a friend drops in the studio and says, "Well, I suppose when you're done with it you'll make him look more like the angry character I know." Or an acquaintance of the sitter blurts out, "I didn't know you had that queer-shaped forehead." To comfort yourself, you recall Goethe's remark to the effect that one is never satisfied with the portrait of a person whom one knows. And you wonder whether Boutet de Monvel was not right in insisting that no one, not even the sitter, see the portrait until it was finished.

262

Very often the comments of friends about the portrait are helpful in achieving a likeness. One can become "blind" in working hour after hour on a painting. The fresh point of view of the outsider is often a boon.

The best course for a client to take is to allow the artist freedom when it comes to the type of picture he is to paint. If the artist is allowed to paint his own pictorial idea, it will inevitably be better than if he is told to do it in a certain way.

Giovanni Bellini upheld this position in a rather brusque way when he told the Marchesa Isabella Gonzaga through an intermediary that the treatment of his proposed picture would be determined by the imagination of the artist, and that no artist liked having limitations put upon him. As for himself, he said, he was accustomed to employing his own ideas.

However, there is another and perhaps a more fruitful solution. I believe that, even if the artist and the client cannot agree at the start on what the picture idea will be, it is an adventure for the imaginative painter to create one hundred ideas, with any one of which he himself will be satisfied; with this storehouse from which to choose, it is not unlikely that the client will find one which will satisfy him also.

This solution reminds me indirectly of a conversation I had with a young farmer from Kentucky who spent the night in our home during World War II. I had been struggling without great success with my small war garden. I said, "How in the world do you handle these bugs that eat the corn?" He answered, "We plant enough corn for ourselves *and* the bugs."

There is, of course, the danger that a prospective client will say that he would like a painting "like the one you did of Mr. X." This is a very natural approach, but if the artist went on, picture after picture, duplicating the one he did of Mr. X, his invention would become atrophied and he would soon sink into "innocuous desuetude."

One of the most disconcerting aspects of portrait painting is the possibility that a finished work may be rejected. There is actually a law in this country to the effect that if, on commissioning a portrait, the client has specified that it is to be a likeness acceptable to himself and, when the work is done, he finds it unsatisfactory, he cannot be obliged to pay for it.

The remedy for a rejection may lie in the painting of a second version, one that is more compatible with the client's idea. Gilbert Stuart was known to have painted two or three portraits of a sitter, the primary reason being to assure himself that he was doing his best. Incidentally, it gave the client an opportunity to choose the one he liked best.

If the artist, after one failure, decides that he will never be able to produce a picture of which his client will approve, it is his privilege to withdraw. One experience which I personally have had might indicate that careful consideration should be given the problem before choosing this solution.

I had painted a portrait of a young boy and, in advance, all the details had been agreed upon—what he was to wear, what the background would be, the possible facial expression, and so on. A week or so after having delivered the picture, I received a call in which my client courteously stated that, having lived with the picture, he believed he would prefer a different pictorial approach. I said I would be glad to do it and would welcome, with his permission, having the first one to show in exhibitions. (Incidentally, a portrait painter always hesitates to ask to borrow a commissioned portrait, since the client, quite naturally, does not like to have it leave his home.)

The second portrait was received with acclaim, an unveiling was arranged to show it to a large number of friends, and, to my surprise and gratification, the client announced that he liked the first one better, the longer he lived with it, and that now he and his wife wanted both portraits.

It is always comforting to know that there have been great artists in the past who have failed to satisfy their subjects. A friend of mine, one of whose ancestors was Mrs. Ithamar Canfield, told me that after Richard Jennys had finished the portrait of her, Mrs. Canfield was so upset by the way he had painted her that she threw her slipper through the canvas. Fortunately, the restorers were able to patch it together.

Even Rodin had such a problem with his friend Puvis de Chavannes, whom he heartily admired. When Rodin had finished the handsome bust of him, the great mural painter said it was "a caricature." This was one of Rodin's bitterest experiences.

Gainsborough, who complained that, though he was primarily a landscape painter, people still came to him for portraits, finally announced, "I'm sick of portraits and wish very much to take my viol-da-gamba and walk off to some sweet village, where I can paint landscips and enjoy the fag-end of life in quietness and ease." And Romney, extremely successful in this field, referred to it as "this cursed drudgery of portrait painting."

An artist's inborn temperament is bound to be a factor in his attitude toward his clients. Some of the early American painters, such as Copley and West, apparently were able to adjust pleasantly in their relations with their sitters. They were instinctively agreeable and easy to get along with. A remark made by Gilbert Stuart, however, might indicate that he was the bristly type. When one of his clients complained that he had not made his wife look truly beautiful, he answered, "You brought me a potato, and you expect a peach!"

Much depends on whether or not an artist really wants to paint portraits. I have often had people say: "How can you accept a commission to paint a portrait when you have not met the person, and do not know whether he or she is a good subject to paint? They may be actually ugly, or just plain uninteresting." This has never bothered me. The real privilege is to paint a human being. Nature herself is the fascinating, inexhaustible, unfathomable source. An ugly face through its very ugliness will have more character than the insipid one. But even the insipid one offers a challenge to express its insipidity. There does not exist a face without expression, and it is this which the true artist delights in capturing.

After all, why should a portrait painter demand to be relieved of problems which, if not identical, are no more trying than those faced daily by the average businessman? The artist's fortitude in solving them, his determination not to allow them to distract him from his goals, cannot but make him a more effective person and, in so doing, a more effective artist.

Aside from the problems of portraiture, there are the indisputable human rewards. Can you imagine how Raphael must have felt when Count Balthazar, standing in front of the portrait he had painted of the count's wife, said to her: "Your image, painted by Raphael's hand, alone can lighten my cares. That image is my delight; I direct my smiles to it, it is my joy; I speak to it and I am tempted to think that it is about to reply to my words. . . . In this way I console myself, and cheat the days of their length"?

Writers over the centuries have made relatively few records of the genuine gratifications of painting portraits. Most of their comments are concerned with the disadvantages and humiliations. Consequently, I wish to mention a few instances which have had real meaning for me. In no sense are they to be interpreted as indicating a pride in accomplishment. They are the kind of experience with which practicing portrait painters are all familiar, and I am mentioning them only because I happen to know the circumstances and background.

When I began to paint portraits, I had no idea how rewarding this aspect of art would be. I remember receiving a telephone call from a lady whose sixteen-year-old daughter I had just painted. The father, I learned later, had not been overeager to have this portrait painted. When he finally saw it framed and hanging over the mantel in the living room, he was favorably impressed. The mother told me that he carried it to the bedroom so that he could continue to look at it. In the morning he said, "This is our most precious possession!"

I know of three families who, every year, take the portraits of their children from their winter to their summer homes and back again.

Two of my close friends have refused to let their portraits be shown in exhibitions because they were afraid that something might happen to them. And one has told me that she has instructed everyone that, if their house were to catch fire, the portrait of their child was to be the first thing to be removed.

After I had painted the portrait of a very distinguished gentleman, he wrote to me, saying: "It took me some time to get used to myself, but the more I studied the face on your canvas, the clearer it became that I would like to be that person. I wonder how many men have become better by trying to live up to their portraits, just as they sometimes become better by living up to the ideal which their religion sets for them."

One afternoon I was showing the finished portrait of a little nine-year-old girl to her mother and her grandmother for the first time. When I had set it up in front of them, the mother threw her head on her mother's shoulder and began to cry. I was mortified with the effect the portrait had caused, until the mother recovered and said, "I had no idea that anyone outside the family would ever know her so well."

In another instance I was asked to paint the portrait of a man who had died a number of years previously. I worked from many photographs of him, assisted by the interpretation of his widow. When the painting was completed, she asked her son to look at it. As she showed it to him, I overheard her say: "He is alive! He is alive!"

I know a portrait painter who, while he was in the hospital, received a cheering note from a friend which concluded, "I love you for all the shining truth and beauty you have given others."

These are experiences which have real meaning for the artist, but it must be admitted that they are peripheral compared with his primary satisfaction, which is the instinctive urge to *paint*. If he can create a picture which will measure up to his standards, this is his main reward. And if, in addition to his deep feeling about it as a work of art, he believes that it is also a likeness of the sitter, then he has achieved his goals.

It will be worth while, I believe, to study various types with which an artist becomes involved in painting a portrait—the ugly sitter, the beautiful sitter, the one whose nature is irascible, the portrait which must satisfy a group, the appreciative patron, and the artistically insensitive patron whose demands for alterations do not weigh the difficulties involved.

Perhaps we should all adopt the point of view of a six-year-old boy who was meeting me for the first time.

"You're an artist, aren't you?" he asked.

"Well," I said, "I try to be."

"I am one!" he said.

I remarked that the older I grew, the harder it seemed.

"It's easy," he said. "I can paint the sun!"

* * *

Every time I walk through the room in the Metropolitan Museum where the Pérussis Altarpiece is hanging I stop and study the kneeling figure on one of the side panels (pl. 129). This, presumably, is a portrait of the donor. As a departure from the classical concept of beauty, his face is a remarkable example. How did the painter (an unknown Frenchman who was active between 1450 and 1490) react when he first saw the donor? Was he shocked, disappointed? He had to face the problem of how he should paint his physical

266

Plate 129. FRENCH PAINTER, UNKNOWN. *The Pérussis Altarpiece* (detail, kneeling figure, 2nd panel from right). Tempora and oil on wood. Metropolitan Museum of Art, New York, Purchase 1954, Bequest of Mary Wetmore Shively, in memory of her husband, Henry L. Shively

peculiarities. If he were to place him with his face pointing toward us, the size of the sitter's nose would not be so evident. But it was customary to pose the donor at one side, and, since he would be looking toward the center of the picture, his nose would be prominent, even in a three-quarter position. Perhaps in the fifteenth century there was a more forthright acceptance of truth than there was three centuries later. At any rate, there is a meticulous recording of each feature to such a degree that we can accept this as a true likeness, or even wonder if it were not slightly caricatured.

Compare the Memlinglike, detailed painting of the face with the stiffly designed, outlined, and rather flat handling of his clothing and that of the figure behind him. It would almost appear that the face had been painted by one artist and the rest by another.

* * *

In one of the intervals between serving terms in prison for his political convictions Jacques Louis David painted the "Portrait of Madame Récamier" (pl. 130). She is dressed in a classical costume which had come into vogue because of his famous "War Between the Romans and the Sabines," on which he had worked for five years. Thousands of Parisians had paid admission fees to see it. Ladies from high society had posed as models for him, and had appeared in public with coiffures and gowns adapted from those he was painting for this picture. Actually, Mme. Récamier's hair, hair ribbon, and gown are almost identical with those of the Sabine Hersilia, who dominates the composition in this huge painting (it is 12½' x 17').

Regardless of the artist's outstanding reputation at the time, Mme. Récamier rejected David's portrait of her, preferring, apparently, one painted by his pupil François Gérard. Consequently, we may learn by this example that a portrait painter's problems with his clients are sometimes a matter of personal whim.

* * *

Often the personal problems in portrait painting are concerned with how to paint a homely person in such a way that the result will not be disturbing. In the case of Marny Ruhm (pl. 131) the problem was the exact opposite. She was so naturally beautiful that a person who did not know her might think that the painting was a conscienceless idealization. I could find no solution, and had to paint her exactly as she appeared.

Instead of a flamboyant dress-of-the-moment, she had selected a dark one of unusually simple design. The necklace forms an excellent line to join with those of the hair and head, and it also points toward her hands, thus helping to bridge the gap between the two light areas. In the background is the handsome retaining wall and tennis court, whose lines repeat those of
268

Plate 130. Jacques Louis David. *Portrait of Madame Récamier*. Louvre, Paris. Phot. Réunion Musées Nationaux

Plate 131. GORDON C. AYMAR. *Marny Ruhm*. 1951.
Water color. Collection of Mr. and Mrs. Herman
D. Ruhm, Jr.

the railing. The sky was painted unnaturally dark, not only to bring out the head, but, hopefully, to avoid what might have appeared to be photographic realism.

* * *

In 1805, when Gilbert Stuart was fifty years old, his portrait (pl. 132) was painted by his good friends Charles Willson Peale (1741-1827) and Peale's son, Rembrandt (1778-1860). This portrait gives the impression of being a truthful likeness. The two artists have gone right to the point; Stuart's tense, volatile nature and his occasional irritability are shown clearly in his expression. They have not hesitated to paint the unkempt look of his hair. Stuart was immediately aware of this revelation of his personality, for he is said to have laughed at the final picture and to have remarked that it made him look like an awkward clown. There are personal problems even when an artist paints his artist friend.

Charles Willson Peale was engaged in a multitude of craftsmanlike activities when he was young. He was not only a clockmaker and saddler, but a silversmith, taxidermist, and dentist as well. His teachers in painting were such distinguished artists as John Hesselius, Smibert, and later, in England, where he lived for two years, Benjamin West. Born in Maryland, he moved to Philadelphia in 1776, but his successful career had begun with a portrait of George Washington, painted upon his return from London.

He was not only an artist, but a well-rounded man of determination and many interests. In 1776 he was made a lieutenant of the militia and, some years later, a captain. To sense his personality it is only necessary to examine his "Self-Portrait in His Museum" in the Pennsylvania Academy Of The Fine Arts, in whose founding he was the guiding spirit. His absorption with zoology and anthropology led him to found this museum in conjunction with his picture gallery.

Rembrandt, his son, was permitted at the age of eighteen to paint Washington's portrait. He went to London to study with West, then to Rome, but finally returned to practice in New York.

* * *

It is interesting to learn that as experienced and successful a painter as John Trumbull (1756-1843) had a very important portrait rejected. This was the fate of his now highly regarded painting of "General George Washington at the Battle of Trenton" (pl. 133). It was painted from life during Washington's first term as President. Washington had resigned from his post in the army nine years before, and this portrait was commissioned by the city of Charleston, South Carolina, presumably to represent him as he appeared when he was still in command. This naturally required a readjustment of the face to make him look considerably younger. No one, how-

Plate 132. CHARLES WILLSON PEALE and REMBRANDT
PEALE. *Gilbert Stuart*. 1805. Oil on canvas. Courtesy, New York Historical Society, New York City

Plate 133. JOHN TRUMBULL. *General George Washington at the Battle of Trenton.* Oil on canvas. Yale
University Art Gallery, New Haven, Connecticut

ever, could be expected to know how to do this better than Trumbull, who had a good reputation as an artist and who had also served in the army as Washington's second aide-de-camp, largely due to his success in drawing a plan of the enemy's fortifications which he had observed secretly.

The painting was rejected, because those who commissioned it insisted that they wanted "a more matter-of-fact likeness." This may have been a courteous way of saying that they did not care for the rather pretentious and artificial pose. Trumbull declared that it was because they preferred to think of Washington in his civilian role, since this was the way they had come to know him when he had visited the city. He added that he had wished to record Washington's heroic military character and that he considered the painting the best of its kind.

The picture shows the general after he had seen the enemy's overpowering strength through his telescope and was deciding on how to escape. Perhaps the prancing horse with the terrified look was intended to suggest the emotional difficulties of the situation. It is a romantic interpretation with little concern for what the actual scene may have looked like.

Perhaps, in order to achieve the effect he was seeking, Trumbull intentionally took certain liberties, for Washington's figure is nine heads high— a fact which makes him look like an unusually tall man. Comparing this with Gilbert Stuart's full-length portrait of Washington in the Pennsylvania Academy of Fine Arts, painted a few years later, one wonders what Washington really looked like. Stuart's gives the effect of a small man with a large head. Even if one concedes the fact that certain liberties may have been taken, how could two such accomplished, well-trained painters, both students of Benjamin West, have painted the figure with such a basic difference? It was customary in those days, as it is today, to instruct students, when drawing from life, to measure the length of the body in terms of the height of the head, a normal figure being about seven and a half heads high. The student holds his charcoal at arm's length and measures not only the total height, but the length of upper and lower arms and legs in relation to the size of the head.

Washington, like many other distinguished men, was forced during his busy life to devote some of his valuable time to sitting for his portraits. Even before he became President he wrote, "I am so hackneyed to the touches of the Painter's pencil, that I am now altogether at their beck, and sit like patience on a Monument whilst they are delineating the lines of my face."

Trumbull had an outstanding career. His father, Jonathan, was a graduate of Harvard and became governor of Connecticut. John graduated from Harvard at the age of seventeen. He then entered the army and, when he was twenty, had reached the rank of colonel. It is extraordinary that, in spite of long interruptions due to his military life, he could have found time to build up such a substantial artistic background that he was able not only to paint portraits, but to combine these with highly complicated pictures of historical scenes.

*　*　*

When we realize that Degas' beautiful portrait of "Mme. Gaujelin" (pl. 134) was rejected by her as unsatisfactory, we are comforted by the realization that even the great are not free from the perils of trying to satisfy the sitter. It is living testimony to the fact that with many people the painting as a work of art is a secondary consideration. Gertrude Stein's attitude was the opposite, and this is why the portraits of her are now in museums.

Mme. Gaujelin's objection may have stemmed from the impression Degas has given of a rather unhappy personality. There is an overtone of dolorous resignation in her expression. This is indicated not only in the mouth, but also in the drooping upper eyelids and the slightly raised eyebrows. Her folded hands also register a mood of acceptance.

Degas has made an interesting design of angular lines throughout the picture—the sofa, the table, the line of the wall, the arms, the hands, and the edge of the figured material. Instead of the customary light face against a dark background, he has kept both equally light. The fingers of the hands are beautifully suggested, and their *lines* give every evidence that he painted them as he would have drawn them with pastel. (He often said that oil paint should be applied in this manner.)

We can be thankful that this picture was not damaged, as was his portrait of Manet and his wife. Degas offered that painting to his friend Manet, who cut it in two, since he did not like the painting of his wife. After a brief quarrel Degas took the remains back to his studio, in order to paint her portrait over again on a new piece of canvas. He never completed this, however, possibly because sometime later Manet painted a picture of his wife, using the same general pose. Perhaps Degas' difficulty in this case was that he had painted her as he declared that he always painted women— without their usual "airs and affectations."

*　*　*

It is surprising that an artist whose success in his profession was so well established as Sargent's should have found himself in such a large number of difficult situations.

However, his flexible style of handling his medium was apparently adjustable to the point that he was able to accommodate his paintings to the inevitable changes required. Sometimes a painting would start out in one direction and end up in another. This, at least, was the case in the "Portrait of Mr. and Mrs. Isaac Newton Phelps Stokes" (pl. 135). Originally, Sargent was going to paint Mrs. Stokes in the customary evening dress, but when

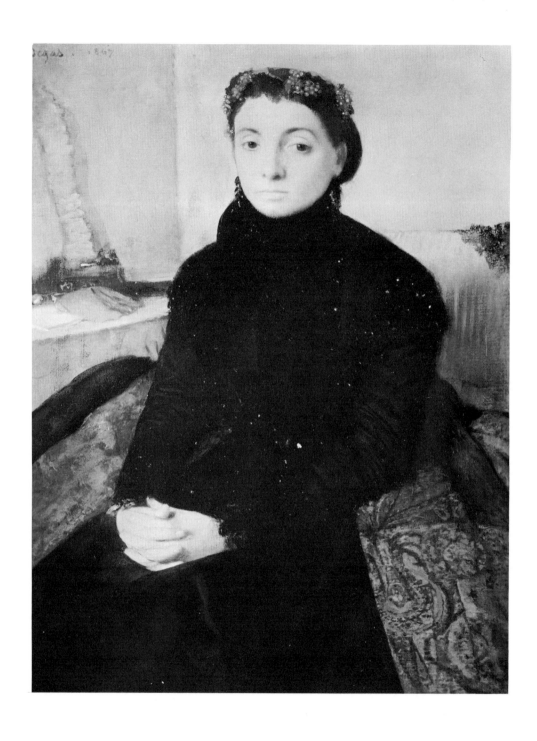

Plate 134. EDGAR DEGAS. *Mme. Gaujelin.* Isabella Stewart Gardner Museum, Boston

Plate 135. JOHN SINGER SARGENT. *Portrait of Mr. and Mrs. Isaac Newton Phelps Stokes.* 1897. Oil on canvas. Metropolitan Museum of Art, New York, Bequest of Edith Minturn Stokes, 1938

she appeared in his studio in tennis clothes, this seemed to him to offer the components of good design. To add to the informality, he started to paint her Great Dane beside her, but, failing to persuade the dog to pose for him, he abandoned this idea. Then he skillfully introduced the portrait of her husband, subduing him by means of a strong cast shadow, which placed him in a properly subordinate position.

There are many instances of Sargent's failing to satisfy his sitters. The famous portrait of Madame X was rejected by her because of the unfavorable comments made about the décolleté effect of her dress when the picture was exhibited in the Salon. Her family even insisted that Sargent remove it while the exhibition was still being held. During one of these difficult periods he wrote to John D. Rockefeller that he would not paint his portrait unless Rockefeller would guarantee that no change would be required.

In the home of a dear friend of ours there hung a Sargent portrait of a close relative, with her young daughter standing beside the chair in which she was seated. It had been painted in London, and was originally a portrait of the lady alone. Two years later she had asked Sargent to add the picture of the little girl. Many years after that, when he was in Boston, she wrote to him, saying that she now wanted him to paint the child out, which would have restored the picture to its original condition. A bristly correspondence ensued, and finally Sargent wrote her a letter which I am able to quote, due to the kindness of one of her descendants. It reads as follows: "I am much surprised at the irritation that my letter seems to have called forth by its sharp illustration of what would be a parallel to an infringement of rules. To disturb the balance of a composition by taking out an important part of it would amount to an embarrassment that an artist cannot consent to be guilty of. The other alternative that you suggest, burning or cutting in two, would be less obnoxious—and any alterations to dresses or surroundings made nowadays would probably not be for the better. I prefer not to make any myself."

In a letter to Lady Radnor, after he had successfully painted a portrait of her daughter and she had requested him to do other members of the family, he remarked, "Ask me to paint your gates, your fences, your barns, which I should gladly do, but *NOT THE HUMAN FACE!*"[4]

His often-quoted remark that every time he painted a portrait he lost a friend, however, did not apply to Mrs. Meynell, who had posed for him. She wrote, in an introduction to a book on Sargent, that he was "one of the family of Velázquez, and no less than his chief heir."

* * *

[4]Federick A. Sweet, *Sargent, Whistler and Mary Cassatt.* (Chicago: The Art Institute of Chicago, R. R. Donnelley and Sons, 1954)

THE CREATIVE IDEA

A PORTRAIT, as I have pointed out, is more than a likeness. It is a picture as well, and while this aspect of it may not be the prospective owner's prime concern, he naturally wishes to have something which will look well on the wall and which will have at least the quality of the furnishings of the room in which it is to hang. Presumably, the sitter hopes that this aspect of it has been taken care of when he has selected a particular artist to paint his portrait.

There are many considerations that enter into the decision as to what the picture will be like. Perhaps the person whose portrait is to be painted has been attracted by a painting of a friend or relative, or he may have seen the artist's work in a gallery or exhibition. He may wish to have one just like it. To avoid this repetition it is then necessary to invent a new and appropriate solution to which the sitter may be attracted. My experience has been that, once the sitter has become involved in various ideas for the painting, he tends to be less aware of the picture which first interested him.

The artist's imagination will be influenced by many things—his training, his respect for the work of certain great artists, ideas which have come to him in the past and are stored away in his mind. He may have wanted to paint a picture according to his own artistic interests, and introduced the human figure as an important part of the composition. On-the-spot discoveries of paintable scenes and poses are among the most important considerations. This last solution was commended by Sir Joshua Reynolds in his "Twelve Discourses": "It is a great matter to be in the way of accident, and to be watchful and ready to take advantage of it."

The *décor* of the room may be a guiding factor—other paintings which are hanging there; a period interior, either current or of the past, which gives the surroundings character. The objects which indicate a sitter's interests are also important factors in making the picture, and, at times, the costume may be the basis of the design.

Many fine portraits have been painted and accepted because they conformed to a currently fashionable style. While this has limited the artist in his creative ideas, it has not always deprived him of the ability to make a good picture.

Then there is the portrait that is born from the sheer joy of getting away from convention and striking out with one's imagination into new fields.

The governing element in all this creativity is the artist's perception of beauty, the potential beauty of the human form, and the objects and surroundings with which he will be working. It is this which will determine whether he will be able to produce a *painting* as well as a *likeness*.

This perception of beauty is as inborn as the color of his eyes, and it manifests itself at an early age. I shall never forget hearing from a friend that when her daughter was about to celebrate her sixth birthday, she said that all she wanted was a dollhouse, perfectly furnished. Her mother, believing this to be true, went to great pains to achieve it. The rooms were properly papered, the furniture was beautifully made, and even the lighting was skillfully arranged. The great moment arrived. The nursery door was opened and the child ran to the dollhouse and sat in silent ecstasy before it. After a long pause she went to her mother, threw her arms around her, and burst into tears. Her parents, heartbroken that it had not met her expectations, asked her what was wrong. She said, "Did you see the shadow of the rocking chair on the wall?" Today she is living in Italy, and is devoting her life to painting.

It is this ability to *see* beauty which is essential, fundamental. The failure of many capable portraitists of our time to devote a substantial part of their talent and energy to this side of art, and their willingness to repeat a commonplace formula, has been one of the reasons for the current attitude of the critics toward portrait painting.

While it may seem presumptuous to assume that we know the background facts involved in the creation of portraits of the past, discussing the subject may serve as a reminder of the various ways in which paintings are invented, regardless of whether or not these assumptions are valid.

280

* * *

I am sure that the large portion of his life which Titian devoted to complicated religious and mythological paintings enabled him to approach portraiture with a natural, inbred imagination. Not that he was an "illustrator" in a derogatory sense, but that in this type of work he was forced to invent and not merely reproduce.

When he painted the "Portrait of a Lady" (La Schiavona) (pl. 136), he used a device which adds considerable interest to the painting. By introducing her profile carved in marble, he has supplemented the definition of the likeness, and at the same time has been able to conceal at least a portion of the width of his rotund sitter. He may have painted the profile from an existing bas-relief, or he could have created it himself, which seems more probable. At any rate, his imagination served to produce a picture which was not a mere repetition of the commonplace.

In studying this painting, I was somewhat at a loss to justify the composition, handsome as it is. It seemed that the shapes tended to emphasize the breadth and shortness of the lady to an unnecessary degree. In a reproduction of this picture when it was in the Crespi Collection in Milan, I discovered one very noticeable difference. If one draws an imaginary line straight upward from the top of the marble just above the carved profile, this will represent the edge of a wall in the earlier state of this picture. Imagine the area to the right of this to be a flat rectangle darker than the wall to the left. This accomplishes several things: the wall line points directly to the profile; it frames her body in a more balanced manner; it repeats the dark of her hair; it completes the steplike design of the marble parapet and unites it with the background. This probably represents the condition of the painting before it was cleaned.

Titian began a picture by painting the outlines and shadows in a thin brown, leaving the primed surface of his panel or canvas as a luminous base for his flesh tones and light areas. He then built his painting up with semiopaque and transparent glazes, all of which enabled him to achieve glowing color. It is these glazes, however, which are so vulnerable when a picture is being restored.

Titian never hesitated to make changes on his paintings. His practice was to carry a picture through its initial stages and then put it aside, sometimes for a matter of months. When he resumed work on it, according to Palma Giovane, who was his pupil, he would examine it with a stern and penetrating look as though it were his enemy, with the intent of searching out its failings.

Some of Titian's contemporaries felt that he had a rather commercial approach to painting in spite of the magnificent quality of his art and his devotion to it. There is a story that one of his patrons received a portrait with which he was not entirely pleased. He was heard to remark that if he

Plate 136. TITIAN (TIZIANO VECELLI). *Portrait of a Lady.*
Courtesy, trustees of National Gallery, London

had paid Titian a few more ducats, perhaps the silks and brocades would have been painted with more care.

Historians differ in regard to the date of Titian's (Tiziano Vecelli's) birth. This ranges all the way from 1477 to 1490. He was definitely active before 1511. Born at Pieve di Cadore of hardy peasant stock, he was sent at an early age to Venice and studied first under Gentile and later under Giovanni Bellini. He worked with Giorgione on a series of frescoes, and, in certain instances, their paintings are indistinguishable. His career was highly successful both in religious paintings and in portraits. He was idolized by his patrons, among whom were Pope Paul III, Philip II of Spain, and Philip's father, the Holy Roman Emperor Charles V.

An entertaining anecdote, told—and perhaps concocted—by his contemporaries, was that at a certain point while he was painting a picture of or for Charles V, he dropped his brush. The emperor promptly picked it up. This, to the notables of that day, so conscious of the rules of etiquette, symbolized the voluntary subordination of the height of temporal power to the superlative talent of the artist.

* * *

Another example of a painter using more than one view of a head is found in the "Triple Portrait of Richelieu" (pl. 137) by Philippe de Champaigne (1602-1674), painted a century later. What could be more infallible in recording the features of an individual than this rendering of three different positions of the head? Posterity now has a complete document as to Richelieu's appearance.

De Champaigne has taken liberties with the direction of light. On the three-quarter face the light is slightly from the right; in the right-hand profile, almost from the front; in the left-hand profile it is a little from the left. It is interesting to see how he chose to join the cardinal's robes at the right, separating them optically by the cord holding the cross.

The color scheme is handsome, due to the splendid red of the robes and caps. The ribbons holding the crosses are a clear blue-green. He has intentionally subdued what was probably a white collar, so that it would not overpower the tone of the face. This has been an accepted custom for centuries.

Van Dyck's "Triple Portrait of Charles I," painted about 1637, is similar, except that the artist shows the subject in profile, full face, and three-quarter face, and includes a right hand and a left hand.

This is the kind of idea that is born in the imagination. There is nothing "accidental" about it. It is the opposite extreme from Ingres' portrait of Bertin, editor of the *Journal des Débats*. After many sketches which did not

Plate 137. PHILIPPE DE CHAMPAIGNE. *Triple Portrait of Richelieu.* Courtesy, trustees of National Gallery, London

satisfy him, Ingres suddenly observed Bertin in a rather belligerent pose which he had spontaneously assumed while arguing with his sons. At this moment Ingres told him not to move, that this was the way he wanted to paint him. This was truly capturing the accidental.

* * *

In talking with Lindsay Findlay (pl. 138) I had no difficulty in discovering that one of her main interests was butterflies. While there were many ways of introducing this into a painting, such as placing them on tall grass beside her, the opportunity of painting a picture in the Memling tradition was what determined the choice of the little box and butterfly. Actually, in posing she was holding a package of cigarettes. The box was an invention, and the species of butterfly was selected because of the size and color scheme of the insect, without regard for its natural habitat.

The little folded paper bearing the sitter's name is characteristic of the old Flemish paintings. Notice that one corner of the little piece of paper on the table meets the corner of the butterfly box and gives it a touch of geometrical design.

Water-color paintings, executed with the finest paints on the best quality of rag paper, should be more enduring than oil, provided they are kept out of direct sunlight.

* * *

"The Bayard Homestead at Alphen, Holland" (pl. 139) is an illustration of how broad an approach can be made in creating a portrait. This was painted by an unidentified Dutch artist about 1644. Landscapes were flourishing at this time. Van Ruisdael, Hobbema, Cuyp, Koninck, and Steen are a few of the well-known names whose distinguished work has come down to us. A century later Gainsborough and his fellow Englishmen were using relatively small figures in large, handsome country settings. The subjects, however, were dressed in the flamboyant costumes of that period, which, to our eyes, look out of place in these rural settings. The Dutch clothing was simpler, but even in this painting the sitters wore the beautiful collars and ruffs which are associated with the portraits of Hals and Rembrandt.

The composition is reminiscent of some of Rembrandt's etchings. A number of them use this diagonal division even more stringently. The slanting line of the trees is counteracted by the slope of the big tree in the foreground and, especially, by the imaginary line connecting the two heads. It is interesting to notice the similarity in the curved outlines of the trees and the shapes of the carefully rendered clouds.

285

Plate 138. GORDON C. AYMAR. *Lindsay Findlay.* 1947. Water color. Collection of Mr. and Mrs. David B. Findlay

Plate 139. UNIDENTIFIED DUTCH ARTIST. *The Bayard Homestead at Alphen, Holland.* c. 1644. Oil on wood panel. Courtesy, New York Historical Society, New York City

The simple, peasantlike look of the homestead with its thatched roofs and distorted lines is a remarkable contrast to the elaborate, palatial settings of the Italian portraits of this period. Since the artist has depicted in the background the simple folk who worked there, he undoubtedly had an affection for them. In many of the English, Netherlandish, and early American group portraits the servants are far more prominently shown, almost equally with members of the family.

In the original painting the characters of the sitters are well defined (which, of course, cannot be seen so clearly in the reproduction). He is a straightforward, masterful type and she is sitting in an overrigid pose, apparently to respond to the demands of propriety and those of the painter.

What a delightful way to have one's portrait recorded—among these intimate surroundings!

* * *

Portraits of people looking out of windows have always interested me. The way they are framed, the natural composition of the body within the confines of the rectangular shapes, the reason for their looking out of the window, which is reflected in their faces—all these considerations have lain dormant in my mind for years.

Lisa Cobb (pl. 140) lives in an old white house on a river; when I went there to study the situation and saw the interesting type of windows, it seemed to me that that was the time to enjoy painting a setting of this kind.

Lisa is looking with keen interest at what is going on on the river. Her body is leaning very slightly to one side to look between the trees—a device which keeps her from being too symmetrical.

Adjusting the rectangular areas in a composition of this kind is exactly as critical as designing their relationships in a good abstract painting. Here the shapes, in addition to their architectural geometry, have various colors to balance them—the dark, warm background, the shutter, and the sky reflected in the glass. The curtains supply a final touch of relief in the stiff design. The curves in the subject's hair, jaw, collar, sleeves, and jumper harmonize with the curtains, and her straight arms are an intermediary between the straight lines and the curves.

A picture of this shape is often suitable to hang over a fireplace; in this case the white woodwork repeated the lines and the character of the mantle.

* * *

The parakeet, which was carrying on a conversation in the dining room in Mary Carton's home, was the guiding factor in this picture (pl. 141). We

Plate 140. GORDON C. AYMAR. *Lisa Cobb*. 1965. Water
color. Collection of Mrs. Samuel Dorrance

selected a simple dress with a collar and cuffs that would contribute to the design. The dress is a modest green, fitting in between the yellow-greens and blue-greens of the bird's feathers. The background is a dark brown, which allows her blond hair to glow with light.

It is probably not necessary to point out that the combined pose was not continued indefinitely. The bird and the girl were separate units bound together by paint rather than pose and patience.

Painting the frame as part of the background of the picture was frequently used in Italian portraits of the fifteenth century. It not only relates the painting more closely with the frame, but also adds a sense of depth.

A beautiful frame, appropriate for the period, was toned in with the dark background of the painting. The corners are dull, rubbed gold, with a rather freely carved, though inconspicuous design.

Mary Carton's portrait is in oil on canvas, which seemed an appropriate medium for a painting of this type.

* * *

In painting a portrait of as distinguished a lady as Madame de Pompadour, the artist must have felt that it was only natural to represent her in a theatrical role. Since interest in the classics was flourishing when Jean Marc Nattier (1685 - 1766) painted her, artist and sitter apparently agreed that she should take the part of Diana (pl. 142). Nothing, however, could be farther from the simple, rigid, unpretentious Greek costume of the ancient goddess than this extravagant silk and satin gown, designed and made according to the ultimate in the French society of her period. In addition to the handsome dress, there are the billowing scarf and the touches of fur, which serve as much as a symbol of luxury as they do to suggest that she has shot the animal which provided it. Her shield and arrows are merely suggested in the background, and have become almost a part of the tree against which they are leaning. This leaves her with the bow alone to symbolize her relationship with the goddess of the hunt and the protectress of womankind. No one but an actress or a ballet dancer could hold the bow so daintily.

Each jewel has been meticulously rendered. The materials of her dress, particularly the *bouffant* sleeves, are objects of beauty in themselves.

Nattier has painted the lady's face almost as a model of classical beauty, while she has assumed the impenetrable veil which protects her from any interpretation of her character. It has often been suggested that posing for one's portrait is a serious matter which tends to make a lady conceal her faults, emphasize her virtues, and summon up her utmost charm. Nattier was apparently able to evoke this mood, and when he was complimented

Plate 141. GORDON C. AYMAR. *Mary Carton*. 1963. Oil
on canvas. Collection of Mr. and Mrs. Laurence
Carton

Plate 142. JEAN MARC NATTIER. *Madame de Pompadour as Diana*. 1752. Oil on canvas. Cleveland Museum of Art, Cleveland, Ohio, John L. Severance Collection

by one of his sitters for his painting, he replied, "It happens because of the magic which the god of grace allows to flow from my mind into my brush."

This was the period in which the arts were flourishing. There is a record to the effect that in 1710 Louis XIV owned 1,299 French and Italian paintings and nearly 200 of other schools.

Jean Marc was the son and pupil of Marc Nattier, and studied also at the École de l'Académie. When he was thirty years old, he was invited by Russia's Peter the Great to paint his portrait. Toward the end of his career his romantic and flattering style was severely criticized.

* * *

The on-the-spot idea is often the determining factor in selecting clothing and background. In the case of Allen Pierce (pl. 143) it was the dark-blue sweater to form a contrast with his blond hair and the Watch Hill lighthouse which juts out into Long Island Sound.

It then became simply a matter of making its general design fit in with that of the figure. Part of the wall parallels his leg. The top of the board on the back of the bench on which he is sitting acts as a continuation of the horizon line.

To offset the stiff lines of the figure it seemed wise to introduce the gulls which were flying overhead. (Incidentally, they are ring-billed gulls, with second-year plumage.) With a little adjusting of wings and legs, they took their place as part of the design leading the eye downward toward the lighthouse.

The strong, dark strip of sky at the top of the picture serves not only to repeat the dark horizontal shape at the bottom, but helps to emphasize the subject's light hair, which is rendered somewhat more roughly than his flesh in order to give it an opposing texture.

* * *

There could not be a better title for the painting by Jean Baptiste Camille Corot (1796 - 1875) than "Interrupted Reading" (pl. 144). It is quite apparent that his model was bored but resigned. It is a good example of the casual, the accidental. And it is beautifully composed, with the right hand and arm curling up to the head in an almost architectural design; the strong diagonal line formed by the left arm ending in the book, which provides sharp light and dark contrasts and repeats the dark of her bodice and hair.

The color scheme is simple and pleasing—the soft flesh color; the dull greenish background, blending slightly into the ocherish skirt; the cool reddish table cover, repeated in the book.

Plate 143. GORDON C. AYMAR. *Allen Pierce*. 1952. Water color. Collection of Mr. and Mrs. William H. Harkness

Plate 144. Jean Baptiste Camille Corot. *Interrupted Reading*. c. 1865/70. Oil. Courtesy, Art Institute of Chicago, Potter Palmer Collection

The forthright, sure touch of the brush was characteristic of Corot, and it was probably due to his having become so involved with landscape painting that he was able to approach the figure with such a fresh point of view and with such confidence. He often declared that he was never anxious to concentrate on details, and that it was the masses and the general character of the picture about which he was most concerned.

He spent much of his time studying and "memorizing" his landscapes. He would make a quick sketch (one of these made in Fontainebleau took fifteen minutes), and would then proceed to make a painting from the study. He used to say that, if necessary, he could get along without having the sketch in front of him. All of which indicates his complete understanding and control of the material with which he was working.

He was an unaffected, honest man not bound irrevocably to any school, but able at the same time to absorb the work of such painters as Manet and Courbet.

*   *   *

It is always an advantage to be able to live in the home of someone you are going to paint; to feel at home with him; to let ideas for the picture multiply. One morning Pamela Rich (pl. 145) came downstairs in her yellow, Sunday-best dress with a straw hat on the back of her head. This was the precious moment; this was the birth of the idea. Since the reasonable place to be wearing a hat is in the front hall, we selected this as the background. The black ribbon of her hat repeated the black of her shoes and the black of the marble floor. The white of the floor and baseboard were repeated in the white part of her dress. The lines in the folds of her dress were stiffened to accord with the geometrical lines of the floor.

The gray wallpaper had to be redesigned, since mermaids, which were an important part of it, did not seem particularly suitable in interpreting the personality of this charming young girl.

*   *   *

The "Portrait of Théodore Duret: Arrangement in Flesh Color and Black" (pl. 146) by James McNeill Whistler (1834-1903) is a convincing example of the idea that is born in a matter of minutes. It seems more than likely that Whistler, with his perceptive eye for the decorative, and his interest in black-and-white design, happened to see Duret with his lady's cloak over his arm and her fan in his hand. This formed the basis of his idea.

It must have been a privilege to paint a portrait of someone so artistically understanding as Duret, who was an art critic and helped promote the impressionist movement. However, there were problems when it came
296

Plate 145. GORDON C. AYMAR. *Pamela Rich.* 1959.
Water color. Collection of Mr. and Mrs. Joseph
Rich

Plate 146. JAMES ABBOTT MCNEIL WHISTLER. *Portrait of Théodore Duret: Arrangement in Flesh Color and Black*. 1883. Oil on canvas. Metropolitan Museum of Art, New York, Wolfe Fund, 1913

to agreeing upon the concept of the painting, and it required many sittings and was redone a number of times.

Duret was a close friend of Whistler. They had lived together in Paris and London years before this picture was painted, and Duret wrote Whistler's biography shortly after his death.

One of Whistler's genuine achievements was his ability to accept the flat, designed character of the Chinese and Japanese, without overemphasizing this characteristic. The feeling for design is definitely present in this portrait; yet there is sufficient modeling in the head, hand, and cloak to give the feeling of unaffected realism. The dress suit, hat, and shoes are executed with almost no sense of form. They make one black pattern. The shadow cast by his body is scarcely defined, and the background is handled with complete freedom from any literal interpretation. In order to avoid a hard line where the wall would meet the floor, Whistler chose what might appear to be a curtain, but while the folds at the bottom are vaguely suggested, the curtain itself is treated as though it were as flat as a wall. The painting is made additionally impressive by its size, which is nearly six and a half feet high.

Whistler's insistence upon regarding a picture as a picture, quite apart from any story it might be telling, commands respect. In naming his paintings "arrangements," "harmonies," "nocturnes," and "symphonies," he was trying to make the public understand this point of view. He declared that "as music is the poetry of sound, so is painting the poetry of sight, and the subject-matter has nothing to do with harmony of sound or of colour."

Two of his most famous paintings, the "Portrait of the Artist's Mother; Arrangement in Grey and Black" and the "Portrait of Thomas Carlyle: Arrangement in Grey and Black" are almost the direct opposite of an on-the-spot idea. They are obviously "arranged." Nothing could be less casual than the stiff way in which their chairs are placed against the wall. For the average person this may appear to be unnecessarily artificial. For the artist, concerned with the perfectly adjusted arrangement of objects, it is of no importance. Carlyle's admiration for Whistler's portrait of his mother determined the basic scheme for his own portrait. It would be interesting to know whether such a close repetition of his mother's portrait was a pleasure or a burden for the artist.

Whistler's early youth and training were far from those of the average American artist. He was born in Lowell, Massachusetts, and went with his engineer father to St. Petersburg, Russia, where he studied in a preliminary way at the Imperial Academy of Sciences. He later entered the Military Academy at West Point (his father was a major), but after three years he was dismissed for a failure in his chemistry course, which he later said was due to a difference of opinion between his professor and himself as to whether silicon was a crystalline substance or a gas. Joining the Coast and Geodetic Survey as a map engraver, he lost this position because he made artistic rather than factual, scientific drawings on the margins of his work. Having thus declared himself as primarily an artist, he studied with Gabriel Gleyre in Paris. He moved to London in 1859 and painted there with considerable success. While some of his paintings were accepted at the Royal Academy, Whistler finally became embittered by refusals and stopped submitting. He was rejected many times at the Salon in Paris until tastes in painting began to change. The critics castigated him for his failure to "finish" a painting. They considered his paintings as sketches and nothing more.

Whistler's reputation has wavered over the years, but it is clear today that he made a definite contribution in a style that was independently his own.

John Ruskin's opinion of Whistler's "Nocturne in Black and Gold" has not stood up through the years. He said, "I have seen, and heard, much of Cockney impudence before now; but never expected to have a coxcomb ask two hundred guineas for flinging a pot of paint in the public's face." This is an instance of the fallibility of contemporary judgments.

* * *

I had not met Johnston de Forest Williams (pl. 147) until I rang the bell of his parents' apartment. When I entered, he ran forward to see the man who was going to paint his picture. We greeted each other as though we were old friends. He said, "Wait a minute!" and away he ran, returning with an excellent drawing he had made of a robin leaning back on his heels as he pulled a worm out of the ground. I asked him if he was interested in birds, and he answered, "Yes!"

At this point my mind flashed back to the giant folio of Audubon prints. Here was an opportunity to paint a portrait entirely in this manner. It did not take long for Johnston's parents to express a similar interest. I discovered that the Baltimore oriole was one of his favorite birds, and that the sweet gum was one of the characteristic trees near their Long Island home.

The crowning touch was that I could use the same water-color paper which Havel used for his copper engravings of Audubon's color sketches. I have always had complete confidence in this paper, which is now over one hundred and thirty years old and as clear a white as though it had been made today. In Johnston's portrait the cold press paper extends, as in the Audubons, all the way to the frame. On it in the same script I lettered Johnston's full name, followed by in-line capital letters with the inscription "Icterus galbula" (Baltimore oriole).

* * *

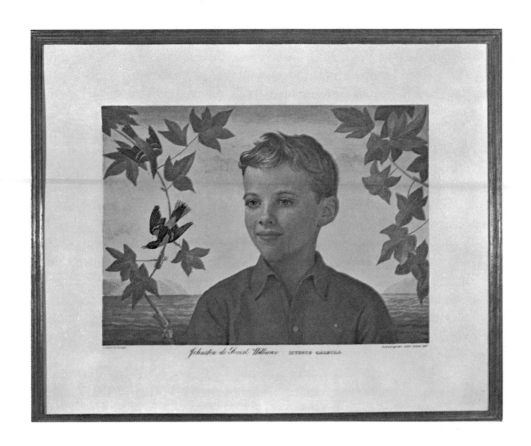

Plate 147. GORDON C. AYMAR. *Johnston de Forest Williams*. 1960. Water color. Collection of Mr. and Mrs. Douglas Williams

There can be no doubt about the creativity of Paul Gauguin (1848-1903). There seldom has been a painter who devoted more hours per day of his painting life to inventing and executing his many-sided works of art. And they had to be *his*. One of his friends referred to him as "ferociously individualistic." He himself said that he wanted to "try everything."

This predilection for forming his own style, however, did not prevent him from admiring the work of other painters and, in some cases, adapting himself to their manner. An illustration of this is his deep regard for Cézanne. In 1890 he painted the "Still Life with Oranges," which shows his interest in the work of this master, particularly in the arrangement of fruit, the crumpled napkin, and the handling of the brush in painting it.

In the same year, when he had retreated to the primitive little town of La Pouldu on the coast just above Nantes, he painted the "Portrait of Marie Lagadu" (pl. 148). His creative idea sprang from a still life of Cézanne's which he had brought with him to the inn where he and his artist friends were staying. This painting, hanging on the wall in the background, dictates the over-all color scheme. When he painted the purplish-red blouse, the green skirt, and the blue chair, he must have adjusted these colors to those in the still life, as he undoubtedly adjusted the still life to the colors in the figure. He often referred in a frustrated, violent way to "that damned Nature." Actual flesh color would have been impossible to use in this scheme and he has made it a mixture of tan, blues, and grays.

With complete disregard for the conventional formula of isolating the head from disturbing neighboring elements, he has used the reds, yellows, and greens in the fruit, and the blue bowl in the still life, as some of the strongest color notes in the composition.

This also was painted in 1890, a year before he left for Tahiti, abandoning his wife and five children to lead the life of a primitive. Having begun his career as a conventional stock broker in Paris, Gauguin began to work seriously as a painter only toward the middle of his life.

When he returned to Paris, hoping to sell some of the sixty paintings he had made in Tahiti, he found that the dealers were not interested and, having inherited some money from his uncle, he entered into a period of debauchery which led finally to his death in tragic poverty in the Marquesas Islands.

* * *

One striking instance of the picture idea coming alive almost instantaneously was the portrait of Ellen Carton (pl. 149). Her mother and I were discussing the various dresses which she might wear. Suddenly the black-and-white striped one appeared, and this became the basis of the design. The delicate, modern chair was appropriate for her to sit on, and, since one

Plate 148. PAUL GAUGUIN. *Portrait of Marie Lagadu.*
1890. Oil. Courtesy, Art Institute of Chicago,
Joseph Winterbotham Collection

Plate 149. GORDON C. AYMAR. *Ellen Carton*. 1958.
Water color. Collection of Mr. and Mrs. Laurence
Carton

of the neighboring rooms was painted with one white and one yellow wall, it was natural and reasonable to use this as part of the geometrical pattern in the background. It seemed important to reserve the use of light and shade for the face, and to suggest the three-dimensional quality of the dress by the rendering of the black stripes in her dress. These were painted with an almost Oriental handling of the brush, by lifting the brush for the thin part of the stripe and pressing down for the thick part. This treatment tended also to add to the designed effect of the painting as a whole. It was to be hung in a room of modern design and furnishings.

* * *

When Sargent was thirty years old, he painted the portrait of Mme Paul Escudier (née Lefèvre) (pl. 150). Her husband was a well-known Parisian lawyer. It is one of the most striking artistic concepts of this talented painter. He apparently agreed with his sitter in selecting the elaborate dress she is wearing, and when he asked her to stand by the window in order to make the most of the full light in this dark room, the unusual composition was formed.

As an abstract painting, quite apart from any connection with realism, it is an outstanding achievement. Turn the book you are now holding upside down and examine the gay, carefree pattern of the light areas which are balanced by the heavy dark form of the chair, the train of her gown, and the Oriental rug. Notice the little, singing echo of the bright window light in the mirror on the wall.

Now, with the book right side up, see how skillfully the artist has placed her figure, and particularly her head, in relation to the dark of the curtain and the light of the window in the rear. The shadow side of her head is clearly defined against the light, and the light side is equally well revealed by the dark of the curtain.

With true perception he has reserved the cleanest, hardest line to define the light side of her face. Her hair above this and her left shoulder blend into the background, and all neighboring edges are softened. On the shadow side of her figure the hard edges are saved for her collar, shoulder, and waist.

Mme Escudier's pose is gentle and unassuming. The clasp of her hands is peaceful, and the slight tilt of her head natural and relaxed. Her expression is one of content.

I find it difficult to accept some of the current criticism of Sargent's work. The assumption seems to be that his financial and social ambitions exceeded his interest in his art and that he failed to use his talents to the full because of this. Critics condemn his paintings as superficial. It is true that his work is somewhat uneven in its merit, but this does not destroy the excellence of a number of his paintings.

* * *

Plate 150. JOHN SINGER SARGENT. *Mme Paul Escudier
(nee Lefèvre).* Held in a private collection, Chicago, Illinois

In the late 1890's and early 1900's, particularly in France, artists were beginning to appreciate the artistic possibilities of the interiors of their homes. This is illustrated in such paintings as "Missia and Thadée Natanson" (pl. 102) and "The Painter Ker-Xavier Roussel and His Daughter" (pl. 151) by Vuillard.

Dutch painters such as Vermeer, De Hooch, Metsu, Steen, and Terborch used their homes as settings for figure painting. They were fascinated by the beauty of the architectural forms of the rooms, the handsome and appropriate design of their furniture, the interesting effects of chiaroscuro offered by the daylight coming through the mullioned windows and open doors.

With the change in taste through the years the decoration of rooms became more complicated. The "nervous," busy patterns of draperies, table covers, rugs, and wallpapers replaced the simple plaster walls and woodwork. The bold, restless brushwork and shimmering colors of the Nabis were well suited to representing this type of interior.

Vuillard, a member of the group, must have observed his brother-in-law, the painter Roussel, sitting by the open window in his unpretentious home. The room appears to be rather small, the ceiling low. At some point he also saw Roussel's little daughter in her large fluffy bonnet. Having placed the child in a reasonable position in relation to the picture as a whole, he pulled the curtains across the window to shut out the outdoor scene and to make their colorful patterns one of the important elements in the design of the picture. This also simplified the source of light, which then came solely from the window back of Roussel.

Here we have a portrait in which the scale of the figures to the total picture is minimal. It is a refreshing point of view. It was painted about 1902 and shows a less strident handling of pattern than in the portrait of the Natansons.

As time went on his manner softened and the original influence of Gauguin disappeared. Gauguin insisted, for instance, that, when there was a suggestion of green in the subject which his students were painting, that green should be made with the strongest green right out of the tube. This point of view had an influence on Vuillard's early paintings, such as the interior entitled "Symphony in Red", painted in 1893.

Three very different approaches are illustrated in the Roussel portrait, the Natansons', and his self-portrait (pl. 89), painted in 1888/90. Each one represents a clear change in style.

His work is well summed up in the article on "Les Symbolistes" written by Aurier. Vuillard, he said, is "a rare colorist full of charm and improvisation, a poet able to communicate—not without some irony—the mellow emotions of life, the tenderness of intimate interiors."

* * *

Plate 151. ÉDOUARD VUILLARD. *The Painter Ker-Xavier Roussel and His Daughter*. c. 1902. Oil on cardboard. Albright-Knox Art Gallery, Buffalo, New York, Room of Contemporary Art Fund

The idea for the portrait of Jane Irwin (pl. 152) came from two different aspects—her personality and her environment. In order to capture her alert, lively look it was necessary to concentrate on her face. A close-up of head and shoulders was a natural solution, and, in order to avoid the stiffness of a rectangular shape, I chose a circle, which is a time-honored device, much respected in the sixteenth century.

The second phase of the creative idea was to suggest that she lived in the woods, and, rather than select a realistic landscape background, it seemed less commonplace to invent the gay, carefree pattern of flowers, which by their very movement appeared to be in sympathy with her animation.

The color scheme was influenced by the fact that her outstanding physical characteristic was her very dark brown eyes, which were emphasized by her blond hair and light-blue dress. The background of green-blue formed a satisfactory harmony, and the pink flowers repeated the color of her skin.

It is always stimulating to invent different solutions for each picture problem. I quite understand Picasso's remark that when you draw, you must close your eyes and sing. It is in this mood that one's ideas are most prolific.

* * *

The basis of surrealism was the utterly uninhibited use of the imagination in creating fantasies which were executed with scrupulous regard for the appearance of nature. Pavel Tchelitchew (1898-1957) became involved in this movement when he was in Paris in 1923. He and his contemporary Eugene Berman were natural exponents of this fresh point of view.

His "Portrait of Gertrude Stein" (pl. 153) gives us an illustration of the surrealist's approach to describing a personality. Gertrude Stein and the artist were fully aware of the symbolism of the globe under her hand and the round objects in the net over her shoulders. These are not likely to be understood by the casual observer, and there is no reason for asking that they should be. A portrait involves an intimate relation between sitter and artist. When Tchelitchew painted this (it is executed in sepia with a pen and washes), he was giving his attention to creating a poem, if you will, which would be the essence of Gertrude Stein. He was not in the least concerned with what it might represent to an utter stranger.

Compare the head on canvas with the sketch below, which was an effort to record her likeness. In the sketch at the top he was treating her head in terms of an oil painting, and was relating this handling to the rest of the picture. In the sketch below he was studying the sculpture of her head as revealed by strong light and shade. He has captured the strength of her

Plate 152. GORDON C. AYMAR. *Jane Irwin*. 1958. Water
color. Collection of Mr. and Mrs. John N. Irwin II

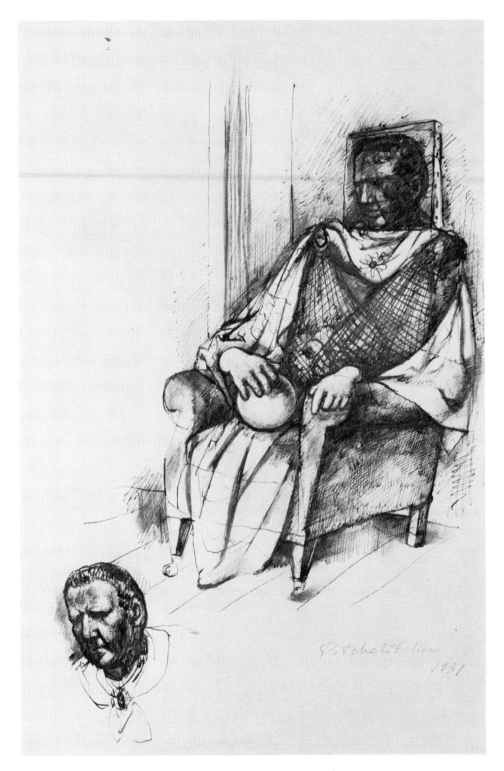

Plate 153. PAVEL TCHELITCHEW. *Portrait of Gertrude
Stein.* Sepia pen and wash drawing. Yale University Art Gallery, New Haven, Connecticut

features, and, when it is compared with photographs of her taken at this period (1931), has given a good suggestion of a likeness.

Twenty-five years before he made this sketch, Gertrude Stein had been painted by Picasso (pl. 56). The two are worth comparing, if only to demonstrate what different ideas can be engendered from the same subject.

Tchelitchew was born in Moscow and studied at the Academy of Kiev. He moved about from Constantinople and Sofia to Berlin, Paris, and London. The Museum of Modern Art in New York was the first to show his work in this country. He lived here from 1938 to 1948 and became an American citizen four years later. He died in Rome at the age of fifty-nine.

* * *

When I first met Thomas Carhart (pl. 154) at his home on Long Island, we walked out on the beach to enjoy ourselves before going through the rigors of posing. As we wandered about, I caught a glimpse of a weathered board fence. The texture and color of old wood have always appealed to me. In the back of my mind I had carried the image of a boy I had seen looking through a hole in a fence. This obviously was the moment to use it. Tommy's light blond hair was a noticeable characteristic, and the natural, outdoor, overhead light focused on this as the lightest spot in the painting.

The room in which the portrait was to hang had several handsome surrealist paintings on its walls. They were beautifully executed and were not disturbing in their subject matter. This further stimulated me to paint something that was not simply an accepted and much-used formula.

Designing the picture as a whole was a real pleasure, and I felt free to work with unevenly balanced shapes. To keep the composition from becoming too random, certain vertical lines are emphasized, such as the one in the upper right-hand corner. This is countered by the sharp, horizontal line of the sea. The finishing touch was to leave the left side of the fence unfinished, thus emphasizing the designed texture of the wood on the right.

* * *

I am sure that Henry Lamb (1885 - 1960) had been waiting patiently for a long time to have the opportunity to paint the beautiful view from his studio window. When Lytton Strachey (pl. 155), the distinguished biographer, posed for him, this apparently gave him the opportunity to do so. Strachey was to set a new style in biographical writing when he published *Eminent Victorians* four years after this portrait was painted.

The typical English bowler and umbrella were placed casually on the chair. Strachey slumped down in the armchair and, at Lamb's request, swung

Plate 154. GORDON C. AYMAR. *Thomas Carhart*. 1956.
Water color. Collection of Mr. and Mrs. H. Whit-
field Carhart

Plate 155. Henry Lamb. *Lytton Strachey*. Reproduced by courtesy of trustees of Tate Gallery, London

to the left so that the light from another source would fall properly on his face. What could have been better? His legs swept out over the board floor, with the umbrella pointed carefully toward his left foot and the blanket pulled out to offset the curve of his legs. As I am familiar with the average spring temperature in an English studio, I would hazard the guess that the blanket served not only as upholstery, but also, upon occasion, as warmth for the shivering sitter.

Lamb was not going to make this a routine, inconsequential painting. He selected a canvas eight feet high, which gave him an opportunity to suggest the size of the studio (notice where the crossbar on the window is placed), and the relation of the figure to the spacious surroundings.

He has taken discreet liberties in exaggerating Strachey's long, thin face and rather strange pose. The light areas of his face and hands are somewhat balanced by the sky, which, with its interesting shape, points toward the figure. The design and rendering of the trees are very satisfying and show a real concern for this aspect of the painting. The fence swings toward Strachey's body, and the two small figures on the walk relieve what might have been a rather uninteresting shape. All in all, it is a stimulating and challenging concept.

During World War II, Lamb was an official war artist for the British army. He was a trustee of the National Portrait Gallery and, for several years, of the Tate Gallery.

*   *   *

Plotinus has a succinct comment to make on the creation of a work of art: "If one attempted to belittle the arts by saying that, in creating, they imitate Nature, the answer should be that the arts create many things by themselves. Where something is lacking, they supply it, because they *own* beauty."

WHO IS YOUR MASTER?

AN ARTIST'S MASTER can come from any one of a number of sources: he may be a teacher who guided him in early youth; one who influenced him when he was in art school; an old or contemporary master whose pictures he has studied on the walls of museums; or, as was the case with Monet and Pissarro, nature herself.

If it is an old master or a contemporary painter, it is important to choose someone of stature. Yet it is surprising how even outstanding artists of the past have failed to recognize those whom time has proved to be great. Michelangelo said of the well-known Flemish painters: "They paint in Flanders only to deceive the external eye. They try to do so many things at once, each of which alone would suffice for a great work, so that they do not do anything really well." And he remarked of Titian that, if he had learned how to draw, he might have become a really great artist. When El Greco visited the Sistine Chapel, he expressed his opinion that Michelangelo was an excellent man, but one who did not know how to paint. If men of this caliber are willing to pass such judgments on painters whose enduring merit has been so firmly established, how can we expect today's opinions to be infallible?

It is my contention that, provided an artist ranks reasonably high in past or contemporary reputation, he should qualify to become one's master. From that point on, it depends upon how much he inspires us to create in his image and with his particular comprehension of beauty. I do not intend that this should be a plea for unthinking imitation, but for inspiration.

In selecting the man or men who are to be your masters, you are opening up a vast field for yourself. You are not only absorbing things which you will apply in creating your own work, but you are having the continuing pleasure of understanding beauty in all its forms through their eyes.

This appreciation of beauty is expressed succinctly and provocatively by Cranmer-Byng in his introduction to a charming book of Chinese poetry. He is discussing the ancient philosophy of the True Way: "To enjoy is to have the affinity to understand, the persistence to enter, and finally the power to reproduce."[5]

* * *

When I painted the portrait of Etain O'Malley (pl. 156), I had in mind the fifteenth-century Italian and Netherlandish device of the simple, dark background behind the figure and the small area devoted to the significant landscape. It adds a characteristic environment, relieves the severity of the head-and-body design, and gives a feeling of a third dimension to the picture. Etain is wearing a dress of lovely hand-woven material, and is sitting in the turf shed outside O'Malley Castle in Ireland.

* * *

There seems to be a variety of reasons which induce a patron to select one portrait painter or another. Probably the most unusual and gratifying experience which has happened to me was the day William Bell (pl. 157) appeared at my studio door, introduced himself, and, with a hidden humor in his eyes, said, "In the absence of Hans Holbein, I wonder if you would consider painting my portrait, Mr. Aymar." What could have been a more engaging first encounter? He had thrown down the gauntlet, and I accepted the challenge with keen interest.

Almost at once William Bell's portrait began to take shape. It was not difficult to select the manner in which the picture could develop. The size should be that of the average Holbein man's portrait. (Mr. Bell's is 16" x 12½".) The interest should be concentrated on the head and hands by keeping the clothing and background dark. (In the actual portrait there is more difference between the value of the background and the coat.) The name and date should be lettered across the painting in the Holbein manner.

In order to delineate Mr. Bell's face with all its gentleness, humor, and strength, and with his penetrating eyes, it was necessary to see his face

[5] J. L. Cranmer-Byng, *A Feast of Lanterns*

Plate 156. GORDON C. AYMAR. *Etain O'Malley*. 1949.
Water color. Collection of Mrs. Richard Roelofs,
Jr.

Plate 157. GORDON C. AYMAR. *William Bell*. 1950. Oil
on panel. Collection of Mrs. Raymond Wing

undisturbed by spectacles. These were placed on his desk, and a letter from his daughter was put in his hands. His watch chain and Phi Beta Kappa key add a decorative touch to this grouping. One's eye is carried from the head to the hands, which form a decorative pattern in the lower part of the picture—a typical Holbein device.

This was a comfortable and absorbing undertaking. I felt at home in the company of this great master and with Mr. Bell, a gracious Quaker gentleman of wide interests and sensitive perception.

*   *   *

"Jamie at the Farm" (pl. 158) was painted before electricity had found its way down the little country road. The light from oil lamps and candles is so much more gracious than that from the one hundred-watt bulbs. There is a warmth, an aura, a romantic air which enriches every surface on which it falls. When I think of candlelight, I think of Georges de La Tour (perhaps the picture should have been called "Hommage à La Tour"), so it was only natural for me to take this opportunity to restudy his work. What a satisfaction it is to paint the human face with the source of light coming from below! To have used La Tour's characteristic accent on sharp, flat planes seemed too contrived, so the light and shade are rendered more or less as I observed them. La Tour in many of his paintings simplified the planes in faces and bodies to the point where they almost suggest the treatment of modern sculpture. This is especially noticeable in such paintings as his "St. Sebastian Mourned by St. Irene," It is a phase of his style which has withstood the passage of time and is thoroughly satisfying. Paintings that have a style of their own, in the proper sense, are those which depart from being a mere representation and become a mode of *expression*.

Jamie is observing the candle flame in a ruminative mood. The painting of him is a study in the hard and the soft—from the hard outline of his profile and the edge of the shadow on his nostril to the soft edges of the sweater as it recedes from the source of light.

*   *   *

The "Portrait of Hendrickje Stoffels" (pl. 159) has been attributed to Barent Fabritius (1624-1673). He was the younger brother of the more famous Carel, who was also a pupil of Rembrandt. They were both properly called "disciples" of the great master.

It is quite obvious from this painting that he was concentrating on the effects of light in the manner of his master. The high studio light falls on the subject's head at an angle which enabled the artist to place the eyes in shadow. Reflected light illumines her jaw and the front of her neck. Avoiding the obvious, he has not painted her hands in the light, but has reserved

Plate 158. GORDON C. AYMAR. *Jamie at the Farm.* 1963.
Oil on canvas

Plate 159. Barent Fabritius (?). *Portrait of Hendrickje Stoffels*. Oil on canvas. Metropolitan Museum of Art, New York, Bequest of Benjamin Altman, 1913

a touch of it for her wrist, which repeats the main light on her face, breast, and ruche.

Barent was never the draftsman that Carel was, and, of course, did not even enter the realm of his master. But it is interesting to see what artistic subtleties can be imparted by a teacher and how much at home a pupil can be in the particular field which absorbs his master. This was not simply a matter of how to set a palette or apply a brush stroke. What Rembrandt was able to convey was a point of view—a way of observing nature and abstracting from it certain qualities of light which were made to come alive and were emphasized by the omission of many other qualities, such as line, clear-cut pattern, and a broad color palette.

*   *   *

Kathleen Thompson (pl. 160) came into my studio dressed in white. As she stood in front of the white wall on the beige-colored rug, Whistler's "Portrait of Mrs. Leyland" (pl. 161) came at once to my mind, followed, of course, by his "White Girl." Why not enjoy studying the problems Whistler was interested in solving with his concern for symphonies of value and color?

After the first sitting I hastened to the Frick Collection to study his approach to "white on white." Actually, he has used more of a cool pink-gray on Mrs. Leyland's gown and the wall, with a cool gray reserved for parts of her dress. The dark notes of the flowers on her clothing are warm brown, and the only opposing colors are the very small green touches of the leaves at the side of the picture.

One of Kathleen's most noticeable characteristics was her long hair; so her pose is based on the body in profile. The number of colors in the painting are reduced to a minimum. The curtain was a pure invention to relieve the monotony of the white wall. Shadows from her body cast upon the wall were for the most part eliminated, to preserve the original concept of the picture.

This is a charming age at which to paint a girl. Her inherent characteristics are all there, but unmodified and undamaged by the strenuous experiences of life. Her look is a combination of wonder, confidence, and interest.

The high key of the whole picture enables the head to stand out, which is just the opposite of the time-honored use of an all-dark background, with the head isolated by its contrast in value.

Incidentally, it was Whistler who maintained that, while so many artists strive to make the model "stand out" from the frame, they should realize that the model actually stands *within* the frame, at a distance equal to that between the artist and his model.

*   *   *

Plate 160. GORDON C. AYMAR. *Kathleen Thompson.*
1954. Water color. Collection of Mr. and Mrs.
Fred D. Thompson

Plate 161. JAMES ABBOTT MCNEIL WHISTLER. *Portrait of Mrs. Leyland*. Oil on canvas. © Frick Collection, New York

Immediately after being released from the hospital to which he had been confined because he was deliriously convinced that someone was trying to poison him, Vincent van Gogh began to resume his work on a painting of Mme. Roulin, the postman's wife. He called this picture "La Berceuse" (pl. 162). The subject is presumably rocking a cradle and watching her baby. The artist was moved to paint this picture because he wished to give it to an Icelandic fisherman to hang in his cabin, so that it might console him during his rugged life by making him feel cared for and mothered.

There was another guiding motive. Van Gogh said that he wanted to capture all the *music* of color. Nothing could better express the essence of his painting. It *is* music—strident, rhythmic, cacophonous, a symphony for brass. In "La Berceuse" he has balanced the violence of the contrasting green skirt and red wall with the insistent, wind-blown design of the upper wall. The subject's ocherish face and hands, by their very lack of accurate color representation, are in harmony with the free treatment of the rest of the picture. The red of the baseboard is carried in a more subdued tone on the chair back up into the predominantly cool color of the upper wall. Van Gogh painted five versions of this picture. The one in the Rÿksmuseum Kröller-Müller in Otterlo shows an entirely different flower design.

There is a certain crudity in the handling of Mme. Roulin's picture, but, as Van Gogh wrote to his brother Theo apropos of his painting "The Potato Eaters," he did not believe it was appropriate to give peasant pictures an unfitting smoothness and that the one thing peasants did not need was a perfumed look.

It would appear that in painting this picture the artist first introduced the broad outlines, then the flat color areas, and finally the modeling in strokes that followed the forms and made rhythmic patterns as well.

Undoubtedly, the work of other artists influenced him to a degree, but the tempestuous creativity of his own artistic concepts was the dominating factor in his life.

* * *

Robert Henri (1865 - 1929), in addition to his ability as a painter, served as a teacher whose enthusiasm and convictions about the function of art in our lives and the technical methods of expressing oneself have seldom been surpassed. George Bellows, his pupil, wrote that only the notes of Leonardo da Vinci and the "Twelve Discourses" of Sir Joshua Reynolds could be compared with *The Art Spirit* written by Henri, in which he condensed the philosophy and technical knowledge of a lifetime.

Henri's belief that America had reached a point where the material for a painting lay before one's eyes in its people and street scenes was conveyed in many of his own paintings. While he respected the influence of the school

Plate 162. VINCENT VAN GOGH. *Madame Roulin Rocking the Cradle*. 1889. Courtesy of the Art Institute of Chicago, Helen Birch Bartlett Memorial Collection

of Paris, which had predominated for many years, and while he was one of the genuine appreciators of impressionism, he wanted to declare his independence of any past movement.

"Himself" (pl. 163), painted in 1913, represents this forthright approach. His model is obviously an Irishman straight from the "old country." He is looking at the viewer with a gaze that could be accompanied by a caustic jibe or, a moment later, by a hearty laugh. The color scheme is rather somber—a warm gray wall and shadows on it, greenish-gray sleeves, a warm brown sleeveless jacket and trousers, a lighter, reddish-brown vest, which serves to bind together the flesh color of head and hands. The scarf is a strong, dark green, used to offer a contrast next to the violent color in the face. Henri has applied a bright red with bold brush strokes to the nose and cheeks. It is exaggerated to the point of becoming, in this respect, a caricature. Without any hesitation he has made the shadow on the wall follow exactly the line of the rod in the subject's hand.

Henri was passionate in his regard for the brush stroke. In *The Art Spirit* he devotes over ten pages to a vivid description of the various strokes, good and bad. He believed in getting the full swing of the body into each stroke. His appreciation of the infinite variety possible corresponds with the use of the bow by an expert cellist. It must be admitted that at times Henri sacrificed draftsmanship to the spontaneity of his brush strokes.

He was born in Cincinnati, and his real name was Robert Henry Cozad. He studied at the Pennsylvania Academy of Fine Arts and also in Paris. It was during his three years there that he acquired his admiration for Velázquez and Hals, from whom his brushwork is largely derived. He admired this quality also in Manet and Renoir. In 1908 he established the Henri School of Art in New York, and had a deep influence on such students as Edward Hopper, Rockwell Kent, Eugene Speicher, Stuart Davis, Yasuo Kuniyoshi, and George Bellows.

*   *   *

There are artists like Andrew Wyeth (1917-   ) who are their own masters. While Wyeth greatly admires the work of such men as Eakins, Hopper, and Homer, he has stated that he is not a realist in the sense in which they are. He has said that he is actually an abstractionist. This implies that he is more concerned with the abstract qualities of tone, color, and design than he is in the representational characteristics of his painting. The ordinary museum visitor is impressed by the meticulous care with which he has painted each blade of grass in a landscape, but *he* is concerned more with making these individual strokes form a *tone*.

This abstract approach interests me very much because I spend an appreciable part of my time in painting my portraits upside down. This

328

Plate 163. ROBERT HENRI. *Himself*. 1913. Oil. Courtesy,
Art Institute of Chicago, Walter H. Schulze Memorial Collection

is the best way to detach oneself from representing details—an eye, a nose, a finger—and to be able to view the picture as though it had no responsibility to represent anything concrete. It then becomes simply an amalgamation of colors, lines, modulations, patterns. No painter who understands this point of view and lives for it will ever leave a painting until this primary aspect has satisfied him.

Wyeth's painting of "Christina Olsen" (pl. 164) is, to me, one of his most exciting pictures. The original concept is expressive of the simple, austere, Maine environment—the weathered wooden door, the bare floor, the subject's simple, country look. Christina, crippled with polio, sits in a quiet but determined pose, accepting life, absorbing nature.

As an abstract pattern it is a masterpiece—the clean-cut, angular space devoted to the light areas and the remaining strong, dark pattern of the shadows. This is not photographic realism. If it were, the edges of the shadows, which are most distant from the objects casting them, such as the top of the door opening and the subject's figure, would be progressively softer. Wyeth was interested in maintaining a firm, equally hard edge for these shadows in order to emphasize pattern.

Her light flesh tones are echoed by the singing note of the white door handle. The dark triangle of her dress and shadow is amplified by the explosive forms of the trees, and the slanting grass below them leans to the left to oppose the various shapes leaning to the right. The beautiful textures of wood, grass, and trees are accentuated by the flat, even tone of the sky.

Wyeth associates himself with movement. The effect of wind appears in many of his paintings—the coat of the old man sitting on a dead tree in "April Wind," the curtain blowing in "Wind from the Sea," and Christina's hair in the accompanying picture.

Incidentally, he has painted three pictures of his friend Christina, the one shown herewith being the first, the famous "Christina's World" the second, and "Miss Olsen" the third. He has painted several pictures of her bleak, three-story house.

N. C. Wyeth, his father, was one of the great illustrators of our time, and his work shows the direct influence of his instructor, Howard Pyle. Elizabeth Shippen Green, also a pupil of Pyle's, felt so strongly the desire to impart the substance of his teaching to the next generation that she voluntarily formed a class in her home in Cambridge for a group who were studying at the school of the Boston Museum of Fine Arts. The point that remains in my mind above all from this series of talks was that Pyle kept telling his pupils: "You must *be there!* You must *become* the person and the thing you are painting." This point of view was passed on to his son by N. C. Wyeth, and the son's painting is the very essence of this requirement.

Andrew never went to art school, nor has he felt any compulsion to go

Plate 164. ANDREW WYETH. *Christina Olsen*. Collection
   of Mr. and Mrs. Joseph Verner Reed

to Europe to study the masters. His world is his own. He became a member of the National Academy of Design at the age of twenty-seven. He is today one of America's most respected artists.

* * *

The really vital factor is for an artist to select a master with whose work he is instinctively at one. Some years ago I had the pleasure of meeting Edmund Dulac, whose work I had always admired. I expressed my admiration for his paintings, particularly those influenced by Persian miniatures, and he responded by declaring in clear terms his art creed. It was the simple awareness that now we are not tied down, as our ancestors were, to the circumscribed area in which we live and study. We are not limited in travel to an exhausting trip from Flanders to Florence, or Pisa to Paris, to examine the works of contemporary sixteenth-century fellow painters. Our masters can be any distance away, and can be alive or dead. Dulac had found in Persian miniatures of the sixteenth century the most congenial environment for his work.

This point of view gave me confidence. From an early age Holbein had been my idol, and from him my interest spread to Jan van Eyck and Memling. For them, visible nature herself provided the greatest, immutable inspiration. God's creation was infinite, ever new. With a flair for design, they recomposed her, for the elements of beauty are always present but not necessarily arranged with the inherent beauty of the objects themselves.

Seeing beauty through the eyes of these great men was *being myself*. To be sure, there is another level and a higher one—that of the artist who creates a new beauty, as, for example, Van Gogh. I console myself, however, for not being able to achieve these heights by remembering that Titian and Giorgione were so profoundly influenced by the paintings of Giovanni Bellini that even the experts cannot determine which one of them executed certain pictures. Tintoretto, also, felt it no disgrace to admit his allegiance to sources outside himself. On the walls of his studio he lettered the inscription "The drawing of Michelangelo and the color of Titian."

If the concept of selecting for your masters those painters whose work was especially congenial was carried to its ultimate conclusion, it might mean that you would render one sitter in the manner of Degas, with a pastel handling of charming color; another would immediately suggest Rembrandt; and still another, Goya or Van Gogh. What a challenge to learn to speak all these visual languages, instead of being limited to interpreting entirely different personalities in the same tone of voice!

Fortunately, today the works of art of all countries and periods are available, not only in museums but in books on art as well. It is truly the day of André Malraux and his *Museum Without Walls*.

INDEX

334

337

GORDON C. AYMAR

He received his A.B. degree at Yale University, and then studied at the School of The Museum of Fine Arts in Boston, with the intention of making portrait painting his career. He left there to join the Navy in World War I, and served as Signal Officer aboard the U.S.S. *Utah*.

At the close of the war, in order to raise a growing family, he became an art director. During this period he was president of the New York Art Directors Club, and later was elected charter president of the National Society of Art Directors, from which, in 1951, he received their award for "Distinction in the Practice of His Profession." He finally gave up his work as an art consultant, to return to the fine arts field.

His paintings have been shown in many museums, galleries and art associations in this country and abroad, among which are the American Watercolor Society, the National Academy, the National Arts Club, the Century Association, the Dayton Art Institute, the Columbia, South Carolina, Art Museum, the Phoenix Art Museum, the Montreal Art Museum, and the Royal Society of Painters in Water Colour in London. He is also represented in the collections of the Brooklyn Public Library, Pratt Institute, and the Yale University Art Gallery. His photographs of St. Patrick's Cathedral are in the Permanent Study Collection of the Museum of Modern Art in New York.